# The
# Compact History
# of the
# Indian Wars

**John Tebbel**

*With Illustrations*
*by Gil Walker*

# THE

# COMPACT HISTORY

# OF THE

# INDIAN WARS

HAWTHORN BOOKS, INC.
*Publishers*

NEW YORK

1260

# Contents

# Part One:

# The Conquest of
# the East

# 1

★ ★ ★ ★ ★ ★

# First Encounters

As THIS AWESOME CENTURY moves toward its closing decades, Americans are preoccupied at home with the Negro's struggle for civil rights, and abroad with the clash of ideologies precipitated by that word which has held so many meanings for so many men—freedom. If there are still those among us who believe we are without sin, they need only examine once more the dismaying record of the real American tragedy: our conquest of the North American continent, in which a nation presumably conceived in liberty systematically destroyed the rights, civil and otherwise, of a whole population numbering a million, reducing it to less than half that number, and making the "freedom" of those who survived a mockery of the word.

The literature of this tragedy is formidable. Its monuments are Francis Parkman's magnificent epic of the great contest between France and England for control of the continent, and William Hickling Prescott's splendid narrative of the Spanish conquest. The story of the long war between white men and red in the continental United States has been told piecemeal, for the most part, but in its totality it is a record of nearly four centuries of virtually constant warfare, roughly from 1500 to 1900. For the sake of convenience, we call this aspect by a collective title, the American Indian Wars. In reality, it was one great war. And to the hopelessly huddled and often starving survivors in the concentration camps we choose to call reservations, it is a war that has never ended.

Like all clashes of arms, the battle between the conquering Americans and their slowly retreating Indian adversaries had its heroes.

As always, brave men fought and died on both sides. Their leaders were sometimes brilliant and courageous, sometimes stupid and cowardly. Neither side enjoyed a monopoly of good or evil. If the cruelty of the Indians is better known to us, it is only because white historians have glossed over the cruelty of their fellows. The dashing figure of the United States cavalryman riding to the rescue is almost overly familiar to us through motion pictures and television. History has obscured, for the most part, the equally heroic figure of the Indian, fighting against superior numbers and firepower, as he did more often than not.

In one respect, however, the four-century war differed from nearly all the others in which the United States has engaged. From the beginning there was no doubt of its outcome. "The inevitable march of progress" is the phrase used most often to describe it, and with these comfortable words we justify the destruction of a culture and a people. True enough, it was inevitable. From the beginning of history, nomadic and pastoral peoples have been conquered by more advanced and better organized societies. Certainly, too, the shaping of the American nation from beleaguered colonies to world power is one of the splendid stories in human history, and we are justifiably proud of what we have achieved. The tragedy, though, lies in the manner of the conquest, the way in which we took this marvelous continent from those who inhabited it before we came, and our subsequent treatment of them as a subject people. We need to understand this story better, in our day of the world-wide struggles for freedom, however men may interpret the word. Once we see our own conquest in perspective, it may help us to perceive the ideals we profess to live by in a truer light.

It is helpful to recall, for example, that one of the first acts of those who came to explore the New World was to enslave some of the trusting natives and take them back to Europe, either as proof of their voyages, or to work in European mines, or both. In what may be the first recorded encounter between white man and Indian, the Portuguese explorer Gaspar Corte Real tells us that in 1500 (or 1501) he kidnapped more than fifty Indians to be sold into slavery.

Another early explorer, the Florentine navigator called variously Verrazano and Verrazzano, repaid the kindness and admiration of the Indians who met him as he scouted the shore from North Carolina to Newfoundland with various acts of calculated brutality, until the word spread to New England, where the natives would not let him come ashore. Parkman accurately describes Verrazano and his men as kidnappers of children and ravishers of squaws. We have honored this man today by giving his name to the great bridge connecting Staten Island and Brooklyn.

The cruel and sanguinary conquest of Mexico and Peru by the gold-greedy Spaniards, so vividly described by W. H. Prescott, was repeated on a minor scale along the northern shores of the Gulf Coast, and in what is today Florida and Georgia. Spanish forays into these lands are replete with tales of abduction for the slave trade, rapine and murder, all in the name of God. It was in these skirmishes that Indians understood for the first time the nature of the white man's invasion. They saw that he meant to enslave, kill and exploit, and for the first time they fought back. They decimated Ponce de Leon's followers before that superstitious Spaniard died in Cuba, and they did away with nearly half of the 620 followers of Hernando De Soto, a man "much given to the sport of slaying Indians," as a later historian describes him, before the surviving Spaniards reached the Gulf after an incredible three-year march, leaving behind them a trail so bloody that the fires of hatred lit among the tribes along the way were not extinguished for generations. In one senseless show of force, De Soto's men killed a hundred helpless, sleeping warriors in a village.

This was the pattern wherever the gold-crazed Spaniards penetrated in the New World. In Georgia they seized slaves, burned villages and murdered those who resisted them. Sometimes a conquistador appeared who seemed more human, as Coronado did, but in the end even Coronado hanged the Indian guide who had brought him safely into the interior of the continent. Nonetheless he left behind him a tradition of moderation and general good will, while De Soto's legacy was one of pure hatred.

The English gentlemen who penetrated America farther north were not much more civilized. Sir Richard Grenville, landing in Virginia in 1585, was received with warm hospitality by the Indians— a hospitality which he repaid by burning and plundering a village in revenge for the theft of a single silver cup.

Such were the preliminary skirmishes before the white men made

Jamestown

their first attempt at colonization in Jamestown, beginning with the
landing of April 26, 1607, when three ships of the London Company
tied up to trees in what is today Hampton Roads, Virginia. No more
than twelve hours later the embryonic colonists were fighting a brisk
but indecisive engagement with the Indian inhabitants of the region,
who had no doubt heard by this time, as most of the Indians along
the coast had learned, what treacherous, dangerous men the invaders
were. For their part, the new arrivals expected to find a savage foe
who was also, by reputation, treacherous and dangerous. The seeds
of mutual hostility had been well sown.

At Jamestown, however, two outstanding leaders confronted each
other for the first time, and successfully prevented the indiscriminate mayhem that might otherwise have resulted. For the colonists
were largely riffraff adventurers, drawn by the promise of gold, as
the Spaniards had been, while the Indians of Virginia were members
of the powerful Algonquin Confederacy and inclined to be extremely
short-tempered with anyone, white or red, who invaded their territory. They would have slaughtered each other had it not been for
Captain John Smith and his opposite number, Chief Powhatan.

In strength of character, John Smith stood head and shoulders
above those he commanded. His purpose was to impose a stern dis-

cipline on the colonists and by united effort establish an outpost in the wilderness from which further exploration and colonization would be possible. His intentions toward the Indians were peaceful; he meant to be firm but just with them.

Somehow this intent must have penetrated the naturally suspicious brain of Chief Powhatan, who was the local warlord. Otherwise it would be difficult to explain why he did not destroy the struggling little colony, as he could have done with the greatest ease in the first two decades of its existence. Captain Smith recorded that Powhatan had "a sower looke," and in fact he was a grim, cruel man, but of more than ordinary intelligence. He probably understood perfectly well what the white men were up to, but did nothing about it except for an occasional perverse refusal to sell them corn or a bland denial that his braves had murdered some lone wanderer too far afield from the colony.

Smith was a diplomat as well as a good soldier, and that led him to have Powhatan crowned as king of the territory in 1609. The chief apparently did not understand, or pretended not to understand, what the crown meant and stubbornly refused to bow his head, at first, to have it put on. He had no trouble understanding the gifts that went with it.

captain John Smith

If there is any truth in the Pocahontas legend, which is doubtful, Powhatan may have had an added reason for not disposing of the troublesome colonists. At the least, his daughter's marriage to John Rolfe must have been a factor in the peace treaty he made with the colonists in 1613. It came none too soon. Captain Smith had been recalled to England in 1609, after a dispute with the London Company's managers, and without his firm control there had been four tense years of sullen, intermittent hostilities between the colonists and the Indians, although there was no general outbreak.

The long and sometimes troubled truce came to an end, however, in 1618 with Powhatan's death, and the accession to power of his brother, Opechancanough, a tough old man whose obsession was hatred of the English. He had dedicated what remained of his life to driving them into the sea.

As an Indian general, Opechancanough was the most able foe the white men had yet faced in their invasion. He was a careful strategist, discreet to a fault, a wily planner who waited four years in utmost secrecy while he fashioned the blow he meant to deal the English.

But this careful man made a single mistake, and it proved to be fatal. He waited too long. Not only had the colonists employed the comparative peace of Powhatan's reign to build up their power, but they had spread their colony for 140 miles along the bay of the James River; the Indians had been forced above tidewater. The colonists were also much more numerous by this time, and they were entrenched and well-armed.

Nevertheless, when Opechancanough led the tribes of his Confederacy in their long-delayed assault, on a March morning in 1622, he was nearly successful. The colony took a staggering blow. By the time the Indians were through with torch and knife and tomahawk, only eight of the colony's eighty settlements remained; 347 men, women and children had been massacred in a single hour.

Opechancanough's strategy would have succeeded only if the devastation had been complete. By leaving survivors, and inexplicably permitting them to survive although he could have easily wiped them out, he laid the groundwork for his own destruction, which was not long in coming. The colonists, after the first shock of the massacre, were imbued with a full measure of the old chief's hatred, and like him, they even neglected their crops as they planned to strike back. In his fashion, too, they pretended to seek peace and convinced the chief he had utterly intimidated them, so that he suspected nothing when the white leaders invited him and other chiefs to a proposed treaty council. There the colonists pounced on them, repaying treachery and murder in kind.

The chief escaped their slaughter, along with a few followers, and now his rage against the white man consumed him. Yet his cautious nature led him to wait and plan for another twenty-two years before he considered himself ready for revenge. By that time he was reputed to be a century old, and so infirm that he had to be carried to battle on a litter. But ironically Opechancanough had made the same mistake a second time—waiting too long while the colony built up a well-equipped force of militia. History was repeated. The chief struck with his forces on an April morning in 1644, with such fury and skill that nearly 500 settlers were killed, and it appeared for a time that the white men might indeed be driven into the sea. But they recovered quickly. Governor William Berkeley led his militia in a counterattack, in which superior firepower brought him the victory after a brief, savage struggle in which both sides fought with exceptional bravery.

Opechancanough was captured and taken to Jamestown. Near death, he was held prisoner under guard in a building where a curious, morbid, hating crowd tried to get at him. According to a story in which legend and fact are inextricably mingled, one of the guards turned his gun on the helpless chief, perhaps in revenge for a slain relative, but the indestructible old man did not die at once. Instead, he pulled himself erect from the bed, stood swaying beside it and, with his customary imperious air, demanded that Governor Berkeley be brought to him. Before this gaunt, dreadful figure the governor must have stood transfixed as Opechancanough pointed a shaking, accusing finger at him and cried: "If it had been my fortune to take Sir William Berkeley prisoner, I would not have meanly exposed him as a show to my people." Whereupon, with the utmost dignity, he lay down again and died.

Opechancanough's reproach, if it was actually made, may be taken as a sample of the florid rhetoric which so distinguished some Indian chiefs' speech, occasionally soaring into pure, eloquent poetry. It can be safely assumed that if the governor had indeed been the chief's prisoner, he might not have been made a show for the crowd, dragged through the streets triumphantly on a litter while he was spat upon and reviled, but he would almost certainly have been tortured with the most exquisite cruelty, had his heart torn from his body and his blood drunk if he died bravely, and quite possibly have been eaten, since cannibalism was not uncommon among the Algonquins. The fires of hatred had been lit on the continent from Canada to Florida.

Meanwhile, farther up the Atlantic Coast, in rugged New England, a drama of a different sort was being played out. There the colonists from the *Mayflower* had proved to be of a better sort than the Jamestown breed. By and large, they were purposeful and intelligent, and they made an effort to get along with the Indians. In this they were helped considerably by a mysterious epidemic, which had already been raging for three years before the colonists landed. It had so shattered the Indian tribes all the way from Rhode Island to Maine that they did not have the strength to resist the invaders, even if they had desired. Consequently the Pilgrim leaders quickly made friends with the local chiefs—Massasoit, his brother Quadequina, Samoset and Squanto.

Of these Indian leaders, Massasoit was by far the most important. A chief of the powerful Wampanoags, he ruled a large territory which embraced Massachusetts, Rhode Island, and westward nearly to the land of the Six Nations. He was, as one of the Pilgrims described him, "a very lusty man, in his best years, an able body, grave of countenance and spare of speech."

Massasoit made a treaty with the invaders on March 22, 1621, and for the first time, by its terms, Indians gave land freely to the white man, an act they lived to regret. It was land that had been depopulated by the plague. Massasoit told the treaty-makers eloquently: "Englishmen, take that land, for none is left to occupy it. The Great Spirit . . . has swept its people from the face of the earth." The chief followed up this generosity as time went on by helping the colonists in every way he could in their struggle to establish themselves in a strange and difficult environment.

As long as the intercourse between white men and red was confined to the modest outposts of the Plymouth and Massachusetts Bay Colonies, peace was maintained and Massasoit loyally adhered to the treaty he had signed, although he was not without provocation to violate it from time to time. But as colonization spread, inevitable frictions began to develop. The Connecticut Colony established itself at Hartford in 1636, and two years later the New Haven Colony took root, about the same time that the New Hampshire Colony established itself in Exeter. It was in 1636, too, that Roger Williams began to organize his colony of dissidents from Massachusetts Bay, in neighboring Rhode Island, which resulted in 1643 in the establishing of his Providence Plantations, along Narragansett Bay.

With this spread of colonization, the white men pushed inland away from the territory of the Wampanoags which Massasoit controlled and began to impinge on the lands of the Pequots, who lived in the Connecticut River Valley. These Indians found themselves also beset by the Dutch moving up northward from Manhattan Island and eastward from the Hudson River Valley. Thus the Pequots were being caught in a squeeze between two steadily encroaching waves of colonization, and the peace which Massasoit had maintained for so long began to show signs of crumbling.

It ended at last in the Pequot War, which began in the summer of 1636 with a strange naval engagement between two fishing boats off the shores of Block Island. One of the boats had been captured by a party of Indians when it was sighted, sails flapping and apparently deserted, by a Boston fisherman, John Gallup, who commanded a force of one man and two boys. Nevertheless he attacked the other boat, which contained a small party of Pequots who had obviously pirated the craft. All but two jumped overboard, and their fate is unknown.

The bush war this incident touched off, however, was the first in a series of bloody New England encounters, and a dramatic demonstration that for sheer savagery the opponents were well-matched. Up in Boston, Governor Vane heard about the incident of the fishing boats and on this slender evidence apparently concluded that the Pequots were about to fall on the colony from their villages on Block Island. He sent ninety militiamen down to the Island, and with commendable dispatch they killed every Indian who had not fled, burned the towns and then retired without loss.

Thus the unequal Pequot War began. As would always be the case, it was unequal because the white men possessed nearly all the firepower. The Indians had few guns of any description. Their chief resource was the advantage possessed by guerrilla fighters to this day—mobility. Like the Viet Cong of our times, they skipped in and out of the wilderness, attacking wherever they thought they had an advantage, then slipped back into the bush.

It would, of course, have been sheer folly for them to attack any

such fortified position as Plymouth. There the Pilgrims had installed
a three-inch, 1,200-pound cannon called a minion, cumbersome but
enough to intimidate a whole tribe of Indians. Along with it they
had another big, awkward gun known as a saker, whose range was
only 360 yards. Then there were two small pieces, called bases, which
fired half-pound balls. As weapons of war, this armament had every
imaginable deficiency, including a tendency to blow up and exterminate the gun crews, but to the Indians it was awesome.

Captain
miles Standish

A more decided advantage was the presence in Plymouth of Captain Miles Standish, an extremely able soldier, who had brought some
military order into his rough-hewn corps of militiamen. He had
taught them how to shoot, and he had his little army separated into
four companies, or "trains," each one designated to guard a wall of
the fortifications.

Like the cannon, the light arms these soldiers possessed would
not have been enough to deal with a professionally equipped enemy,
but they were more than adequate to oppose the bow and arrow. For
the most part they were the fowling pieces the colonists used to
hunt their food; muskets so absurdly long they had to be fired from
props; and the blunderbuss, a weapon about the size of a carbine
with a bell like a trumpet and a short barrel into which could be
stuffed a pint or so of whatever ammunition might be desired—anything from small rocks to slugs. Naturally, it was deadly at short

range but of little value for any other kind of action. Like the cannon, however, it made a tremendous noise, and that—when taken with the shower of slugs it sprayed into the landscape—was enough to terrify most Indians.

Nevertheless, in spite of the inequities of armament, the massacre at Block Island stirred up every Pequot in New England. Like Opechancanough, the Pequots were filled with a murderous hatred and the desire to push the white man into the sea. More sophisticated than the Virginia chief, they realized that they must have strong allies to do it, and they turned first to their old enemies, the Narragansetts. Roger Williams frustrated this piece of diplomacy. In his eloquent way, he pointed out to the Narragansetts that they had nothing to gain by fighting the Pequots' wars for them.

With or without allies, the Pequots began a sniping guerrilla campaign of pillage and murder among the scattered settlements and farms of Connecticut, until there were a thousand or more of them on the warpath and the white inhabitants were so alarmed that they appealed to neighboring Massachusetts for help.

Massachusetts sent a professional soldier, John Mason, in command of a small but well-equipped force consisting of eighty colonists and about a hundred Indian allies of doubtful loyalty, under a Mohican chief named Uncas. Setting off on his expedition in May, 1637, Mason tarried in the country of the Narragansetts long enough to persuade them to add a large party of warriors to his army, after which the whole force embarked in three small boats from Saybrook, en route to a landing below the fort of the Pequots, on a hill looking down upon what is today Groton, Connecticut.

The Pequot fort was in command of Sassacus, who happened to be the father-in-law of Uncas. Mason thought that would be an advantage, since Uncas had an inside knowledge not only of the fort but its defenders as well. What Mason did not know was that Uncas could not be trusted, as little by his own people as by his white allies. Nor had the Massachusetts captain yet learned that as fighters Indians were opportunists and pragmatists, who fought only when they were reasonably certain of winning. When the Mohicans and Narragansetts viewed the Pequot fort for the first time, they had serious doubts about whether Mason could take it, and politely offered the white men the opportunity of leading the assault, while they waited at a distance. Uncas, too, seemed doubtful, and it appeared that he meant to wait until he saw how the battle went before he decided to which side he would give his help.

Saybrook Fort 1636

Fortunately for Captain Mason, Sassacus was no strategist and he also had a poor opinion of his enemy's ability, which led him into further errors. He held a strong enough position. The Pequot fort had a stockade twelve feet high. The posts were separated enough to fire through but too narrow for an invader to squeeze past. Mason crept up on this establishment in the twilight of May 25th without being seen. His scouts informed him there were two entrances, and Mason decided to split his force and strike at both gates just before dawn.

From a military standpoint, the attack could not have been more successful. Caught by surprise, the Pequots fought back with the courage for which they were celebrated, and for a time it seemed as though the fears of Mason's Indian allies might have been justified. But the Captain himself turned the tide by flinging a burning branch into the wigwams, an action emulated by his men, and soon the whole interior of the fort was a howling furnace. Those Indians who managed to get out were picked off at leisure by Mason's men, who had retired outside and ringed the fort as soon as it was ablaze. The destruction was total. Some estimates place it as high as 1,000 Indians killed, men, women and children, but probably it was somewhat less. Cotton Mather estimated that "no less than six hundred Pequot souls were brought down to hell that day," while an eyewitness wrote with satisfaction of the Indians "frying in the fire, and streams of blood quenching the same, and horrible was the stink and scent thereof: but the victory was a sweet sacrifice, and they gave prayer thereof to God," who, they confidently believed, approved this sanguinary bath.

On the way back to their boats, Captain Mason and his men encountered a war party of 300 Pequots, returning to the fort after an expedition of their own. Now the slaughter might have been reversed, or at least avenged, but the militiamen fought a skillful rearguard action, putting themselves between the Pequots and the water, and got back to their boats with scarcely any casualties to add to the two men killed at the fort.

Mason was, if anything, a thorough man. The Governor had told him to exterminate the Pequots, if possible, and he did. The war party he had encountered on the way back was the bulk of what remained of the nation, and after resupplying his force, Mason set about with energy to hunt the others down, ranging the country between New London and Saybrook until he had either killed or captured every surviving Pequot. The captives were sent in chains to Bermuda as slaves, except those who remained in the same status in Connecticut and Massachusetts. Of the few who escaped Mason, nearly all found refuge with other tribes, but Sassacus made the mistake of appealing to the Mohawks for sanctuary. These practical men cut off his head and sent it to Boston as a proof of their loyalty.

The destruction of the Pequot nation had, understandably, a depressing effect on the resentments and ambitions of other tribes. It was plain that these white men were not going to be pushed into the sea, consequently a policy of uneasy accommodation was pursued by the Indians. It lasted for forty years—four decades during which the growing white settlements continued to push out into Indian lands to the accompaniment of cheating by the traders, forced unilateral treaties, and an overall contempt which generated a smoldering rage in the tribes up and down New England.

If the Indians were so long in striking back, it was simply that they lacked a strong leader. The influence of the aging Massasoit, perennial friend of the white man, was still strong. But Massasoit died and was succeeded in 1660 by his son, Philip. In him the Indians at last had their leader.

Philip (or Metacomet, to use his Indian name) was a man of exceptional intelligence and resourcefulness. He had an immediate ally in his brother Alexander, or Wamsutta, another strong figure, but like the other leaders before him, Philip understood that he must have the united and enthusiastic support of other tribes if he hoped to wage a successful war. Philip viewed the Indian situation realistically. He realized it was virtually hopeless, but he held the dogged hope, as so many Indian leaders would in later years, that if only the tribes would unite they would be powerful enough to drive the white man back. Certainly, he knew, it had better be done as soon as possible in New England, or it would be forever too late.

Consequently Philip laid the groundwork for war in the general pattern of what had been done before, but he did it with much greater skill. Small wonder that he was known as King Philip. He and his envoys were so persuasive that even the Narragansetts, who had never shown any enthusiasm for fighting white men, agreed to join the secret army now forming. That was a highly important acquisition, since the 4,000 Narragansetts comprised nearly a quarter of the 20,000 or so Indians remaining in the southern part of New England. There were 3,000 Nipmucks and 1,000, more or less, of the belligerent Wampanoags. The remaining 12,000 were scattered among more than a half-dozen tribes.

These 20,000 Indians faced an already numerically superior population of 17,000 Massachusetts citizens, 10,000 Connecticut colonists, 5,000 members of the Plymouth Colony and about 3,000 Rhode Islanders. Obviously, Philip would need all the strength he could muster if he were to save the New England tribes from being crushed between the westward-moving colonists on the East and the mighty Iroquois Confederacy to the West. Philip saw clearly that the time had come to defend these ancient lands from the white man's church, laws, ideas and physical presence, all of which represented the colonist's profound conviction that God had ordained him to live on the land of the Indians, who in any case were an inferior people, without rights under English common law.

For their part, the colonists were not unaware that something was brewing among the Indians. They summoned Alexander to Duxbury in 1662 and tried to extract information from him. When he died a few days later of a fever, his widow and probably Philip as well believed he had been poisoned. In any case, the Indians generally blamed the white man for Alexander's death.

In 1671 it was Philip's turn to be summoned for questioning, this time to Taunton. As sole chief of the Wampanoags, he was the chief suspect in the growing unrest the colonists could feel among the Indians. The Plymouth authorities treated Philip as a small-town Southern sheriff might treat a Negro suspected of civil rights activities. They demanded that he and his party surrender their guns on the spot, and that their fellow tribesmen give up all the guns they possessed as soon as possible. Then they demanded peace, and presented Philip with a treaty to sign, filled with the usual unilateral clauses.

Angry as he was, Philip had no choice at the moment. His plans were not yet mature. He signed the treaty, agreed to give up the weapons and went home. Not unexpectedly, the other Indians refused to give up their guns and Philip was soon called back, treated even more rudely and compelled to sign a more humiliating treaty.

For four years the affronted King held the peace and his temper, until a bizarre incident in January, 1675, precipitated the war he had prepared for so long. John Sassamon, a Christian Indian, was found murdered beneath the ice of a pond southwest of Plymouth. Sassamon had studied at Harvard, returned from the white community to serve as Philip's secretary, so to speak, then changed his loyalties again and gone back to Plymouth, where he had become a preacher and, as it proved, a spy, since he took advantage of his status and his old friendships to frequent the Indian towns as well as the white communities. Shortly before his murder, it turned out, he had told the authorities everything he knew about Philip's war plans.

On the testimony of an Indian witness, three Wampanoags were arrested and hanged for the murder. When the rope slipped on one of them, he sought a reprieve by gasping out a confession, but the authorities pulled him up again anyway. One of those hanged was a trusted counselor of Philip's.

Whether or not the victims were guilty—and it was not improbable that they were, no doubt punishing Sassamon's spying by the immemorial method—their death infuriated the Wampanoags. Philip may not have been ready for war, but he could no longer hold back his tribesmen. The storm broke at last, over Swansea, Massachusetts, on June 24, 1675. It was an inevitable first target, since the Indians could not enter the peninsula and swarm up into Massachusetts and Rhode Island without first overrunning this town.

Swansea had no chance; it was looted and burned, and nine of its settlers were killed before the Indians swept onward, meting out the same treatment in the next few days to the towns of Taunton, Middleborough and Dartmouth. Those who survived in these villages sent frantic alarms to Plymouth and to Boston, where 110 men responded in the first three hours to the drum beats on the Common for volunteers. Captain Samuel Mosely, commanding this force, moved out of the city only two days after the destruction of Swansea and two days after that he and his men stood in the ruined settlement.

On the morning following his arrival, Mosely was challenged by a superior force of Wampanoags, who dared him to fight. The Captain was not a man to refuse a dare, which apparently astonished the Indians, who fled after a brief skirmish. Mosely pursued them as far as Philip's village, where he found nothing but the staring heads of eight white men, hung on poles. These victims were avenged two days later by a young lieutenant bringing up troops from Rehoboth to Swansea. Surprising a party of Indians, he killed a few before they could escape and, reversing the usual procedure, scalped them (the first scalps of the war) and sent his grisly trophies back to Boston.

The war produced new leaders. One was a Plymouth soldier named Benjamin Church, residing with his wife at Little Compton, Rhode Island, and until then a sincere friend of the Indians. But Church was outraged by the savagery of the Swansea affair and, one may assume, seriously concerned for the safety of the colonies. Putting friendship aside, he took the field and joined the other commanders in what had now become a vast game, whose object was to find Philip.

The fast-moving King, more elusive than the Pimpernel, was believed by Church's superiors to be on the Mount Hope peninsula, jutting down into Narragansett Bay. Church thought he was on Pocasset Neck, and advised concentrating the colonial force there. He was overruled and the other officers set off on a fruitless expedition to Mount Hope. As soon as they had departed, Philip emerged from Pocasset and began marching toward Plymouth, plundering and burning as he went.

Hoping to circumvent him, Church split his forces and with only nineteen men advanced on Tiverton, another of the numerous land fingers poking into the Bay. There he encountered no less than 300 Indians, who nearly massacred his little force and would have if a sloop had not suddenly appeared offshore and removed the besieged white men by canoe, two at a time, in a Dunkirk lasting six hours, including the initial engagement, during which not a single one of Church's men was killed. The indomitable Captain, who had commanded his tiny army with extraordinary bravery, was the last to leave, his hair creased by a bullet.

The other half of his force, oddly, had gone through somewhat the same ordeal. They had been trapped in an old waterfront house farther along the shore, and had also been taken off in boats.

In all this confusion, the quarry had escaped. The white men pursued him with whoop and halloo through the Rhode Island and Massachusetts landscape, until at last, near the end of July, it appeared that they had trapped the King and a large body of his men in a swamp near Taunton. But Philip cleverly led his pursuers into the swamp and ambushed them. They barely escaped. Meanwhile, the wily King slipped out undetected, leaving the unsuspecting militia to besiege the empty swamp—once more against the advice of Captain Church, who asserted bluntly that it was foolish to build a fort where there was nothing to defend and no one to attack.

Having floated his men out of the swamp in a flotilla of canoes, Philip slipped inland to the Connecticut River country, where he joined with the Nipmucks in a destructive march up into Massachusetts. There he besieged Brookfield, whose inhabitants were saved only by the timely arrival of fifty mounted men commanded by a seventy-year-old veteran, Major Simon Willard, but not before every house in the village had been burned except the small fortress in which the settlers had taken shelter. The rescuers swept into the

ruins of Brookfield on the third day, and in the sharp struggle which
ensued, eighty Nipmucks were killed.

Philip's raiding parties ranged from settlement to settlement,
spreading ruin and death. Hadley was attacked, then Northfield and
Deerfield, Medfield, Wrentham and a dozen others. By this time the
colonies were thoroughly alarmed. It appeared that Philip might
threaten even the larger cities, particularly because the Narragansetts,
convinced by Philip's successes, finally forsook their neutrality and
joined him.

An army was quickly organized to put into the field against Philip.
A force of 520 men came from Massachusetts, 150 more from
Plymouth and 300 from Connecticut, along with 150 rather reluctant
Mohicans. Governor Josiah Winslow, of Plymouth, was in command
of this army, whose slightly more than 1,000 men were called upon
to confront the considerable force Philip already had—a force which
had just been augmented by 3,500 Narragansetts, who were concentrated in a virtually impregnable fort at Kingston, Rhode Island.

Winslow saw that this fort must be the main target. There was
little point in pursuing the elusive Philip about the countryside if
the Indians' largest concentration of strength, and the only one capable of doing fatal damage to the big settlements, could be successfully attacked. It would not be an easy task, the Governor realized.
The Narragansetts had built their fortification with an engineering
skill that would have done credit to their more sophisticated white
enemy. It was on high ground in the midst of a swamp, reached only
by a log bridge and surrounded by thick, firm palisades not likely
to be breached. Winslow marched his army against this rugged bas-
tion on December 19, 1675.

It was the strategy of Captain Mason and the Pequot fort all over
again. Winslow led the Massachusetts Bay men in an assault on the
front gate, while Captain Church took the Plymouth and Connecticut
men around the fort and attacked at the rear. The Governor's men
were thrown back by a curtain of fire which almost devastated them,
but Church was more successful. Wounded three times, he forced the
rear gate and led his men into the village.

There was a quick strategy conference. Church, in a true humanitarian spirit, was against burning the village, with its vital supplies

of corn, but he was persuaded to put the torch to the wigwams and, as Mason had done, he ordered them set ablaze—a giant torch of 600 Indian habitations flaming against the black night sky over the swamp. Once again the Indians had to flee for their lives, and fight as they sought to escape. They fought with the utmost bravery, retreating slowly into the swamp with Winslow's army in pursuit, until they reached open country. There the survivors melted away.

It was a decisive victory. Six hundred Narragansetts, including twenty chiefs, lay dead. Winslow had lost only eighty men, and about twice that many wounded. Others on both sides no doubt lost their lives in the bitter cold which was the relentless enemy of white and red men alike.

With this engagement, the war had reached its turning point, but it was not over. Philip was still at large, and no victory could be final until he was captured or killed. Apparently he thought himself in no immediate danger, for his men planted crops in the deserted fields of Deerfield and gave such clear evidence of taking over the village permanently that a hundred men were sent to dislodge them. A Boston captain named Turner, who was in command, achieved another stunning victory in a dawn surprise attack which cost Philip 300 men and resulted in the death of only a single militiaman. But the victors were in turn surprised by a war party of Indians which had been within gunshot of the engagement, and as a result Turner's force had to fight hard to save themselves from extinction, losing a third of their men, including the Captain himself.

Such was the give-and-take in this last stage of King Philip's War, as it rambled about the fields and forests of Rhode Island and Connecticut. Sometimes it was impossible to tell the pursuers from the pursued. But the inevitable end was approaching, and Philip could only postpone it by furious stabs here and there, as more soldiers were impressed by the colonial governments and all trade with the Indians was cut off.

Captain Church, having recovered from his wounds, was now in the field again, leading the chase to hunt down Philip.

Church attacked Philip's headquarters on August 1, killed or captured 130 Indians including the King's wife and son, and seized a large quantity of wampum. Philip himself had escaped with a few followers, who left him one by one in the days that followed until he was almost alone, a desperate but still proud fugitive, skulking in the swamps. When one of the faithful who remained urged him to surrender, Philip committed the worst crime of his life, which also proved to be his greatest mistake. He clubbed the unfortunate brave to death, and the brother of the victim, enraged and probably fearful of his own life, went to Captain Church and guided a party of militia to Philip's last hiding place. On the morning of August 12, 1676, the chase ended.

The King eluded the detachment sent to seize him and dashed from the swamp, only to meet, head-on, an Englishman accompanied by an Indian. Ironically, it was the Indian who killed King Philip with two musketballs at pointblank range, after the Englishman's gun had missed fire.

Sometime humanitarian though he may have been, Captain Church saw in the tragic figure of the slain King only "a doleful, great, naked, dirty beast," and ordered him beheaded and quartered (again with irony) by an Indian executioner attached to the colonial army. Thus, killed and hacked up by his own people, all that remained of King Philip—his gory head—was carried to Plymouth and displayed on a gibbet for the next two decades as an object lesson to other chiefs who might be considering resistance to the white conquest of America. One of his hands was similarly on exhibition in Boston, and what was left of his dismembered body was left to rot where he fell, because the Plymouth authorities would not permit its burial.

The war Philip had planned so carefully and fought with such bravery petered out with a few desultory skirmishes in New Hampshire during the year after his death. The price of peace was heavy: several thousand of the colonists had been killed, twelve of their settlements burned, and 100,000 pounds of debt had been incurred to put down the rebellion.

As for the Indians, they had lost the war and their last great leader in New England as well. Worse, they had lost what successive tribes would lose in the westward march of the white man's civilization—the privilege of living as free men.

King Philip's War left a bitter heritage. In the coming struggle between France and England for possession of North America, the treatment of the Indian tribes by the colonies, in New England and elsewhere, pushed valuable allies into the willing arms of the French. The long narrative of suspicion and hatred, of treachery and death was only beginning.

# The Struggle Between France and England

T HE SEVEN YEARS' WAR was a vast drama played upon a world stage, an epic contest between the British and French empires in which the struggle for North America was no more than a sideshow, despite its fateful import. We call its American phase today by an inaccurate and meaningless name, the French and Indian War, and our principal concern with it is the role it played in launching the career of George Washington.

Yet it remains one of the most dramatic wars in our national history, much neglected and little understood today in spite of what Francis Parkman and recent writers have done to underscore its historic importance. It was a giant bush war, fought up and down the eastern half of the continent by a motley collection of antagonists—raw militia from the colonies, ragtag regulars from Britain, the largest Indian armies yet seen, and eventually by the best men and commanders the two antagonists were able to send over, when it was realized how important the outcome would be. For at first, in its supreme effort to preserve an empire from the encroachments of the French, Britain did not seem to understand what was at stake in the wilderness across the ocean. It was nothing less than whether the continent would be French and Catholic, or English and Prot-

Iroquois

estant. Religion and commercial greed were intermingled in the fierce emotions aroused by the war.

In this complicated and farflung conflict, the Indians appeared to be the true losers—as usual. The ground England and France were fighting over was, in fact, theirs. The wisest of the Indian leaders never doubted that, in the end, when the shooting was over, it would not be the Indians who emerged with wealth and power, no matter which side won. Two great nations were fighting over *their* land, and strangely enough, these nations expected, or at least hoped for, loyalty from those who were about to lose what they possessed. The result was a history of treachery and shifting allegiances unmatched in our national story.

At the center of this drama within a drama was the mighty Iroquois Confederacy, the most highly developed Indian culture on the continent. In some respects it was more than a century and a half ahead of the white colonies. The women of the Confederacy could vote and inherit property and, in political structure, the tribes of the Confederacy had fashioned something remarkably close to the framework that later united the colonies. It was a loose federation, in which elected representatives met in the Long House to decide common problems. The members also contributed to the common defense, on occasions when the Confederacy felt itself threatened.

There was nothing east of the Mississippi to threaten it seriously. The nations of the Confederacy—Mohawk, Oneida, Cayuga, Seneca, Onondaga and, in time, the Tuscaroras—were the unquestioned rulers of a territory which stretched from Albany to the Great Lakes. Yet the Iroquois considered themselves surrounded by enemies, and from time to time they chastised their neighbors, which were the tribes speaking the various Algonquin languages. These spread out over what is now northeastern United States and Canada, from Nova Scotia to the upper Great Lakes, southward as far as Kentucky, back east through Pennsylvania, Virginia and New Jersey, and up through New England to Nova Scotia again.

Along the undefined boundaries of the Algonquin empire, which had no political or military organization, the Iroquois fought desultory wars. They chopped away at their southern neighbors, the Andastes, who lived along the Susquehanna, until a smallpox epidemic removed them as a threat, which had never been more than imaginary in any case. On Lake Erie's shores, the Eries and the Neutral Nation were too weak to be a menace. In New England, what remained of the tribes after King Philip's War—Mohicans, Pequots, Narragansetts, Wampanoags, Massachusetts and Penacooks —were controlled by only one of the Five Nations, the Mohawks, who kept them terrified. In the West there was a vague impinging on the territory of the powerful Illinois, who had a confederacy of their own, but these mighty neighbors respected each other enough to confine themselves to occasional raids-in-force.

There was only one other Algonquian nation, the Hurons, living in western Ontario and along the eastern shores of Lake Huron. They represented no more of a threat to the Iroquois than any of the others, but for reasons which remain inexplicable to this day, the Confederacy selected them as its prime target and in about 1630 they began a war of annihilation against the Hurons which continued for forty-five years until they had reduced this prosperous nation of 22,000 people to a ragged band of fugitives seeking shelter wherever they could find it on the Upper Great Lakes. The cost of this senseless war was entirely out of proportion to anything the Iroquois could possibly have gained. Their own strength of more than 3,000 warriors was cut to 1,400, not including 800 Hurons, Eries and other captives who had been adopted.

There were more serious consequences. By nullifying the strength of the other tribes, the Confederacy had precluded any chance of uniting them in a coalition powerful enough to resist the westward expansion of the colonists. Moreover, although they stood supreme among all the Indians of the East, they had weakened themselves for the struggle which now began to develop as the French pressed down upon them from Canada and the English surged upward from the south and east.

Both the French and English were adroitly dividing them wherever and however they could, seducing them with religion, money, goods or rum, or any combination of these which might be effective. Thus, when a French and Indian raiding party swept down out of Canada in the winter of 1689 to attack the British stronghold of Albany, there were ninety-six Christian Iroquois in the expedition. These Indians could not have been persuaded to fight their own people, but they were happy to set upon the English.

Other Iroquois, however, had been attracted first by the Dutch and then by the English merchants of Albany and New York, and had developed such a profitable trade with them that they were quite willing to join their partners in fighting any effort by the French to intrude upon it. If the Iroquois were compelled to make a choice between French and English, there were many more who would have chosen the English, even though their record of honest dealing was hardly better than the French. This general allegiance of the Confederacy was more or less legitimized by the Treaty of Utrecht in 1713, which climaxed several decades of desultory border warfare between England and France. The treaty ceded Arcadia, Newfoundland and the Hudson Bay Territory to England and, in passing, acknowledged the Five Nations to be British subjects. No one, of course, had consulted the Confederacy on this matter, but its members raised no serious objection.

The treaty failed in what should have been its chief objective, that is, to define the boundary between the colonies and French Canada. Thus, skirmishes between the two nations continued until 1744, when King George's War (or the War of the Austrian Succession, as it was known in its more important European phase) served as an excuse for the French to swoop down once more with their Indian allies on the northern settlements in the colonies, pillaging and killing. That period ended with the successful British assault against the French fortress of Louisburg on Cape Breton Island, until then considered impregnable. But the Treaty of Aix-la-Chapelle in 1748 restored to both countries most of what had been taken away before, including Louisburg, and the colonists were left with their rage and frustration over this senseless turn of events. Needless to say, the treaty also failed to settle boundaries or old disputes, and did not even begin to deal with the most dangerous issue between the two great powers—who was to own the rich valleys of the Ohio and the Mississippi.

Thus the stage was set for a real war, to which the previous conflicts had been only a prelude. In the coming struggle, the Iroquois hoped they could remain neutral. They did not consider themselves really British subjects, much less the "British slaves" that the French contemptuously called them. They had no love for either side, and they were conscious that temporarily, at least, they held a precarious balance of power between the two nations. They acted as middlemen–agents between the English buyers of the East and the Indian fur trappers and sellers of the Great Lakes, and were consequently valuable to the British. While the French would have liked to get this trade for themselves, they did not dare antagonize the Iroquois for fear the whole Confederacy would side openly with the British and present a united front that might well be unbeatable.

Nevertheless, conflict was inevitable. Two great colonial powers confronted each other along a frontier stretching from Quebec to the prize they both wanted, the Ohio Valley. Church and State had united in Canada to carry out a grand scheme that would establish a string of French posts from Quebec to the Mississippi and thence to the Gulf. (The Jesuits meant to go all the way to Peru.) The strategy of the French high command was to execute a vast sweeping movement, with its hinge in Quebec, which would close like a door against the English colonies, pushing them back against the Alleghenies or possibly over and beyond to the Atlantic itself. In this far-flung campaign, Indian allies were to play a major part.

Such was the French dream of North American empire. Opposed to it was a group of quarrelsome colonials, who could barely govern their own territories and were always embroiled in disputes with each other. The Iroquois stood in the way, too, but the French were content to have them neutral, unless they could be wooed to join the grand plan. Obviously, there was good reason for the French to feel confident.

There was little to shake their confidence in the obscure skirmish which touched off the war. The French had been busy trying to secure the Ohio Valley and had made good progress in that direction by capturing the Ohio Company's fort on the strategic site where Pittsburgh rises today, and renaming it Fort Duquesne. They had built another on the present site of Erie, Pennsylvania. Using these two strongholds as anchor points, they meant to begin closing the door by taking possession of everything possible from the Alleghenies westward.

In this critical phase of the larger contest, the Indians once more stood in the middle. Their center of population had already shifted from the Mohawk Valley to the Ohio, as a result of constant pressure from the East. Both the French and English had been wooing them, and for a time it appeared that the English traders were better at it. The French had improved their position in 1752 by sending the noted French *voyageur,* Charles Langlade, at the head of a canoe fleet of 250 Ottawas and Ojibwas to attack the seat of English intrigue, a place called Pickawillany, today near the site of Piqua, Ohio. A chief with the unlikely name of Old Britain, or the Demoiselle, as he was often called, lived there and generated plots against the French with the traders who gathered at his place.

Langlade struck the Demoiselle's headquarters early on a June morning, killing fourteen Indians, including the chief, stabbing a wounded trader to death and capturing three others. After this morning's work, his men occupied the rest of the day by boiling Old Britain's body, which they had for supper that night.

This had been the opening gun in the French campaign of conquest. It was followed by a far more impressive expedition—1,500 men, who floated down the St. Lawrence to Lake Erie, bent on securing the Ohio. It was this expedition that had built the fort at Erie, naming it Presq'Isle, and another on nearby French Creek, which they called Le Boeuf. The forts gave them a supply link to Duquesne.

These moves alarmed Governor Dinwiddie of Virginia, although they seemed to have little enough effect on the governors or legislators of the other colonies in the path of the French. It remained for Dinwiddie to do something about it by sending a young major of militia, George Washington, with a message for the veteran officer, Legardeur de Saint-Pierre, who was in command at Le Boeuf. The message was couched in the language of diplomacy, but its meaning was clear. The French were ordered, in effect, to withdraw because the land they were occupying was English land. Neither Dinwiddie nor Washington understood that the French honestly believed the land was theirs by right of discovery, since the explorer La Salle in the previous century had claimed virtually all of Eastern America for the French King.

It was on his rugged winter journey to Le Boeuf from Williamsburg, and on the return, that young Washington learned about Indians at first hand. What he learned did not incline him to love them. He understood how important it was to win their support and, inexperienced as he was, he did his best to negotiate the allegiance of Half-

King, the Indian leader in the region, who seemed to be the best hope of the English. But Washington saw how adroit the French were at wooing the Indians with rum and presents, and he saw too how uncertain the loyalties of the red men could be. There was implanted in him then a distrust of the Indian that was fortified by later experiences and led to his stern policy toward them as President.

After Washington returned to Williamsburg with the French reply, which was in essence a plain defiance, events moved rapidly toward a showdown. Dinwiddie sent Washington into the field as a Lieutenant-Colonel of militia, in command of a reluctant and poorly equipped force with which he was supposed to oust the French from their strong position at Duquesne. In pursuit of this vain objective, Washington encountered a French patrol at the Great Meadows, not far from where Uniontown, Pennsylvania, stands today and killed the French commander, Jumonville, along with nine of his men.

It was this relatively trivial skirmish which, as Parkman put it, "set the world on fire" and led directly to the declared outbreak of the Seven Years' War, two years later. For the French asserted that Jumonville had been leading a peace mission (although captured documents proved that it was nothing of the kind) and they called Washington an assassin. Jumonville's brother, the Sieur de Villiers, hurried from Montreal with reinforcements and an expedition was assembled at Fort Duquesne to punish the English.

How successful the French had been in enlisting Indian allies could be seen in the words addressed to this expedition by Contrecoeur, the commandant at Fort Duquesne, before they marched away: ". . . And now, men of the Saut St. Louis, men of the Lake of Two Mountains, Hurons, Abenakis, Iroquois of La Présentation, Nipissings, Algonquins and Ottawas—I invite you all by this belt of wampum to join your French father and help him to crush the assassins. Take this hatchet, and with it two barrels of wine for a feast." And he added, speaking to the Delawares, who had not yet made up their minds, "By these four strings of wampum I invite you, if you are true children of Onontio [as the Governor of Canada was called by the Indians] to follow the example of your brethren."

Washington, meanwhile, had much less impressive support. After the affair at Great Meadows, he had retreated a short way and built, with the greatest speed, a defense he called Fort Necessity, which was little more than an entrenched camp. Half-King joined him there, with a noted queen named Alequippa, thirty families and forty warriors from the Ohio country, who later turned out to be spies.

In the end, however, it was not the superior French strength nor their Indian allies that decided the issue, but inadequate supplies and a steady downpour of rain that soaked the colonists' powder and muskets and left them defenseless. They were compelled to surrender and abandon the fort on July 4, 1754.

This modest success strengthened the French cause considerably by persuading doubtful Indian allies of their strength and giving them time to consolidate their positions. It also gave the Iroquois an additional importance. Now they were all that stood between the colonies of the seaboard and the Ohio Valley, and they were potentially a barrier to further French expeditions from Canada. Yet the colonies were so disunited, and so inept in their dealings with the Indians, that they did nothing while the French seduced the Senecas and Onondagas; nor could they prevent the Dutch settlers of the Hudson River Valley from further angering the Mohawks by constantly nibbling away at their territory. Moreover, they stupidly antagonized the great Mohawk chief, Hendrick, one of the most impressive Indian leaders on the continent, when he came to New York and attempted to get some compensation for the wrongs his tribe had suffered.

Only the efforts of one man saved the English from losing the Indians entirely. That man was Sir William Johnson, an almost legendary figure in the Mohawk Valley while he was still alive. He had created there a rural barony, living like a noble in the splendid house he had built at Amsterdam, yet beloved by Indians from one end of the Valley to the other because he could live as they did with equal ease. Hendrick's daughter had once been his mistress (they were married by Indian law) and another famous chief, Joseph Brant, had given him his lovely seventeen-year-old daughter, Molly, as a wife.

This genial, ambitious, redhaired Irish giant, who liked good living and believed in fairness and justice to all men, whatever their color or status, had such control over the Iroquois nations that he was able to pacify them and save the English from themselves. The Indian state of mind was expressed eloquently by an Onondaga chief

Mohawk Chiefs

who declared to Johnson: "We don't know what you Christians, English and French, intend. We are so hemmed in by you both that we have hardly a hunting place left. In a little while, if we find a bear in a tree, there will immediately appear an owner of the land to claim the property and hinder us from killing it, by which we live. We are so perplexed between you that we hardly know what to say or think."

Johnson's anxiety to resolve this bewilderment led to the calling of a grand council at Albany, after the provincial governors had responded to his urgent pleas. The Iroquois leaders met with representatives of New York, Pennsylvania, Maryland and the New England colonies—Benjamin Franklin was among the delegates—and argued their cause, while the commissioners sought to win them to the British side.

Hendrick delivered a speech to the delegates which was to make him an even more distinguished figure. Always friendly to the English, this dignified chief who had once been presented at court to Queen Anne, promised first to "renew and brighten the covenant chain" binding the Iroquois to the English, but then he said: "You ask why we are so dispersed. The reason is that you have neglected us for these three years past. You have thus thrown us behind your back," he went on, throwing a stick behind him to illustrate, "whereas the French are a subtle and vigilant people, always using their utmost endeavors to seduce and bring us over to them. The governor of Virginia and the governor of Canada are quarreling about lands which belong to us, and their quarrel may end in our destruction."

Then Hendrick turned the full power of his sarcasm on the listening colonists. "Look about your country and see," he advised them. "You have no fortifications; no, not even in this city. It is but a step from Canada here, and the French may come and turn you out of doors. You desire us to speak from the bottom of our hearts and we shall do it. Look at the French: they are men; they are fortifying everywhere. But you are all like women, bare and open, without fortifications."

This speech, later reprinted and widely discussed in England, had an immediate effect on the delegates, who could not help feeling that Hendrick had spoken the truth about their situation. In response, Franklin laid before the congress his plan for a union of the colonies, which foreshadowed the creating of the American nation. But the time was too soon. The Crown thought this plan gave the colonies too much power, and the individual colonies had no intention of giving up any sovereignty. Consequently the only positive result of the congress was that it convinced the colonial governments of their danger and impelled them to make an effort to save themselves.

They importuned the Crown to rescue them from the French, and the British ministers responded by sending Major General Edward Braddock, in command of two regiments totaling 1,000 men. Two hundred more were to be enlisted in Virginia.

The often-told story of General Braddock's expeditionary force has seldom done credit to this brave officer, except when the accounts have been given by professional historians. In the popular mind he comes down to us as a pigheaded Britisher who would not have lost his campaign and his life if he had only listened to Washington. He has been commonly pictured as a man of ungovernable temper who would not listen to advice and came to a disastrous end because of poor generalship.

If Braddock was often in a temper—and that much was true—he had ample reason to be. A highly competent professional soldier who had served with the best armies in Europe, he found himself late in his career in command of two regiments of riffraff regulars from his own country, and another of colonial militiamen who were little better and could not be depended upon to fight a minute after their enlistment terms ran out. He was confronted by problems of supply that he could scarcely bring himself to imagine. The population he had come to save showed little inclination to act in its own behalf. They cheated his quartermaster outrageously, and habitually produced too little, too late. Politically, he found the provincial governors a bickering, jealous lot, and in the case of Pennsylvania, downright opposed to his efforts. He liked Washington and took him into his official family of young officers, but the Virginian had no authority and could not help him with these larger problems; in any case, he did not have the experience to cope with them, having tried vainly to do so in his own small command.

The Crown, in sum, had given Braddock an almost impossible assignment, to be accomplished with far less than adequate means. To the unhappy general it must have seemed that he was swimming through a sea of molasses. Nevertheless, he pursued his dogged course with energy and no little talent. As for his military ability, later scholarship has established that he did everything a commander could do or should have done to prevent the famous ambush, and in fact he was not ambushed in the conventional sense. His forward elements made contact with the advancing French well ahead of the main body, and if his men had known anything of wilderness fighting, a subject of which the general was equally and understandably ignorant, the massacre would not have occurred.

The enemy he met was predominantly Indian, the most formidable collection of warriors yet assembled to confront white men. There were Caughnawagas, Abenakis and Hurons; mission Indians, including some Christian Iroquois; Potawatomies and Ojibwas, under the command of the redoubtable Langlade; Shawnees and Mingoes from deep in the Ohio Valley; and a detachment of Ottawas under a young and ambitious chief, Pontiac, whose name would soon be known to everyone in Eastern America.

To this savage force, the French contributed only seventy-two regulars from Fort Duquesne, where the expedition had assembled, and thirty-six officers, to which 146 Canadians had been added. Contrecoeur, the fort's commandant, was in supreme command, but the force was to be led by Captains Beaujeu, Dumas and Ligonier. (Beaujeu had been sent to succeed Contrecoeur, and therefore was in actual command.)

The French officers, after a council, concluded that it would be better to go out and meet the advancing British rather than stay in the fort and allow themselves to be besieged. But when this idea was offered to the Indians, they rejected it flatly. "Do you want to die, my father, and sacrifice us besides?" they asked Beaujeu.

The French captain made exactly the right response. "I am determined to meet the English," he said. "What! Will you let your father go alone?"

That was the kind of appeal they understood. When the column was ready to march next morning, the Indians were prepared. It was their victory, too, in the slaughter that followed, because they were fighting the kind of war they knew best against an enemy that had no idea of how to defend itself. There were acts of exceptional bravery on both sides. The courageous Beaujeu fell in the first exchange and Dumas, taking command, rallied his momentarily wavering army, until the Indians could flank the British column and begin the murderous enfilading fire that eventually caused them to panic. If the British regulars ran in terror before long, it was not hard to understand, but less could be said for the North Carolina militia. The Virginia militia fought well, but nothing could have saved the day after the debacle began. Washington's personal heroism was almost beyond belief. So weak from a severe illness that he could scarcely sit in the saddle that morning, he was in the thick of the engagement, had two horses shot from beneath him, helped remove the stricken Braddock from the field, and then rode all night through the black forest, with the cries of the wounded in his ears, carrying Braddock's call for help to the regiment bringing up the rear.

When the expedition counted its losses, they were indeed staggering—853 men killed and wounded, more than seventy-five per cent of the total force. They had escaped complete annihilation by a miracle.

Braddock's campaign had been part of a master plan devised by the Duke of Cumberland to drive the troublesome French out of America. While Braddock was traveling his course to ruin, other commanders were occupied with other aspects of the plan. One was Sir William Johnson, who had been made a general as well as placed in charge of Indian affairs. It was Johnson's mission to march against the French stronghold of Crown Point, and for that purpose he hoped to assemble an overwhelming Indian army by exercising his celebrated influence with them. Calling a meeting at his great house, he was gratified to find himself playing host to 1,100 Indians, all of them apparently ready for the war trail. Yet, when the time came to march, only 300 appeared. Disappointed though he was, Johnson knew the reason. The Iroquois anticipated they would be called upon to meet their fellow tribesmen who had gone north to join the French, and they had no heart for it.

Fortunately, Johnson did not have to depend on his Indian friends for an army. Although he was without military experience, he had been placed in command of nearly 4,000 New England farmers who were as green as he was at the art of war. These militia and the Indians regarded each other with mutual contempt. Hendrick, Johnson's good friend, was doubtful about the expedition from the first, and when the general would have divided his army, Hendrick warned him against it. The chief by this time was nearly seventy, so old and fat he had difficulty getting into the saddle, but he knew more about warfare than all the others combined. Of Johnson's force he remarked, "If they are to be killed, they are too many; if they are to fight, they are too few."

Opposing the provincial army was a German, General Dieskau, of high professional competence, who had enjoyed a distinguished career in Europe but now, for the first time in his life, found himself commanding Indians, an experience he was not enjoying. "They drive us crazy from morning till night," General Dieskau wrote. "There is no end to their demands. They have already eaten five oxen and as many hogs, without counting the kegs of brandy they have drunk. In short, one needs the patience of an angel to get on with these devils; and yet one must always force himself to seem pleased with them." These were the Iroquois whom Hendrick and his warriors were so reluctant to meet.

The forces of these two troubled generals met in the engagement known as the Battle of Lake George. Hendrick lost his life in the first volley. Legardeur de Saint-Pierre, who had met Washington at Le Boeuf and now commanded Dieskau's Indians, was also killed. The Indians on both sides showed little inclination to battle each other, although they were quite ready to slay any white man they encountered, and would have done away with the wounded and captured Dieskau, as he lay in Johnson's tent, if Sir William had not prevented it.

In the end the victory was Johnson's, but his provincial troops had had enough of fighting. He could not persuade them to stay together and advance on Crown Point; as a result, the expedition had to be entered as another failure.

The third phase of Cumberland's plan was an assault on Fort Niagara, which was to be led by the redoubtable Massachusetts governor, William Shirley, whose son Will had been one of Braddock's aides and had shared the General's fate. Shirley, who was the epitome of energy and purpose, was no more successful as a general than the others. His expedition ended in failure without a single battle, because Braddock's captured papers had disclosed Cumberland's entire plan to the French and they were so well prepared to meet Shirley and his army that the governor realized it would be folly to attack Niagara and the other French strong point on Lake Ontario, Fort Frontenac.

Thus the campaigns of 1755 came to an indecisive end, with the French still in possession of all their forts. But in the following year the two great powers declared war on each other officially, and the complexion of the conflict in America changed at once. The plight of the Indians was lost in the dramatic sweep of large armies across the face of the continent. Commanders of stature appeared on the scene: Montcalm in command of the French forces and Earl Loudon at first at the head of the British. In 1757, Montcalm assembled a terrifying army of 8,000 regulars and more than 1,600 Indians and attacked Fort William Henry, at the head of Lake George. The veteran Colonel Munro, who was in command, had to capitulate, and in spite of everything the French General could do, Montcalm's Indian allies slaughtered the women and children, the sick and wounded, and eighty of the troops who had surrendered.

During the march down Lake George, Montcalm had been irritated by his Indian legions, just as Dieskau and every other European commander had been. Like them, he could build no bridges from the military tradition which he had known all his life to this strange and wholly alien culture. In fact, the milling, restless throng of nearly 2,000 Indians in Montcalm's army was far from homogeneous. The French had gathered them in from points as far distant as the Mississippi, and the Iowas, farthest from home, found no white and few Algonquin-speaking interpreters who could understand their language.

In the end, Montcalm and his officers found themselves frightened by this savage assemblage. After the massacre at Fort Edward, which was appalling enough in European eyes, the Indians appeared at Montreal with 200 prisoners that Montcalm had been unable to take from them. Vaudreuil tried stern remonstrance first, without effect, then made a ghastly mistake by exchanging some kegs of brandy for a few of the prisoners. Quickly drunk on this powerful brew, the Indians, before the horrified eyes of the governor and the citizens of Montreal, killed one of their prisoners, put him into a kettle and compelled other prisoners to eat him. Another eyewitness swore they made mothers eat their own children. Afterward they roamed about Montreal, knives in hand, threatening and insulting citizens. The governor loaded them with presents to get rid of them, and at last they left after a fortnight of debauchery.

This was the high water mark of Indian influence in the fortunes of that war. While they continued to maraud on the frontiers, the battles were now being fought primarily by regulars of both sides, under the command of professional officers. Lord Jeffrey Amherst once more took the impregnable French fort at Louisburg in 1758, and General John Forbes captured Duquesne in the same year. Montcalm still held strategic Ticonderoga, after a battle during which 300 Mohawks who had come with Sir William Johnson sat on the slopes of a hill and watched the white men slaughter each other through a bloody afternoon. But that was not important, from a military viewpoint. The forces of the contenders were now so large that it was irrelevant what Indian forces were involved. Even the Five Nations were no longer a strategic factor.

The war came to an end, as everyone knows, with the high drama on the Plains of Abraham, where Montcalm met his match at last in James Wolfe, the strange little military genius who now commanded all the British forces. With both Generals dead on the field, and Quebec, the French citadel, fallen, there was only Montreal to conquer, which occurred the following year, in 1760. The Treaty of Paris ended hostilities officially in 1763.

In the aftermath, the great issue had been decided. The colonies were to remain British and Protestant. But the Indians were left in a more divided state than ever. Most of them had fought on the losing side, which only added to their hatred of the British. Those Indians who had aided the victors thought them unappreciative, as indeed they were. There were some tribes which despaired of any future but living off the white man's bounty, but these were in the minority. Among the others, from the villages of the Iroquois to the country of the Illinois, there was a profound apprehension about the future. Now that the white men had stopped killing each other, they would be free to do away with any Indians who resisted their western advance.

It was this fact, clearer than ever in the cold light of peace, which stirred Indians everywhere to sullen, angry resentment. The war had brought more white men to the continent than any of them had ever thought would be there, and not all of them had gone home. Moreover, the end of hostilities meant that the English were free to colonize the Ohio Valley, or anywhere else they chose. If they were ever to be stopped, the time was now. Again, the Indians only awaited a leader.

# 3

## Pontiac's Conspiracy, and the American Revolution

**E**VEN BEFORE THE TREATY ending the Seven Years' War was signed in Paris, the bold figure of Pontiac stood in the wings, ready to step onto the stage of history. He was the leader the tribes of the East had been waiting for. His early history had to be accepted on the basis of hearsay, but tradition held that he was the son of an Ottawa mother and a Chippewa father, born in an Ottawa village sometime between 1720 and 1725.

Whether he first came to notice as one of the architects of Braddock's defeat is not fully established, nor is it certain that he was one of the chiefs who met with Major Robert Rogers after the fall of Montreal in 1760, when the intrepid Ranger leader was commissioned by Lord Jeffrey Amherst to take over the French forts on the western Great Lakes. But certainly he was one of the Indian leaders who, even before the war ended, had become convinced that British policy toward the Indians was even worse than the French had been. The British would not sell them rum and, what was worse, would give or sell them only a bare minimum of powder. That was a serious matter. One of the few blessings of civilization the white man had brought was the gun, as a means of getting enough food to eat when it was not being used for murder. The Indians regarded powder as essential to their livelihood and they thought the British should share it with them, as the French had done. The British thought it was private property, and no doubt meant to give the Indians as little as possible of the means to kill white men, in case they were tempted.

The commanders of the British forts in the west, in brief, ran a tight ship and the Indians were angry and resentful. The Senecas tried to organize a conspiracy against the British, but the tribes around Detroit, which included Pontiac's, refused to go along with it. New impetus was given to the idea in 1762 and immediately afterward by a mysterious Indian evangelist known as the Delaware Prophet who appeared in the Ohio Valley and began preaching a religion of Indian self-sufficiency, which he asserted would give them the strength to push back the white man from their lands.

Pontiac was one of those who heard the Prophet's words, and absorbed some of his messianic zeal. Pontiac was no mystic, however. He was highly intelligent, tough-minded, capable, a splendid physical figure of a man, lighter than most Indians. Invariably he impressed white men as well as Indians with his natural air of command.

It was Pontiac who determined to put into motion the idea the Delaware Prophet was preaching and that the Senecas had failed to carry out—a comprehensive conspiracy to attack the British strength in the west at several points, and destroy it. He had no intention of attacking the French who remained.

At a grand council on an island in the Detroit River, in April, 1763, Pontiac followed in the footsteps of King Philip and Opechancanough and formulated a plan of attack. The force of 460 warriors he could muster immediately was composed of Ottawas and Potawatomies, with a sprinkling of Hurons. Pontiac thought it would be enough for the first stroke, an assault on Fort Detroit. It was planned that the Indians, with their guns concealed under their robes, would get into the fort on pretense of a council with Major Gladwin, the commander, and at a signal they would fall upon the unsuspecting white men.

Unfortunately for this ruse, the plot leaked to Major Gladwin. Legend says it was disclosed by an Ottawa maiden who was the Indian mistress of the major and sought to save his life, but it is more likely that Gladwin heard the news from several different sources. In any case, he was armed and ready when the Indians came, and Pontiac had to retire in frustration, with a few presents. He tried again two days later, with the same result.

Seeing his leadership challenged by Gladwin, a British empire

builder of the down-to-the-last-man stripe, Pontiac knew he would
have to take positive action, and therefore ordered his warriors to
destroy everything they could outside the fort and cut it off. This
was done, to the accompaniment of some incidental murder and pillage, after which Pontiac laid siege to the fort.

While this was going on, another part of Pontiac's conspiracy was
being carried out by a party of Ottawas and Hurons, who took nearby
Fort Sandusky, killing all but one man in its garrison. This development encouraged the Detroit besiegers and stiffened the resistance of
Gladwin, who had been assured unequivocally by Pontiac that all
125 men in the garrison would be tortured to death, the major first.

As the warm days of May ended, other segments of Pontiac's plot
were carried out, and other British outposts began to fall as the war
spread. Fort St. Joseph, near the present site of Niles, Michigan, was
next to go, then Fort Miami, now Fort Wayne, Indiana, and on
June 1, Fort Ouiatenon, where Lafayette, Indiana, now stands, was
captured. These were small forts which fell easily. Fort Michili-
mackinac, larger and much better fortified in its strategic position on
the Straits between upper and lower Michigan, was a more difficult
problem, but the Chippewas took it by employing a ruse. Apparently
playing a peaceful game of lacrosse outside the walls, they permitted
their ball to go through the open stockade gate. Following it, they
produced hidden guns and began a frightful massacre, which chilled
the blood of the British who had not yet felt Pontiac's wrath. The
British commander at Fort Edward Augustus, on the site of Green
Bay, Wisconsin, decided to abandon it when he heard the news.

That departure appeared to make Pontiac's victory virtually complete. Except for Detroit, which was still under siege and seemingly
in a hopeless state, no more British forts remained in the western
Great Lakes. By this time, too, the Delawares were caught up in
Pontiac's war, along with the Mingoes, and these tribes were raging
through Pennsylvania. They even laid siege to Fort Pitt, which was
much too strong for them to take. Senecas joined in the struggle
and destroyed Fort Venango, on the site of Franklin, Pennsylvania,
slaughtering the entire garrison, and then moved on to take forts
Le Boeuf and Presq'Isle—once the seat of French power—in company with Ottawas, Hurons and Chippewas sent by Pontiac to help
them. In all these engagements the soldiers were brutally murdered,

and sometimes eaten.

Captain Ecuyer, an astute Swiss in command of Fort Pitt, saved this stronghold by an expedient which enraged generations of Indians. He gave the Indians presents—two blankets and a handkerchief from his smallpox hospital. The resulting epidemic raged for nearly a year among the Delawares, Mingoes and Shawnees, decimating their nations and removing them from the war.

By this time, however, the news from the West had alarmed British headquarters in New York, where Sir Jeffrey Amherst was waiting impatiently for orders to return home and leave a country he had come to loathe. The dispatches convinced him that he was confronted with a major Indian uprising, and he must do something about it. Characteristically it did not occur to him that the Indians had any real grievances. He had the British military man's contempt for them, and meant to suppress them by any means necessary. In London, the King's ministers were wiser. They conceived the idea of establishing a boundary along the Appalachians to separate Indian lands from colonists' lands, and made it official policy in a proclamation issued on October 7, 1763. This intelligent, if wholly inadequate move, was much too late. Neither side could be expected to observe boundaries.

Meanwhile, Amherst was resolved to send relief for Detroit. The siege there had gone on long enough to insure Pontiac's eventual defeat. If he had stormed it, the story might have been different, because he could then have turned his armies around and confronted the relief expeditions with overwhelming strength. But Indians did not storm forts if they expected to lose heavily. Moreover, the siege had lasted so long that the inevitable defections were beginning. Indians were incapable of giving their undivided attention to long sieges.

A relief expedition miraculously penetrated Pontiac's siege ring late in July, 1763, bringing 220 badly needed men under an energetic captain, James Dalyell, and including Major Robert Rogers with a party of Rangers. Dalyell organized an attack immediately, and in a savage battle outside the fort in the darkness before dawn, was badly beaten by Pontiac, who had been informed of the plan by his French friends. Dalyell himself was killed, and his head was hoisted on a pole by Pontiac's braves. A gruesome legend adds that the remainder of the captain's body was served to the chief's French allies under the guise of young beef.

This melancholy defeat nevertheless left Gladwin with additional manpower in those of Dalyell's men who managed to escape, and early in August he was further reinforced by a schooner which contrived to run the blockade and bring in sixty more men, along with supplies. Another of Amherst's relief expeditions, under Colonel Henry Bouquet, was meanwhile coming to the relief of besieged Fort Pitt. Surrounded by a force of Mingoes and Hurons, east of Pittsburgh, the accomplished Bouquet routed the Indians at Bushy Run by luring them into his circle of defenders and then surrounding them in turn, although the victory cost him fifty dead and sixty wounded. Then he went on to the relief of Fort Pitt. In western Pennsylvania the war had ended.

While these sanguinary battles were going on, there was a constant game of hide-and-seek between settlers who lived away from the forts and small parties of marauding savages. This disorganized warfare generated deep hatreds and resulted in atrocities on both sides. The frontiersmen were fully capable of killing and scalping Indian men, women and children. In this kind of war, hatred bred hatred, atrocity led to atrocity. Nor was it confined to the white ragtag of the frontier. Amherst, when he heard about Captain Ecuyer's smallpox trick, advised Colonel Bouquet to use it with infected blankets, and to "try every other method that can serve to extirpate this execrable race. I should be very glad if your scheme for hunting them down by dogs could take effect. . . ." Amherst's instructions to the relief expeditions he sent westward were to take no prisoners but put to death every Indian who fell into their hands. Killing Pontiac himself would be worth 200 pounds to the man who did it.

Pontiac was having difficulties of his own. Defections were increasing. Winter was not far off, and many of the Indians were ready to talk peace with Gladwin. The war was disintegrating before his eyes, but Pontiac was a proud and stubborn man—curiously, much like his enemy Gladwin—and he would not give up. He still hoped to get some help from the French, who had no serious intention of giving it.

With the first hard freeze and snowfall, the end was near. These portents of winter arrived almost simultaneously with a messenger bearing a letter from Major de Villiers, French commander at Fort de Chartres, in Louisiana Territory, addressed to all the tribes of the region, urging them to bury the hatchet and to live peaceably with the English as the French intended to do. This letter convinced Pontiac as no military gesture could have done. If the French would not help him, there was no hope whatever. He sat down and addressed a note to Major Gladwin, in which pride and dignity could not wholly mask his despair.

> The word which my father has sent me to make peace I have accepted [Pontiac wrote]. All my young men have buried their hatchets. I think you will forget the bad things which have taken place for time past. Likewise I shall forget what you may have done to me, in order to think of nothing but good. I, the Chippewas, the Hurons, we are ready to go speak with you when you ask us. Give us an answer. I am sending this resolution to you in order that you may see it. If you are as kind as I, you will make me a reply. I wish you a good day. Pontiac.

With stiff military correctness, the major replied that Amherst, not he, was empowered to negotiate a peace, and said he would send Pontiac's letter to headquarters. He did not say that he would send a letter of his own, advising Amherst to wait until spring for a peace treaty because by that time the Indians would have so little powder that there would be no danger of their breaking out again. If the Crown wanted really to demoralize them, he suggested, and without further expense, they had only to permit the free sale of rum, "which will destroy them more effectively than fire and sword."

Gladwin need not have worried. Pontiac's war had collapsed, and the chief himself was a stunned and broken man. His good friends the French had made common cause with the English; his Indian allies had given up the struggle too; his own village had turned against him. He was dazed and alone, scarcely able to comprehend that these incredible misfortunes had befallen him. Late in November, accompanied by a few loyal warriors, he left the scene of his defeat and spent the winter on the Maumee River with some Ottawa families, with whom he formed two villages. In the spring, his hopes reviving somewhat, he made a long journey to Fort de Chartres, talking to the tribes along the way and trying to stir them up. De Villiers, waiting at the fort until he was ordered home, was cordial but could do no more than confirm what he had already written. Only among the Illinois did he find any enthusiasm or support for renewing the war.

It was a vain hope. As summer came on, more and more of the tribes were asking for peace and it was clear that there would be no more hostilities for a long time. Nevertheless, Pontiac doggedly journeyed about the Midwest, exhorting any chieftain or tribe who would listen to him, and it was not until the following April, 1765, that he at last gave up. He was still a powerful enough figure to compel the negotiations for a treaty to be conducted through him.

Once more a shabby peace was signed. Implicit in its language was the British (and the white man's) view that Indians had no rights, and that gifts and meaningless promises would keep them from being troublesome nuisances. Pontiac, however, took the treaty seriously. He went so far as to help the British subdue any lingering resistance and, as time went on, he gave them every aid he could. This gained him no particular favor with the British, but it alienated many of his own people, so that in the end he stood alone. No one listened to him; only a few relatives and friends were faithful to him, this man who had once been a chief among chiefs, feared and respected by everyone. Although he no longer had any power, apparently he could still excite jealousy or suspicion. No one knows the exact motivation which led an obscure village of Peorias to decide on assassinating Pontiac while he was visiting them in the spring of 1769. The brave selected to do the job was named, aptly enough, Black Dog. He struck down Pontiac from behind as the chief was peacefully trading in the little village of Cahokia.

The Peorias and the Illinois, who did not understand how completely Pontiac had been shorn of his power, were apprehensive that a storm of revenge would break upon them. But nothing whatever happened, except that in the following year, one of Pontiac's best friends and allies, the Chippewa chief Minavavana, arrived in Cahokia with two braves and, by way of revenge, murdered two innocent workers in the trading company with which Pontiac had been doing business when he was killed.

In this irrational manner, Pontiac and his conspiracy disappeared from contemporary history, although not from the annals of the nation, which has named seven towns and lakes after him, as well as one of its best known automobiles.

Pontiac's passing, on the eve of the Revolution, was like a dividing line between eras. The long era of colonial warfare had ended, and a longer one was about to begin in which the enemy of the Indians would be the United States and its newly created Army. By one of the ironies of history, the tribes had no sooner ceased their brutal struggle with the British in Pontiac's war than they found themselves allied with England in the Revolution. Paradoxically, Pontiac had been the bridge between the allegiances, because the treaty which ended his war meant, in effect, that the Indians had ended their loyalty to the French king and transferred their wavering affections to the Great White Father in London. This in itself was a recognition that they had nowhere else to look for help, whether in trade or in any other respect. An attack on this source of help and authority, therefore, was an attack on them. Consequently the Revolution was a war between the British and the Indians against the American settlers, who had now been in the country long enough to lose their identity as Englishmen, at least as far as the Indians were concerned. The great political issues of the war were lost on the Indians. Once more it was a conflict between two possible masters, in which they thought to gain more from the British, if the redcoats won, than from the Americans. In this expectation, futile as it was, they could hardly have been more optimistic. There is no reason to believe that one side would have treated them any differently than the other.

In fact, the British made one of the major strategic mistakes which helped to lose the war for them when they failed utterly to realize that the Indians could have been decisive, if they had been properly armed, organized and commanded by trained officers, and had then launched a coordinated assault along the Western frontier while the British fleet and armies attacked on the Atlantic frontier, from Charleston to Boston. Instead, the British high command pursued a policy of opportunism toward the Indians, and since this was the Indians' own policy, the tribes' contribution to the Crown's war effort was one of unorganized terrorism. Most tribes swore allegiance to Britain, with varying degrees of enthusiasm; a few remained loyal to the colonies. In neither case did they prove to be a major factor in the Revolution's shifting strategy.

There were those on both sides who believed the Indians should not be "used" as a matter of principle, but it was not long before both successfully overcame their consciences. The Americans were first to do so, even before Lexington. There was also a good deal of windy rhetoric on each side about the Indians. So august a document as the Declaration of Independence was sadly in error when it accused George III of "endeavoring to bring on the inhabitants of our frontiers, the merciless Indian Savages whose known rule of warfare is an undistinguished destruction of all ages, sexes and conditions." The King had been no more assiduous in this regard than the colonies, although somewhat more successful. As for the "known rule of warfare," the white men had demonstrated often enough that they, too, followed this rule if the victims happened to be Indians who stood in the way. The mercies they showed in warfare were directed toward each other. Indians were generally regarded as undeserving of such Christian qualities as mercy. It was, moreover, pure fiction that the Indians invariably murdered women and children. The practices of war varied widely from tribe to tribe, and from circumstance to circumstance.

There were some curious parallels between the Seven Years' War and the Revolution, as far as the Indians were concerned. Again the Iroquois nations lay between the colonies and Canada, where the British were organizing a drive southward. Again there was a Johnson among the Iroquois, but now it was Sir William's son-in-law, Colonel Guy Johnson. Sir William had died of a heart attack after haranguing the Iroquois to fight for the British and, even before hostilities began, the Colonel was carrying on this policy, in spite of the fact that he was nominally Superintendent of Indian Affairs. Guy did not have William's influence, however, and the Iroquois were wavering. The Continental Congress, in the belief that a neutral Six Nations was infinitely better than a hostile one, proposed neutrality directly at a council in Albany, and the Iroquois gave a candid reply: "This, then, is the determination of the Six Nations: Not to take any part, but as it is a family affair, to sit still and see you fight it out." Unfortunately for the Americans, the sentiment of this council did not truly represent the united beliefs of the Iroquois. More than half the nations were even then plotting in Montreal with the British.

Thus, at the beginning of the war, there was little definite concerted movement among the Indians in either direction, even though they were in their hearts overwhelmingly sympathetic to the British.

But almost at once the Crown's commanders exhibited their inability to understand and employ what was offered to them.

No one demonstrated this ineptitude more than "Gentleman Johnny" Burgoyne when, in the summer of 1777, he began the march from Albany which was part of Lord George Germain's grand plan to cut the colonies in two by sending Burgoyne from Montreal to Albany, and Lord Howe from New York to the same point. On the maps in London it seemed a splendid plan. On the ground it was a different matter. There was a vast difference in terrain between the two routes; the road from Montreal to Albany was wilderness travel, that from New York much easier. Burgoyne, in any case, was ideally unsuited to command this kind of expedition. Finally, liaison was so bad between the two armies and London that General Howe never got his marching orders.

Burgoyne's most easily discernible talents were for theatrics and bombast. He proclaimed before the march began that he would send "thousands" of his Indian allies to hunt down the Americans if they did not cease their rebellion, although at the moment these allies did not exceed 400 in his army of 7,213 men. Then, addressing the Indians, he exhorted them to "strike at the common enemies of Great Britain" and in the same breath "positively forbid" them to cause bloodshed if they were not opposed, and if they were, to spare aged men, women and children and prisoners. This led Edmund Burke to inquire sarcastically in the House of Commons what the Keeper of His Majesty's Lions would do if a riot broke out in the Tower Hill menagerie. "Would he not fling open the dens of the wild beasts and then address them thus? 'My gentle lions—my humane bears—my tender-hearted hyenas, go forth! But I exhort you, as you are Christians and members of civilized society, to take care not to hurt any man, woman or child!' "

Not being aware of this high level policy quarrel, the Indians followed their usual custom of doing what they pleased. As Burgoyne advanced, they killed and looted where they could; and when Colonel John Stark confronted the advancing British at Bennington, they vanished at the first sound of battle, taking the Canadians with them.

Only a few weeks before this battle, however, Burgoyne's Indians committed one of those acts of sheer brutality which, because it involved a young girl, did more than anything else to turn the hearts of both the British and Americans against the Indians—but an act which, of course, did not prevent them from continuing to use Indians as allies whenever they could.

Burgoyne had fancied that his Indians were under control because he had placed them under the command of St. Luc de la Corne, a French nobleman with a formidable reputation for leading Indians in the Seven Years' War. At seventy, this incredible soldier was a rugged physical specimen, skilled in woodcraft, who could scarcely be told from those he commanded, so much did he live as they did. Burgoyne was as uncomfortable with him as he was with the Indians.

There was consternation in the British camp on July 27, 1777, when a Wyandot warrior named the Panther arrived with a white woman's scalp of long black hair, and tried at once to sell it. The British were known to trade beads, weapons and rum for enemy hair. But this hair had come from a lovely young 23-year-old girl, Jane McCrae, who lived near Skenesboro, New York, and was engaged to Lieutenant David Jones, attached to a Tory contingent in Burgoyne's army.

Jenny had refused to seek the safety of Albany, and instead had gone to stay with her neighbor, the widow McNeil, near Fort Edward. That July morning four Wyandots had broken into the house and seized both women, announcing that they were taking them to the British camp. Jenny was ready to go quietly, apparently in the expectation of seeing her fiancé, who would rescue her, but the fat and talkative widow went under loud protest, promising that her cousin, the British general, Simon Fraser, would have their hides. The Wyandots had two horses but they were unable to lift Mrs. McNeil on the back of one of them, so two Indians remained to take her through the forest on foot and the other two went ahead with Jenny.

As nearly as it could be reconstructed later, since there were no eyewitnesses except the Indians, the Wyandots quarreled over whose prisoner the girl was and, realizing that neither could have sole possession, they settled the matter by killing Jenny and scalping her. Later amplifications of this story asserted that she was also stripped and raped, but no one who knew the Indians believed this version because Indians almost never committed rape on any woman, white or red. In the outrage and excitement which followed the murder, however, rape was readily accepted as a part of poor Jenny's fate.

When the Panther brought his trophy to camp, Mrs. McNeil recognized it at once, as did Lieutenant Jones, who would have killed the Indian on the spot if Burgoyne had not intervened and sentenced the Wyandot to be executed. At this juncture, St. Luc intervened and advised the general that if he did not turn the Panther loose he would lose the entire contingent of Indians. Having just learned that Howe was not marching from New York to meet him, as he had supposed, Burgoyne was confronted with a difficult choice. He could ill afford to lose the Indians, deep in enemy territory as he was, with no support, but all his instincts as a British gentleman urged him to hang the Panther. Putting the safety of his army first, he concluded it would be better to release the Wyandot.

The story of Jenny McCrae, and what had happened to her murderer spread everywhere like a raging fire, and its psychological effect was profound wherever men heard of it. The Tories were dismayed that a British general could let such a deed go unpunished. Burgoyne's own men found it hard to understand and many were indignant, which did not help morale. At home in England, Parliament was outraged and all those who had virtuously argued against using the Indians in the first place considered themselves justified. On the American side, politicians and generals used the incident as a bludgeon to belabor the British further. General Horatio Gates penned a hot letter to Burgoyne, who unwisely tried to answer it but only made matters worse by admitting that the Panther had been pardoned. Newspapers were full of the story, and it became a major propaganda weapon in the American armament, strengthening the morale of American troops as it diminished that of the British. It was unsettling, to say the least, for the redcoats to find their dead sentries with notes pinned to their uniforms reading, "For Jane McCrae." It was less disturbing, no doubt, to see the same note fastened to the bodies of Indian allies, scalped by the Americans. No one can estimate the subtle, pervasive effect of Jane McCrae's death on the men of both sides who approached Saratoga, where for the first time in British history an entire army was surrendered to the enemy, in what would be one of two decisive battles which decided the Revolution.

During that fateful summer of 1777, the United States Army was beginning to take shape. For the first time, in the men of the

Smallwood's
Maryland Rg.

Haslett's Delaware

Continental Line, the Army had regular troops. They would be fighting Indians for the next century and, more immediately, this hard core, which never exceeded 10,000 soldiers, was what the Americans needed to defeat the British. They were volunteers. Their officers, commissioned by Congress, were appointed by the governors. They were paid ten dollars a month when they were paid, which was the constant subject of letters between Washington and Congress. Land was portioned out as an additional inducement to serve, with 500 acres guaranteed to colonels, and so on down to a hundred acres for privates. To qualify, a soldier had to serve for the duration—and, of course, the war had to be won.

The names of the best outfits in this army are still legendary: Glover's Marbleheaders, who made the retreat from Long Island and the passage of the Delaware possible; Haslett's Delaware Blues; Smallwood's Marylanders; Morgan's Virginia Riflemen, those famed sharpshooters and accomplished woodsmen; Greene's Rhode Islanders; Wayne's Light Infantry; Knox's Artillery; and Light Horse Harry Lee's Cavalry.

Between the regulars and the militia lay the gulf which always exists. In this case there was ample reason for the regulars' contempt. Militia members were completely undependable; having enlisted only for short periods, they would leave for home on the hour these enlistments ran out, even if it was the eve of battle. "We strike for our country while they strike for home," the regulars sneered. Nevertheless the militia on occasion fought bravely and well, as touched with heroism as any regular.

One of those occasions was the struggle for Fort Stanwix, a strong point left over from the Seven Years' War, lying between the Mohawk River and Wood Creek, which connected the Mohawk to Lake Ontario. The Indians called this the Great Carrying Place.

Stanwix was the first objective of Burgoyne's two-pronged assault on Albany. While the flamboyant commander himself was descending from the North, in the advance that was to be crushed at Saratoga, another army was to sweep in from the West through the Mohawk Valley. This army was to be commanded by Barry St. Leger, one of Burgoyne's most trusted veterans. It included a Tory regiment, the Royal Greens, under Colonel John Johnson, Sir William's son; and a similar outfit, the Tory Rangers, under Colonel John Butler, a bold but utterly heartless soldier. These forces accounted for only 875 men. They were considerably augmented when they reached Oswego by 1,000 warriors of the Six Nations, under their greatest chief, Joseph Brant.

Fort Stanwix, which had been rebuilt as Fort Schuyler although most people still called it by the old name, stood on the site of Rome, New York. Its strategic value was inestimable because it controlled the passageway from the Hudson and Mohawk valleys to the Great Lakes. It was the only real protection the prosperous settlers along the Mohawk enjoyed, and they in turn were invaluable to the American cause for the supplies of cattle and food they provided. Further, Fort Stanwix could successfully prevent reinforcements reaching Burgoyne from the Lakes and Canada.

A young colonel, 28-year-old Peter Gansevoort, was in command at Fort Stanwix, and to him fell the task of defending it in the bloodiest battle of the Revolution. Lieutenant Colonel Marinus Willett, second in command, was nine years older and brought to the post his experience in the Seven Years' War. Under these talented officers was a force of 750 men, most of them from New York and Massachusetts, and all regulars in the Continental Line. It was these soldiers who had rebuilt the fort and named it Schuyler. When they saw St. Leger's men and Brant's Indians outside the walls, they understood that the safety of all the inhabitants of the Mohawk and Hudson Valleys depended on them, and they determined to die rather than yield it.

St. Leger sent in a cleverly worded ultimatum: "Deliver up your garrison and your people shall be treated with every attention that a humane and generous enemy can give. The Indians are becoming very impatient. I am afraid it will be attended by very fatal consequences, not only to you and your garrison, but the whole country down the Mohawk Valley." To this Gansevoort returned a note of blunt defiance and the battle was on.

First the British tried to burn out the fort with fire bombs and arrows, but Gansevoort's four-pounders on the walls prevented any rush and the fires were put out after one barracks was burned. Firing back with his eight pieces of light artillery, St. Leger saw that they were not enough to breach the walls, and his troops dug in for a siege. Gansevoort had already sent messengers to get help, and the duel now settled upon whether aid would get there before the British and Indians succeeded somehow in overrunning the fort, as they inevitably would, with their superior strength.

Help was on the way. Back in Tryon County, the militia had mobilized for the rescue at the call of a tough man, a 60-year-old Palatinate German, Nicholas Herkimer, veteran of the Seven Years' War. He had mustered 800 men at Fort Dayton, and with an advance guard of Oneida scouts, had begun the march toward Stanwix. He estimated it would take him two days.

As he marched, Herkimer plotted his strategy. He would advise Gansevoort to attack as his militia approached the fort and they would crush St. Leger's army between them. This admirable plan was foiled, as Herkimer should have known it would be, by St. Leger's Indian scouts, who patrolled the countryside around the fort, alert for just such a possibility. They discovered the advancing relief force, and St. Leger immediately planned an ambush at Oriskany, six miles from the fort. The Indians, with a few detachments from the Tory battalions to support them, were given the assignment.

With enough time to do it, St. Leger had selected an ideal place for the ambush, at a point where the corduroy road traversed a deep S-shaped ravine which a creek made into a bog on both sides of the road. Herkimer's column, strung out through the defile, would be sitting ducks for an enemy perched on the heights above them. No doubt St. Leger remembered Braddock's disaster and had high hopes of duplicating it.

Herkimer, however, was no Braddock. He was a wilderness man himself. As his creaking, squealing oxcarts approached the ravine, he stopped the column and a brief dispute arose. According to plan, signal guns from Stanwix were supposed to be fired at this point, but the general had heard no sound. The other officers persuaded him to push on, since the fort lay just ahead. The Oneida scouts, drawn into the argument, did not fan out far in advance as they had been doing, and so they missed discovering the ambush, although they were uneasy.

It was 10 o'clock on the morning of August 7, 1777, when the column began to move into the ravine. Brant's Indians, tense and eager for blood, ignored their chief's orders and sprang the trap too soon, before the rearguard had entered. Nevertheless, the initial assault was deadly, and it seemed like the Braddock massacre all over again. Herkimer was struck in the first moments of the battle. A bullet shattered his leg and killed his horse. Calmly, the superb old veteran dragged his saddle over to a tree, sat it as though he were still astride, and leaned back against the trunk. He lit his pipe and deployed his men, who had immediately taken cover, unlike Braddock's panic-stricken soldiers. Only the rearguard, outside the ravine, fled with the Indians in pursuit, leaving their dead behind them in a bloody trail two miles long.

The others, under Herkimer's calm direction, covered each other in pairs from behind trees, pulling into the classic circle of the besieged around the hillock where the general sat. By means of the pair arrangement, one man kept firing while the other reloaded, thus preventing the Indians from swooping in on them. Nevertheless, since there were 1,500 men jammed cheek-by-jowl into the narrow ravine, it was quickly a matter of the bloodiest hand-to-hand combat, a chaotic, howling frenzy of knife, club and gun and, in desperation, even bare hands grabbing at throats. In the midst of it, the three signal guns were fired at the fort, as planned. No one heard them.

To add to the horror, a violent thunderstorm suddenly blew in from the lake, darkening the ravine like night, flooding it with torrents of rain and lighting it intermittently with weird flares of lightning. Firearms were soon useless. The combatants fought each other in the gloom with knives, tomahawks and their clubbed weapons, scarcely able to tell friend from foe.

The summer squall passed as quickly as it had come, and in the dim sunlight that followed, Brant's Indians surveyed the battlefield and concluded that the struggle was going against them, whereupon, characteristically, they retired abruptly, leaving 500 killed and wounded men behind them.

Momentarily Herkimer's army was too exhausted to follow them. At Stanwix, meanwhile, the garrison had heard the noise of combat and Gansevoort, realizing what must be occurring, sent out a sortie in force under Colonel Willett. It poured from the fort with such driving energy that it swept over the depleted British camp like a wave, so abruptly that Sir John Johnson barely escaped with his life —in his shirtsleeves and without his papers. His troops departed as hastily, without their baggage, arms and ammunition. Willett's men destroyed everything that was not useful and withdrew, before St. Leger could organize a counterattack.

Thus the fate of the fort was still in doubt, although its position had improved. Herkimer's relief force was too badly hurt to continue and fell back to Fort Dayton, where the valiant general died from his wounds and an attempted amputation. St. Leger's Indian allies, the bulk of his force, were bewildered and sullen, shaken by their heavy losses, but the British general nonetheless reestablished his siege lines and sent in another ultimatum. Gansevoort again refused, and realizing that his position was precarious, sent once more for help, this time to General Schuyler, who at that moment was engaging Burgoyne. His emissaries were Colonel Willett and a Major Stockwell, both veteran frontiersmen, who made a daring escape through the enemy lines by night. In two days they had reached Fort Dayton, and soon after were in Schuyler's camp.

When Schuyler called for volunteers, the first to offer was General Benedict Arnold. He was the best man Schuyler could have hoped for to lead the relief expedition. Not only was he popular with the men, and admired by them, but the Indians far and wide were more in terror of him than of any other American leader, possibly because of his exploits in Canada, unsuccessful though they had been. Consequently when Arnold called for volunteers, in his turn, 1,200 responded. By the next morning they were on their way, making forced marches. In a week they were at the German Flats, twenty miles from Hendrix.

There Arnold conceived a scheme to outwit St. Leger, one which did full credit to his agile intelligence. He enlisted the service of a Tory spy who had just been captured, one Hon Yost Schuyler (Herkimer's nephew), a poor dimwitted fellow whose mentality was not so retarded that he could not get himself arrested for trying to enlist Valley men in the British cause. Schuyler's mother and two brothers beseeched Arnold not to hang him, and the general graciously consented if, he added, Hon Yost would consent to carry out a plan against the British. Even if he had not been retarded, Hon Yost would have embraced this opportunity eagerly.

Arnold then unfolded his plot. Commanding Hon Yost to take off his coat, the general had it shot through with bullets, after which the boy put it back on and set off for St. Leger's camp. He was to rush in as though the devil were after him, and swear that he had come to warn his red brothers of the approach of a great American army, from which he had just barely escaped. An Oneida, who was to trail him into the camp at a little distance, would then come forward and confirm everything Hon Yost had said. Arnold counted not only on the effect this story would produce by itself, but the superstitious awe with which the Indians regarded Schuyler, as they did anyone whose brains were addled. As an added incentive, Arnold told Schuyler that if he failed one of his brothers would be hanged in his place.

The plot worked to perfection, exactly according to Arnold's script. It was given strength by the fact that the news of Burgoyne's defeat at Saratoga reached St. Leger's camp just before Hon Yost appeared. Since the supposed fugitive was well known as a Tory, his tale was accepted at once, and when the Indians heard that it was Arnold who was marching at the head of the advancing American army, they panicked. St. Leger could not stop them, with gifts, threats or promises. Half the warriors left immediately. The chiefs among those who remained virtually forced St. Leger to make a general retreat.

Fort Stanwix and the Mohawk Valley were temporarily saved, but under the circumstances it was only a question of time before the British, having been tricked once, would make another attempt. They did so the following spring of 1778. St. Leger had been recalled by that time, but Colonels Johnson and Butler were aching for revenge, as were the Senecas who had suffered such a beating from Herkimer. Near the end of June, from their base at Fort Niagara, on Lake Ontario, the two Tory regiments sallied out again with about 900 men, including 500 Senecas. This time they did not try to assail Stanwix, but bypassed it to the south and entered the lovely, fertile Wyoming Valley of Pennsylvania, in Luzerne County, on the north bank of the Susquehanna. There occurred what has been called, in a much used phrase, "the surpassing horror of the Revolution."

The Wyoming Massacre, as it came to be known, was perpetrated on defenseless towns, whose men had gone off to fight for General Washington. One of the few soldiers home on leave was Colonel Zebulon Butler, who had quickly gathered up what strength was available as soon as the first rumor of the invasion reached him. He established a garrison of 300 men, most of them old men and boys, in Forty Fort, on the site of Wilkes-Barre. But these unprofessional soldiers were restless and impatient. They were afraid that while they sat in the fort the British and Indians would desolate their homes. Against Zeb Butler's pleas and better judgment, he gave in to their pressure and set out with most of the garrison on July 3 to meet the enemy head-on.

They marched straight into John Butler's hands. The Tory Rangers and Royal Greens met the Wyoming men's assault, while the Senecas filtered through the woods on both sides. After the first volleys, the Senecas came rushing out to attack the Americans' flanks. Outnumbered and outmaneuvered, the settlers missed their only opportunity to retreat in good order toward the fort, gave ground and then fled in a wild panic.

It was nothing less than annihilation. The Senecas and John Butler's men killed 227 of the 300 outright, and all but sixty of the others were either wounded or prisoners. Only two Rangers and a Seneca were killed; eight Indians had been wounded. Zeb Butler was one of those who escaped.

After this bloodletting, the invaders swept into the Valley, burning houses and mills, laying waste the fields, carrying off livestock and property. Those inhabitants who had not fled were summarily murdered. Prisoners were tortured and burned by the Senecas. It was as though a floodgate had been opened. The marauders moved up into the Mohawk Valley in September and burned the village of German Flats, where Herkimer, New York, stands today. The inhabitants had fortunately been given enough warning to flee. This depredation was added to the Wyoming devastation, where a thousand homes had been burned. In turn, the German Flats settlers burned the Senecas' town of Unadilla, fifty miles away.

Even as Butler, accompanied by Brant, made his way toward winter quarters at Fort Niagara early in November, he found time to enter Cherry Valley, a village only fifty miles from Albany, near Otsego Lake, where white men and Indians combined to butcher thirty villagers and burn every house in town in one morning's work.

When the winter was over and the spring of 1779 brought warm weather, Brant and the Senecas resumed where they had stopped in September and began a new reign of terror in the Mohawk Valley and in nearby Pennsylvania. As news of fresh outrages reached Washington's headquarters, the Commander-in-Chief realized that, hard-pressed as he himself might be, it was necessary to divert some strength and make a determined attack on the coalition of Indian and Tory raiders. If he did not, the Hudson River Valley itself would again be in danger.

What Washington planned—and he did the planning himself—was a full-scale campaign against the Iroquois, or at least against those of the Six Nations which had allied themselves with the British, principally the Senecas, Cayugas and Onondagas. He gave the command to General John Sullivan, of New Hampshire, a quick-tempered Irishman whose judgment was not always sound but who had proved himself to be a driving, daring general.

Washington's instructions were explicit. He wanted "the total destruction of their settlements and the capture of as many prisoners of every age and sex as possible." Moreover, he wanted the country of the Iroquois not only *"overrun* but *destroyed."*

Sullivan had 4,000 troops at his disposal to do the job, half of them from the Continental Line. They were men from New York, New Jersey, New Hampshire, Massachusetts, Pennsylvania and Maryland, and a detachment of Morgan's Riflemen. They were well supplied with munitions and equipment, even including pontoon boats for portages. There were eleven pieces of artillery, two-, three- and six-pounders, and two 5½-inch howitzers. The attack was to be three-pronged. Sullivan's route lay up the Susquehanna to the New York border. General James Clinton was to proceed through the Mohawk Valley, then down Otsego Lake and the Susquehanna, while Colonel Daniel Brodhead moved from Pittsburgh up the Allegheny.

The campaign was entirely successful from a military point of view, and proved once more that there was little to choose between white men and red for sheer brutality. Sullivan began by burning the Indian town of Chemung, after which he found himself confronted by a large army of 1,000 Indians, under Brant, augmented by five companies of about 500 Tories under Johnson and Butler. Brant had prepared another ambush, which he hoped would be more successful than the one at Oriskany.

But this time Brant and the Tory leaders had made a profound and fatal mistake. Their reconnaissance had not informed them cor-

Morgan's Virginia

rectly of the force advancing to meet them. They were not told that the scouts ranging before Sullivan's army were Morgan's sharp-shooters, widely celebrated as the best Indian fighters in the colonies. Nor were they aware that these were veterans of the Continental Line moving in, and that they were supported by artillery.

By the time the British and Indians learned these facts it was much too late. Morgan's scouts had uncovered the ambush, and Sullivan's column had deployed for the attack, centering first on the Indians, who were in an ecstasy of terror as the artillery threw a barrage of round shot, grape and canister at them. Worse, they were outflanked and nearly surrounded. Brant could not prevent them from flying for their lives. Sullivan then turned his attention to the Tories, who by this time had some idea of what had befallen them and were already on the heels of their fleeing allies, leaving dead and wounded behind them. In the aftermath, according to the journal of a young New Jersey lieutenant, he and another officer found two dead Indians and "skinned [them] from their hips down for boot legs; one pair for the Major and the other for myself." Not even the Senecas had thought of this piece of savagery.

With this defeat, Indian resistance to Sullivan's army crumbled. The general was then free to carry out his orders from Washington, and he did so with a thoroughness not entirely characteristic of him. He burned every Iroquois village to the ground, more than forty of them; in one town alone 130 buildings were destroyed. These were not tepees. The Iroquois had built frame and stone houses, as well as log cabins; some had fireplaces and glazed windows. Around the towns the fields were set on fire; 160,000 bushels of precious corn, which the Indians needed desperately to live through the winter, were burned. Sullivan's men even hacked down the fruit trees.

Colonel Brodhead's column never succeeded in joining the main army, but it was just as thorough in its work of destruction, destroying hundreds of houses and burning more than 500 acres of corn. White captives were rescued, showing the effects of starvation and torture, which inspired the soldiers to new brutality against any Indians who fell into their hands. In turn, soldiers captured on patrol were subjected to horrifying treatment by the Indians and Tories.

Sullivan's expedition failed in one respect. Without Brodhead, the general did not dare attack the British stronghold of Detroit, which remained the rallying point and refuge for the defeated, devastated Indians. There and at Fort Niagara they spent a winter of abject misery, one of the most severe the old inhabitants could remember. This time the British were more astute. It was good policy to nurture these miserable refugees until they could take the warpath again in the spring, so food and blankets and 10,000 gallons of rum were provided.

When they emerged again in the warm spring weather, it was clear that, for all its destructive power, the Sullivan expedition had also failed to end Indian resistance in the Ohio Valley. The survivors were, if anything, more virulent than ever in their anger against the Americans and firmer in their loyalty to the British. The frontier was aflame again as Joseph Brant, fighting as much for the survival of his own people as for the British cause, scourged the Mohawk Valley from one end to the other until, in the autumn of 1783, Colonel Marinus Willett, one of the heroes of Stanwix, dealt them and their Tory allies another crushing blow at Johnstown. Willett pushed them back to Oswego, and effectively ended the Indian phase of the war in the Mohawk Valley.

In the West, operations were in the hands of young George Rogers Clark, only twenty-three when the Revolution began. Clark, a tall, redheaded, Viking figure of a man, belonged to an adventurous family; his brother, William, was later Meriwether Lewis's partner in the famous expedition which bore their names.

As a Virginian, Clark had been busy exploring and surveying the Northwest Territory as part of the commonwealth's attempt to stake out its land claims in fierce competition with Massachusetts, Connecticut and New York, all of which claimed land extending to the Mississippi. The "Territory" itself was still not well defined. In the Revolution it was regarded as the Ohio Valley, Indiana and Illinois, and parts of Michigan and Wisconsin. On the other side of the Mississippi, Spain was the claimant.

The news of Burgoyne's surrender gave Clark a magnificent idea. With that threat to the interior removed, he thought, it would be possible to seize these British lands, with undoubted profit to Virginia as well as the nation. Governor Patrick Henry agreed, commissioned Clark a Lieutenant Colonel, gave him the authority to raise several companies, and set aside 1,200 pounds to finance the expedition.

A man better qualified to carry out this campaign could not have been found. Besides his personal attributes of abundant energy and courage, Clark was a natural strategist, an inspirational leader and (uncommon among colonial military men) he understood Indians. He saw that Sullivan's failure to capture Detroit was the key to the situation in the Northwest. That base must be destroyed, but first he would have to attack and overcome the three forts protecting it— Kaskaskia, where the Kaskaskia River and the Mississippi met; Cahokia, at the site of East St. Louis, Illinois; and Fort Sackville, at Vincennes, on the banks of the Wabash River.

Unlike other conquerors who had come storming into Indian territory with shot and shell, Clark first tried reason with the tribes of the Territory, hoping to win as many as possible to neutrality before hostilities began. He went about the country as a visitor to tribal council fires, where he would argue persuasively:

> The Big Knives [Americans] are very much like the redmen. They do not know well how to make blankets, powder, and cloth; they buy those things from the English (from whom they formerly descended) and live chiefly by raising crops, hunting, and trading as you and your neighbors, the French, do. The English became angry and stationed strong garrisons through all our country (as you see they have done among you on the lakes, and among the French). They said we must do as they pleased and they killed some of us to make the rest afraid . . . The whole land was dark . . . At last the Great Spirit took pity on us and kindled a great council fire that never goes out at a place called Philadelphia. He struck down a post there and left a war tomahawk in it. You can judge who is in the right. I have told you who I am. Here is a bloody belt [enemy] and a white belt [friend]. Take whichever you please.

After a gratifying number of tribes had chosen the white belt, Clark decided it was time to make his move against the British forts. In the course of this campaign, one of the most remarkable of the Revolution, Clark was never able to put more than 200 men in the field at any one time, but the results he achieved were far out of proportion to his strength. Beginning on June 26, 1778, he moved down the Ohio River to the mouth of the Tennessee, and after a double-quick, four-day march, he fell upon Kaskaskia in a successful surprise attack and captured it without any loss to his own meager force of 178 men. Cahokia and Vincennes were the next to fall.

george Rogers Clark

When news of these victories reached Detroit, a shudder of apprehension stirred the British. The key point in the declining British empire of the Lakes was now vulnerable to attack, and if it were lost, control of the Northwest Territory would go with it. Colonel Henry Hamilton, the fort's commander, was not a man to wait passively for disaster to approach. Known as "The Hairbuyer" and hated on the frontier, perhaps unjustly, as one who bought American scalps, Hamilton was nevertheless a bold and vigorous soldier. It did him no good to insist that he meant to pay for prisoners, not scalps. The Indians had discovered that if they brought scalps instead and asserted that the prisoners had been shot trying to escape, Hamilton would have to pay anyway because he did not dare to antagonize them. The colonel had no idea how many scalps in his collection were French, Spanish or even British, but once embarked on this wilderness con game, the Indians would not let him stop.

Hearing of Clark's approach, Hamilton energetically proposed to go out and meet him. With only 170 men and sixty Indians, he set off in late October of 1778, ignoring the imminence of winter weather, which might upset his plans, and after a rugged seventy-day march, descended on helpless Vincennes and retook Fort Sackville with no difficulty, since Clark had not even left a garrison, thinking it safe.

At the moment, Clark was in Kaskaskia. When he learned what had happened, he in turn decided he must make a quick move. To wait until spring would give Colonel Hamilton a chance to consolidate his positions and assemble an overwhelming force to oppose him. He estimated that the British commander would not expect a counterattack so late in the season. Indeed, to anyone else such a movement would have seemed foolhardy. There were 170 miles between Clark and Vincennes, and much of it might well be flooded, as it often was in winter. These were the "drowned lands," as they were called, likely to be covered with anywhere from two to four feet of water, dotted here and there with soggy hummocks.

Nonetheless, Clark ordered the march. Although he had only 180 men in his command, he sent fifty-three of them up the Ohio and Wabash Rivers with his light artillery and reserve supplies, while he prepared to move overland. The forces were to come together near Vincennes.

The weather had been so cold that Clark had some hope the drowned lands might be frozen. But a spell of unseasonably warm weather ended that possibility. By the time he reached the Little Wabash, on February 13, he could see the sodden land stretching before him—"drowned" indeed.

There was no alternative but a primitive amphibious operation. Men waded in the icy water, holding up their rifles and powderhorns. Supplies were ferried on a pirogue. Pack horses stumbled and swam as best they could. Canoes carried the sick. The advance went on, while the rations began to run out and the men shivered all night in camps made on what unsubmerged land they could find. Some help came from five Frenchmen captured in a canoe, who gave up their supplies and the information that Hamilton had strengthened Sackville. Clark and his men struggled on. A detail was posted at the rear of the march with instructions to shoot any who tried to turn back. It turned colder, but that was no help because now the soldiers had to contend with thin ice that cut at their legs as it was broken. They pulled themselves out at last, within sight of Vincennes, and refreshed themselves with fire and food before beginning the last drive to the goal.

In the streets of the village of Vincennes, within sight of the fort, Clark paraded his little force, doubling it from front to rear where it could be seen best so that the British would think they had a larger body to deal with. Meanwhile a party of Indians was sighted on the way to the fort, and Clark's men pounced on them, killing some and capturing five others, whom the American commander ordered tomahawked when he discovered they were carrying American scalps intended for Colonel Hamilton. He meant this to be a salutary lesson to other Indian allies when they heard about it.

Inside the fort, Hamilton believed he could hold his position with his small garrison, backed by five cannons, although he had been taken in by Clark's deception and thought himself confronted by 1,000 men. For his part, Clark was compelled to attack at once; he could not afford to wait for his cannon to come up out of the drowned lands. But he had another weapon—companies of sharpshooters, possessed of a skill the British had never seen. These riflemen proceeded to amaze and terrify the garrison by picking off its artillerymen whenever they opened a gunport, and even killing soldiers who fired through loopholes.

This was the kind of deadly fighting calculated to shake the morale of the defenders. Moreover, Hamilton saw no sign of the relief he had expected from his Indians. On February 23, 1779, he concluded that he could hold out no longer, and surrendered. The Colonel, spirited away under heavy guard to protect him from the American settlers who would have gladly killed him, sat out the rest of the war in Virginia.

Still the prize both Sullivan and Clark had sought—Detroit—remained tantalizingly distant. Like his predecessor, Clark did not have a large enough force to assault it, and he was not reinforced, as he had hoped. Intrepid soldier that he was, he might have made the attempt anyway, if it had not been for a senseless massacre which stirred the Indians out of the neutrality Clark had taken such pains to establish before he began his campaign. There had already been enough trouble after a Shawnee chief held as a hostage had been murdered, sending his tribe on the warpath. But this was followed by a horror perpetrated on ninety Christian Indians from the Moravian towns of Ohio who lived together in a small village called Gnaddenhutten. A roving band of bloodthirsty Pennsylvanians, out for revenge against any Indians they could find, invaded this peaceful community, whose inhabitants had taken no part whatever in the Revolution, and murdered every man, woman and child.

The tribes Clark had pacified rose in savage retaliation. They first came upon a party of 300 men under Colonel William Crawford, Washington's old friend, on the Upper Sandusky and hacked them to pieces, torturing the Colonel to death in the most horrible manner. That was in June of 1782. A month later the largest Indian war party of the Revolution, 1,100 braves, swept into Kentucky and moved toward Wheeling, which they would have demolished except for a rumor that Clark was coming to intercept them. The Colonel's reputation was so formidable by this time that the mere rumor of his presence was enough to cause the defection of all but 300 of the Indian army.

This remnant encountered Colonel Daniel Boone and a band of Kentucky frontiersmen at Blue Licks, on August 19. Boone would have waited for help, seeing himself outnumbered, but his wild recruits would not wait, insisted on attacking, and were cut to pieces for their recklessness. But they were more than revenged by Clark, who sent out a force which struck the Shawnees' great town of Chillicothe, burning it to the ground, after which he destroyed five other Shawnee villages and a quantity of corn and provisions. That was enough to take the Shawnees out of what remained of the war.

It was also the end of Indian participation in the great struggle between the British and their rebellious colonists. The war came to a more or less official end with Yorktown, but in the Northwest Territory a stalemate remained. The British still held Detroit, although Clark was in precarious command of everything south and east of it. The Indians, too, were still largely on the side of the British; the massacre of the Moravians had seen to that.

The treaty John Jay negotiated with the British was, in one sense, a tribute to Clark. By its terms Britain ceded all the Northwest Territory to the new United States, whose new government rewarded him and his soldiers with promises of land grants of 150,000 acres each. These promises were largely unfulfilled. Worse, Clark was never given his back pay, nor was he ever reimbursed for money he had advanced to his men and officers when the Continental Congress was slow to pay, or failed to pay at all. Clark died poor and all but forgotten in 1818.

If the new nation turned its back on Clark, a hero, what could be hoped for in its treatment of the Indians, who had once more fought on the wrong side? They had not signed the treaty, notwithstanding that it was their land the white men were parceling out. They were now without allies, since their British and French friends had both been removed from America. As they set about rebuilding their burned villages, pushed ever westward by the rolling tide of settlement, the Indians must have wondered what possible future they could look forward to, now that they were completely in the hands of a government which had already sworn once officially to exterminate them and, in any case, had rarely shown them anything but deception, hostility and aggression.

The Indians' nineteenth-century twilight was approaching.

# 4

★　★　★　★　★　★

# War and Exploration
# in the Ohio Valley

Seven years after the close of the Revolution the new nation and the Indians of the East confronted each other with a mutual hatred which could only lead to an explosion. The center of Indian power had moved westward from the Six Nations to the tribes along the Miami and Wabash rivers, but the grievances were the same. To these old scores had been added the bitter disillusionment produced by the Seven Years' War and the Revolution. The tribes no longer trusted anyone. They were engaged in a constant guerrilla warfare against the advancing frontier, particularly along the Ohio where, between 1783 and 1790, they had succeeded in killing, wounding or taking prisoner about 1,500 men, women and children, stolen 2,000 horses and committed $50,000 worth of property damage. Not to mention interference with river traffic, which made it dangerous to transport goods by water between the interior and the Atlantic coast.

When it appeared that England and Spain might go to war, making the Mississippi a lifeline certain to be hotly contested and raising the possibility that the tribes in that region would be stirred up anew, President Washington, no Indian lover in any event, concluded that he would end the danger and punish transgressions by sending an expedition under a competent commander, as he had employed Sullivan during the Revolution.

The means at hand were not what they might have been, but that was not Washington's fault. Before his election to the Presidency, still riding the crest of adulation as the successful commander-in-chief, he had strongly urged Congress not to break up the Continental Army. Keep four regiments of infantry and one of artillery, he had recommended. But Congress, exhibiting that shortsightedness which had so nearly lost the Revolution, decided that the militia would be sufficient to handle any of the new nation's military problems. Consequently the Continental Line was reduced until, by 1784, it consisted of a West Point artillery company of fifty-eight officers and men, and twenty-nine others at Fort Pitt. In the next year Congress authorized one regiment—the American Regiment (the 7th Infantry, now the 3rd Infantry).

As a result, when he decided upon the expedition of 1790, Washington could not send Federal troops. Instead, he authorized Major General Arthur St. Clair, who was Governor of the Northwest Territory, to raise troops and conduct the campaign. The force St. Clair gathered at Fort Washington, the present Cincinnati, under the command of Brevet Brigadier General Josiah Harmar, was made up of militia from four states, who could not yet be called regulars. The 1st Infantry Regiment was drawn from these men. Privates in this army were paid only two dollars a month; clothing and hospital care were deducted. Professional pride was the only incentive these soldiers had to fight. Harmar, their commander, was a brave officer who had fought with the Pennsylvanians in the Revolution, but there was little else to recommend him. He drank excessively, could not keep order and had no experience in fighting Indians. This force was entirely inadequate for the job it was sent out to do. It was faced by a loose but powerful coalition of Miamis from Ohio and Indiana; the Shawnees, who had good reason to hate the whites with a black hatred; the fierce Potawatomis from Illinois and the country around lower Lake Michigan; and the Chippewas from the eastern side of Lake Huron and northern Michigan. These tribes had a leader who was Harmar's superior in every respect. Little Turtle had the intelligence of Joseph Brant, Pontiac and other leaders of that caliber, and he was a military strategist of distinction. His Indian name was Michikinikwa.

President Washington's intentions toward these and other Indians had modified somewhat since the perilous days of the Revolution. He told Lafayette that "the basis of our proceedings with the Indian nations has been, and shall be *justice,* during the period in which I may have anything to do in the administration of this government." There is no doubt Washington meant it. There was no cynicism in him, no disposition to dispense anything but justice to everyone, yet he did not—perhaps could not—understand the situation of the Indians any more than other white leaders.

Having ordered the expedition, Washington had misgivings from the first about its leadership, based on the stories that filtered back from the scene of action. His doubts were soon justified. First, St. Clair took pains to inform the British at Detroit that his purpose was not to attack them, a piece of information which quickly reached the Indians. Then Harmar set out into Indian country, on September 26, 1790, with a force that had disaster written on it. These militia were badly equipped and untrained. There were 1,133 of them, augmented by the 320 men of the 1st Infantry Regiment, a mounted company and three light cannon. The pack train which followed behind was large and disorganized, and it included a herd of cattle. To move this awkward, shapeless force in a square formation through wilderness country against a mobile Indian army, as Harmar was trying to do, was an invitation to suicide.

Little Turtle exploited this situation masterfully. Slowly, deliberately, he led Harmar's men deeper into his territory, burning some deserted villages himself to encourage Harmar in the belief that the Indians were disorganized and fleeing. Once Little Turtle turned long enough to attack and destroy a reconnoitering party following in his wake. Then, a little farther on, he wheeled again and attacked Harmar fiercely with his superior force. Unexpectedly, Harmar launched a counterattack, whereupon Little Turtle fell back deliberately and permitted the Americans to pursue him until they were strung out. Then he flanked them and struck savagely, killing 183 of Harmar's men and wounding thirty-one others. The general retreated, and because the Indians permitted him to do so without defeat, he was obtuse enough to present the affair as a victory in his dispatches.

Obviously, however, the new United States Army had taken a beating. There were demands in Congress for a court of inquiry, which was convened and exonerated Harmar, asserting he deserved "high approbation." But the echoes of the affair would not die. Harmar resigned his commission a year later; Congress meanwhile had convinced itself that more than one regiment of Regulars was needed in the field. A new unit, the 2nd Infantry, was authorized. Once more green militia were drafted to make up the regiment. The army was now larger but no more fit.

To compound this error, Washington gave the command to Harmar's superior, St. Clair. No doubt he recalled how well the general had fought at Ticonderoga, Trenton and Princeton, but St. Clair was by this time a gouty fifty-five, and he suffered from the difficulty that had hampered so many other American commanders —an ignorance of how to fight Indians. Nevertheless, he was recommissioned to his wartime rank of Major General, making him the new Army's ranking officer. Having been warned against surprise by Washington, an old wilderness fighter himself, he set out on his own course of folly.

His subsequent actions can be viewed more charitably, perhaps, when they are seen against the background of indecision and conflicting views which prevailed in Philadelphia, where the government sat. President Washington wanted to preserve every Indian alliance possible, and those tribes which could not be persuaded would be beaten into submission. That was the mission he had given St. Clair. Jefferson's approach was harsher. He wanted to give all the Indians a "thorough drubbing," without discrimination between friend and foe, and then keep them pacified with "liberal and repeated presents" —certainly, in a man of Jefferson's stature, an incredibly shallow point of view. Washington wanted a firm, permanent peace, and he did not advocate any further white encroachment on Indian lands. Other men in the government were convinced that foreign policy was the answer. Once a settlement had been made with Britain on the forts she still occupied in the Northwest Territory, a major irritation would be removed and there would be peace. Similarly, Indian troubles in the South would be ended if Spain could be persuaded or prevented from supplying them with powder and arms from Florida.

If St. Clair was aware of these policy disputes, it made no difference. He had his instructions from the President, and he was carrying them out with truly formidable ineptitude. His planning was disorganized, his logistics absurd. The troops were often without rations or pay. Reconnaissance was neglected more often than not.

On October 3, 1791, he marched his forces out of Fort Washington in the general direction of a place called the Miami Village, 135 miles away north-by-west. He wanted to build a fort there, which he thought would impress the British and frighten the Indians. The line of march included 600 regulars and 800 militiamen enlisted for six months from Maryland, Massachusetts and Pennsylvania, along with 600 more from Kentucky. Trailing in the rear were 200 wives, mistresses and ladies ambiguously described as laundresses. Some of them could march and shoot a gun as well as the men they followed, but they were a sorry addition to an army about to meet an enemy as professional as Little Turtle.

Morale in this assemblage deteriorated as the march went on. Daily desertions soon brought its strength down from 2,000 to 1,400. The tents leaked in the heavy autumn rains, spoiling good powder. There was little grazing for horses and cattle because of killing frosts. As the sick list mounted, it was discovered that medical supplies were either in short supply or useless.

Nevertheless, St. Clair managed to build two forts, Hamilton and Jefferson, along the way. This was more of a patriotic gesture than a positive strategic advantage, since they were outposts too weak to resist a determined enemy. By November 3, however, he was at the place on the upper Wabash River, fifty miles from the site of Fort Wayne, where he intended to make his stand. It was well chosen. St. Clair would not be criticized later for any failure in that regard. He had selected high ground, with dense forest surrounding it and a creek in front, across which he stationed his Kentucky militia. That there were Indians about was soon made evident by these militia, who found them lurking nearby, but St. Clair had no idea how many there were, and he made little attempt to find out. He did not throw up defensive works, nor did he post any more than the usual number of sentries.

The negligence of this wilderness army was almost beyond belief. When a patrol flushed a large body of Little Turtle's warriors, who had by this time encircled the camp, St. Clair's men barely escaped with their lives, and when the discovery of the warriors was reported to General Richard Butler, the militia officer who was second in command, he inexplicably failed to inform St. Clair. That gave Little Turtle plenty of time to prepare his attack, which he intended to launch at dawn the next day.

A little before sunrise he sprang his trap, catching the Americans as they were sleepily halfway between standing reveille and getting back to their bivouacs. The Kentucky militia across the river caught the brunt of the assault by 1,100 screaming Indians. The militia, instantly demoralized, came stampeding through the water into camp, where their panic spread to the other troops and caused a fatal delay in drawing up any kind of battle line. The efforts of the artillery to win time were nullified by the heavy morning air, which curled the smoke from the guns into a kind of low-lying fog, obscuring the view of the infantry. Poor St. Clair, so crippled by gout he could scarcely get about at all, was helped onto his horse by four men and galloped bravely trying to rally his men, while bullets ripped through his clothing. Ironically, it was this circumstance which saved his life, because he lost his insignia and the Indian sharpshooters did not realize he was an officer, their prime target.

Once they had recovered themselves a little, the militia behaved courageously, charging again and again with their bayonets. But the Indians simply gave before the charge until the men were close enough to be shot down from cover. After every charge, Little Turtle pulled in his encircling line a little closer.

It took no more than three hours of fighting to convince St. Clair that he would be lucky to escape. The help he expected from the 1st Infantry, which had been left in the rear to protect supplies, was not forthcoming because of a mistake understandable in the prevailing confusion. Coming up to aid their comrades, after they had heard the sound of combat from a distance, the 1st met the initial wave of men who had not waited for St. Clair's call to retreat and were busy trying to save their scalps. Hearing a tale of disaster from them, they retired in a more orderly way, having the forethought to take the supplies with them back to Fort Jefferson.

Meanwhile, what remained of St. Clair's army was being hacked to pieces by Little Turtle's slowly closing forces. Before the end, a final desperate thrust broke the Indian line at the rear and those who could do so escaped through it, closely pursued by their enemy, who followed them for nearly four miles. Only 580 survivors reached safety.

Those who were trapped met a horrifying fate. According to one account:

> In that frenzy of victory the Indians inflicted on the luckless captives every species of cruelty that savage ingenuity could devise. They danced and laughed and howled at the screams of prisoners roasting at the stake; they pulled out men's intestines bit by bit; they flayed others alive and slowly hacked or wrenched limbs away. They dashed out the brains of children against the trunks of trees and flung their battered bodies into the brush. Some of the women were stretched naked on the ground and run through with wooden stakes; others were cut in two after their breasts had been hacked away.

The slaughter would have been worse if the Indians had chosen to pursue the survivors any farther than they did. As it was, the retreat "was, in fact, a flight," as St. Clair himself put it, and he added: "The most disgraceful part of the business is that the greatest part of the men threw away their arms and accoutrements even after the pursuit . . . had ceased. I found the road strewed with them for many miles. . . ."

If St. Clair had done nothing else to make his name remembered in history, he had been in command of the worst defeat white men had suffered at the hands of Indians since Braddock's disaster, and in fact it was the worst in the history of the Indian Wars. Where Braddock had lost 725 of his 1,200 men, St. Clair's losses were 900 out of 1,400—thirty-seven officers dead and thirty-one wounded, 593 enlisted men killed and another 251 wounded. By comparison, Custer's later defeat at the Little Big Horn would be mild, with only 211 of his 7th Cavalry annihilated.

It was a humiliation of American arms which shocked the people of the new nation as nothing had done in their brief history. Washington, when he read St. Clair's dispatches, flew into one of the rare fits of temper which he fought all his life to control, according to some reports. In a "paroxysm of passion," he cursed St. Clair for a blundering idiot. St. Clair, said the President, was "worse than a murderer."

Yet the President made no attempt to conceal the magnitude of the blunder. He gave St. Clair's report to the press, in all its unabashed candor, and people were soon reading that remarkable document which began: "Yesterday afternoon, the remains of the army under my command got back to this place [Fort Jefferson], and I now have the painful task to give you an account of as warm and as unfortunate an action as almost any that has been fought, in which every corps was engaged and worsted, except the First Regiment. That had been detached. . . ."

There was, of course, a demand for an inquiry. St. Clair could not be heard before a military court of inquiry, since he outranked every officer in the Army, so the House of Representatives conducted the investigation, and after repeated hearings the General was cleared, not unpredictably. What was surprising about the verdict was its implicit candor, matching St. Clair's own, in placing responsibility on "lack of discipline and experience of the troops," which of course reflected the failure of Congress to raise and maintain a proper army. As for St. Clair, he was allowed to resign.

The defeat was too public, too crushing to be pushed under the rug, however. There was a renewed debate over what to do about the Indians. Washington's political opponents in the press and elsewhere argued that it was a mistake to invade the Indians' lands in any case, especially when the cost in lives and money was plainly so high. The prevailing opinion, on the contrary, was that peace with the Indians was essential, and the way to achieve it was to raise and equip a force strong enough to crush them unequivocally.

Consequently a Militia Act was passed by Congress which would enlist all free white citizens between eighteen and forty-five in an army that would not be Federal since it left to the states the responsibility of enrollment and organization. Thus, in the zeal to preserve states' rights, the earlier errors were repeated and the United States still had practically no national army. To make a token correction of this situation, Congress authorized a Federal force to be called the Legion, composed of four sub-legions, each one having two infantry battalions, one rifle battalion, a troop of cavalry (Congress called them dragoons) and an artillery company—in brief, a primitive kind of task force.

The new Legion was to be colorful if nothing else. Officers were

1st Dragoons 1851

Cavalry 1800s

to wear cockades of white, yellow, red or green on their hats to distinguish the various units. Enlisted men sported caps with patches of cloth of the same colors, and pieces of bearskin as well. Looking like something from medieval times, the dragoons were to wear brass helmets with horsehair crests. There was also a good deal of sharp metal, including cavalry swords and bayonets.

Naturally the selection of a Major General to lead this dashing force was a political plum of the first magnitude. It went to a hero of the Revolution fully as colorful as the troops he would command, "Mad Anthony" Wayne. There was nothing really mad about Wayne. An excellent disciplinarian, he was simply more daring than the usual army officer, a quality this handsome, rugged fighter had demonstrated at Stony Point, among other engagements. After the war he had struggled unsuccessfully to make a living growing rice in Georgia, and had given it up for politics. For a year he had served that state in Congress until a quarrel over his election and his residence qualifications left him without a job. Wayne was overjoyed to get back to his real love, the army.

Taking command in June, 1792, the new General found himself compelled to deal with the problems which had so frustrated the old generals when they tried to make an army out of militia—drunkenness, laziness, gambling and every other kind of unmilitary preoccupation. Already noted as a disciplinarian, Wayne treated these problems with a firm and heavy hand. When it appeared that the training grounds at Legionville, near Pittsburgh, were too close to a constant supply of whiskey, the General shifted his entire operation to Fort Washington, where liquor was much harder to get. He drove the men hard. They and their camp sites had to be clean. Everyone was expected to know the regulations and present a smart military appearance. Target practice was ordered in all kinds of weather, and Wayne showed infantry and cavalry how to operate as a unit.

Politically, Wayne sided with those who advocated a hardnosed line toward the Indians. He had no patience with the idea of negotiation or accommodation. It was his conviction that the Northwest Territory could not be secured for white men until the Indians there were thoroughly defeated. He believed, too, that something would have to be done about the British forts still in the Territory, some of them on American soil, and about the British agents who were constantly stirring up the Indians. Although it was not his immediate problem, he was undoubtedly also on the side of those who were convinced that a confrontation with Spain was inevitable over their role in pushing the Indian tribes of the South to revolt.

The President nevertheless was insistent on exhausting the possibilities of negotiation before he unleashed Wayne and his new army. At a great council in Sandusky on July 31, 1793, the government made a final effort to achieve peace without war, but the Indians reiterated an old demand, that the boundary of the frontier be the Ohio River, as it had been after the council at Fort Stanwix in 1768. There was not the slightest hope the government would agree to any such concession. The chiefs and the commissioners went home in a mood of mutual recrimination. It was to be war.

No doubt Wayne heard the news with considerable satisfaction, although by this time it was too late in the season for a campaign. There was just time to march his 3,000 men up to the Maumee's south branch and build a fort for winter quarters. He called it Fort Greenville (properly, it should have been spelled Greeneville) for his Revolutionary commander and comrade-in-arms, General Nathanael Greene. During the winter there he had the usual difficulties with desertions, rebellious officers and expiring enlistments, but by spring his force was relatively intact and ready.

This time Little Turtle was faced with a commander whose talents were equal to his own. That they might also be superior appeared possible when Wayne confused the Indian leader by seeming to delay when, in fact, he was advancing. On the very scene of St. Clair's tragic defeat, the general now raised a new, strong fort which he named Fort Recovery. The Indians had hidden the captured six-pounders, four of them, in hollow logs, but Wayne retrieved them and, before the Indians knew they were gone, had mounted them in his fort.

At this juncture the war might have been avoided had the tribes listened to their leader. He had tested the white man's defenses by a sudden assault on Fort Recovery, on June 29, which had been a costly failure. Looking over the new army which faced him and assessing its leadership, Little Turtle wisely concluded that it would be the better part of valor to seek the best possible peace. But when he argued for this solution in council, the younger chiefs would not listen. The memory of their recent triumph was still fresh in their minds, and British agents had seen to it that it remained green. Moreover they did not like Little Turtle, a highly superior leader who could not help showing his contempt for them. A tall, arrogant, morose and arbitrary man, the chief often seemed like an outsider to them, although they could not help but respect his military leadership. Perhaps they suspected him of being too long with the white men, because he had often frequented their towns in earlier days and absorbed some of their civilized ways. He excited jealousy and envy among his own people.

It was this state of mind which led to Little Turtle's overthrow. The other chiefs not only overruled him on the question of how to deal with General Wayne, but they deposed him from his command, appointing a lesser man, Chief Turkey Foot, in his place. Without the genius of the one leader who might have been able to save them, the Indians consequently placed themselves squarely on the road to disaster, with a plan of attack which was foredoomed to failure. Wayne, meanwhile, was astutely engaged in weaning away the British from giving help to Turkey Foot, who confidently expected it. As a result, only a few Canadian militiamen and a smattering of volunteers appeared to join forces with the chief's 2,000 warriors, who were to storm Fort Recovery after St. Clair's cannon had breached the walls. Turkey Foot had not yet discovered that the Americans had found the cannon.

When he did find out, he was not particularly dismayed. A leader possessed of more courage than military talent, Turkey Foot not only determined to carry on without cannon, but permitted himself to be drawn into battle prematurely and without a particular plan. He could not resist attacking a small force setting out from Fort Recovery on its way to Fort Greenville. Something of the surprise Wayne had prepared for the Indians was plain in the way this little detachment reacted. They showed the careful training Wayne had been giving his men, and fought back so well, in spite of their initial losses, that they reached the safety of the fort. Pursuing them, Turkey Foot's men opened battle on the fort itself.

The skirmish had begun in the early morning, and it went on all day. Indian losses mounted by the hour. There were casualties in the fort, too, but the slaughter in the stump-filled clearing around the fort was frightful. Little Turtle would never have permitted such a departure from all the rules of Indian warfare as trying to storm a fortified position, nor would he have sanctioned the even grosser violation which occurred after sunset when the Indians, having pretended to call a retreat, returned under cover of darkness. A sharp-eyed sentry discovered their presence, and the sound of his musket alerted the fort in time. The defenders sent a heavy barrage into the darkness, with telling effect to judge by the screams and cries which rose from the clearing. This time the Indians withdrew to a considerable distance and, again ignoring the strategy Little Turtle might have pursued, waited for the white men to make the next move.

Wayne was soon better prepared to make one. He was joined by 1,400 mounted militia, volunteers of a superior quality who brought to the Indian wars a new element which would in time be more important than any other—cavalry. Their presence now was heartening but it was not an unmixed blessing. Horsemen were not particularly suited to the forested terrain over which this campaign was being fought.

Nonetheless Wayne's army now was 3,000 strong, powerful enough to persuade the general that he should go on the offensive. He marched his men out of Fort Recovery in the direction of the nearest British stronghold, Fort Miami, where Maumee, Ohio, now rises. Wayne thought it would be a salutary thing if he could bring the Indians to a final accounting under the very noses of the British, who would certainly be impressed and perhaps intimidated if the Americans won a decisive victory, which Wayne confidently expected would be the case.

As the Legion marched through the forest, erecting Fort Defiance along the way, it bore little resemblance to previous invasions of Indian territory. This force protected itself by night with redoubts and abatis, thus precluding surprise, and in the daytime marches cavalry covered the advance, while the foot soldiers themselves were on the ready at every moment.

By mid-August Wayne had reached the Maumee River rapids, and there made brief contact with outlying Indian patrols. Wayne sensed that Turkey Foot meant to make a stand in this general area. It was a fitting place for a wilderness battle. Some forgotten tornado had thrown the forest into a wild confusion of felled trees, so that the place had come to be known as Fallen Timbers.

Wayne approached the combat with more caution than he usually displayed, conscious of the importance of this showdown. The United States could not afford another defeat like St. Clair's, particularly at that moment, when John Jay was in London negotiating the treaty which would involve American rights in this territory. Then, too, if he failed, the frontier would once more be in a turmoil and no man's life would be safe.

In this frame of mind, Wayne played a clever delaying game—a strategy which had often confused the Indians. For three days Turkey Foot and his chief lieutenant, Blue Jacket, waited in vain for the white men to attack, and with every passing hour they became more restless. They also had a problem of supply, since it was necessary for some of them, at least, to fall back on Fort Miami, four miles away, every night to get food.

On the morning of the fourth day, August 20, the Indians were convinced that Wayne had no intention of attacking immediately, and nearly 1,300 of them had gone to Fort Miami the preceding night, leaving only 800 warriors and sixty or so Canadian militiamen to hold their position.

At this juncture Wayne, who had kept himself informed of what was going on, mustered his force quickly and struck his enemy by surprise. Oddly enough, he sent in his cavalry first, but they were unable to maneuver in the tangled mass of dead trees and had to retreat under heavy fire. But the infantry, coming up behind them, deployed and began to advance slowly while Wayne's cavalry circled the Indian flank.

Then the General executed another brilliant maneuver. His infantry, advancing and firing at will, choosing specific targets rather than firing volleys, was getting closer to the Indians' wall of timber. The first line let loose a volley at the entrenched Indians, which was returned, but before Turkey Foot's warriors could reload, Wayne's second line charged them. Here the bayonet performed deadly work, and the Indians could not deal with it, hampered as they were by the tangled underbrush. Under such pressure they began to withdraw. The encircling cavalry on the left could not find enough open ground to cut off this retreat, but the right wing was more fortunate. It emerged in a cornfield, and closed on the retreating Indians, sabers swinging.

Those who escaped ran pell-mell through the woods to Fort Miami, where they found, to their rage and astonishment, that the British had barred the gates against them. This piece of perfidy was the end result of Wayne's careful diplomacy. Faced with the choice of abandoning his allies or embroiling himself with the American Army, the British commander had chosen the side of the heaviest battalions. It did not matter to him in the least that he had promised the Indians the safety of the fort if they had to withdraw. Trapped between the fort and Wayne's advancing men, what remained of the Indian force was virtually dissolved, while the Americans tweaked the British nose by burning their trading post and some cornfields before their eyes.

In no more than two hours the Battle of Fallen Timbers was over. Wayne had lost only thirty-three men killed and a hundred wounded. No one knew what the Indian losses were, but they were obviously substantial and the casualties had included several important chiefs.

The General consolidated his victory by ranging over the country-side around the fort, burning Indian villages and destroying crops—more than 5,000 acres of them. It was a crushing, humiliating defeat, so final that it was two decades before the Indians of the Ohio could lift up their heads again. In this demoralized state, 1,100 chiefs and warriors came together on August 3, 1795, at Fort Greenville and there signed a treaty with the American commissioners, giving away a vast territory which included the entire state of Ohio, as it is today, and a good part of Indiana as well. Little Turtle, who could have said "I told you so," was one of the signatories but there was no pleasure in having proved himself right. It is worth noting, however, that he subsequently became a white man's peacemaker, acting on behalf of the government, and something of a popular hero in America as he traveled about the country, meeting such other celebrities as the French philosopher Volney, and Kosciusko, the Polish hero. Naturally, the closer his approach to the white man's civilization the less influence he had with his own people. It was an irony which probably escaped them that Little Turtle died eventually of a disease peculiar to white men—the gout.

The Treaty of Greenville made the Northwest Territory safe for American democracy, at least for the time being, but it did not settle the tangled question of its ultimate control. The Indians were only momentarily discomfited, and the British, who had taken no decisive part in the affair, were only biding their time. It would, apparently, take more than a single brilliant campaign by an able general to win and hold the Territory.

Moreover, the Ohio Valley was not the only place on the continent where the new nation would have to defend itself, or to put down Indian rebellion. With the Louisiana Purchase of 1803, a veritable Pandora's box of future trouble was delivered at the door-step of the American government. Now, by virtue of its doubled size, the western boundaries of the new nation were the great domains of the Oregon Territory, over which the United States was already in dispute with England and Russia. Spain would also now be drawn into the argument because of California and all of the Southwest down to the Rio Grande.

In these disputes among the great powers, the voices of the real owners of the land, the Indians, were not heard at all, yet they had no intention of permitting themselves to be run over. The prepara-tions for resistance among these fierce tribes west of the Mississippi forecast bitter conflict to come.

As President, Thomas Jefferson had the vision to see what could be expected in the future from both the white disputants and the Indians and, in 1804, he began to do what he could to mitigate the effects of westward expansion. His plan was to send out three explor-ing parties to the West and Southwest. While their mission was os-tensibly peaceful—that is, they were to map the territory, note its re-sources, and learn as much about the Indian tribes as possible without antagonizing them—the real purpose was military. The expeditions were conducted by the United States Army, and their character was that of reconnaissance.

The names of the men who led these explorations have become a lasting part of the American story. Zebulon Pike headed two of them. The third was under the command of two veterans, Captain Meri-wether Lewis, the President's private secretary; and Lieutenant William Clark, son of George Rogers Clark, who had been with Wayne at the Battle of Fallen Timbers. Their modest force, purposely restricted so that the Indians would not think of it as an invasion, was com-posed of volunteers. All three leaders were seasoned Army men.

How Lewis and Clark penetrated the West is one of the best-known episodes in American history, an adventure story in the grand man-ner. The journals kept by the leaders are a part of the nation's litera-ture, read with pleasure today by old and young. It is a tale of travel over thousands of miles of wilderness, on foot and on horseback, in blinding heat and in biting cold sometimes as low as forty-three de-grees below zero. As a military operation under such conditions, it was conducted with an astonishingly low casualty rate. One sergeant died of disease, one soldier deserted and two others were dismissed. Inevitably there were many injuries, including one to Lewis, but none were fatal.

Here for the first time, the Army encountered that implacable tribe, the Sioux, which was soon to be its chief enemy. It was a meeting that tested the temper of both sides. A Sioux stole one of the expedition's horses, but after he was summoned to council and reprimanded sternly, he returned it. In a gesture of friendliness, the leaders gave the Indians some liquor along with a few presents and prepared to shove off in their flatboat, but the Sioux were not prepared to let them leave with only a single round of drinks. They held on to the boat's ropes and unlimbered their weapons, whereupon Clark, a no-nonsense kind of man, dressed them down in what his journal euphemistically calls "positive terms," while his men confronted the Indians with upraised rifles. There was a tense moment, but it was the Sioux who gave in. No further trouble with them occurred while the expedition passed through their territory, which they would in time defend at appalling cost.

With other Indians, Lewis and Clark had less trouble and even better relations. They spent the winter of 1804–05 in a Mandan Indian village, where their life with the tribesmen was amicable enough. As they journeyed on westward during the spring, they were careful to spread the word among everyone they met—Indians, British and French traders—that the United States considered this land as belonging to the new American nation. One may assume the claim was received with skepticism and even resentment, but for the moment there was no overt hostility.

The expedition struggled over the mountains, often on the brink of disaster, and at last paddled their canoes down the Columbia River to the ocean. They spent their second winter near the site of Astoria, Oregon, and began the return journey in March, 1806, dividing their force at times into three groups, for purposes of broader exploration.

On the way, Lewis's party had the only untoward encounter with Indians experienced on the whole long journey. It was a familiar kind of dispute. After camping with a party of Blackfeet overnight, it was discovered in the morning that four rifles and some horses had been stolen. The thieves tried to flee, but Lewis shot one after a brief and dramatic chase and a duel with pistols. Another soldier leaped on a Blackfoot and quickly and efficiently killed him with his knife.

Late in September, 1806, the weary expedition reached the end of its magnificent journey and came to rest at Fort Bellefontaine, near St. Louis. As John Bakeless, one of its best historians, puts it:

> They had crossed the continent, braved the Rockies, endured starvation, struggled with lice, fleas, wounds, disease, wild beasts, and evaded the red man's wiles. They had come back safe, alive and healthy. . . . Snugly secured from damp in their tin cases in the boats that waited impatiently for him on the shore, were the records that told the whole story. Mr. Jefferson would be pleased.

Lewis wrote to the President:

> In obedience to your orders we have penetrated the Continent of North America to the Pacific Ocean and sufficiently explored the interior of the country to affirm that we have discovered the most practicable communication which does exist across the continent.

It was joyful news not only for Mr. Jefferson, but for the nation. Lewis and Clark had long ago been given up as lost. Now that their splendid story began to unfold, the imagination of Americans everywhere was stirred as they understood for the first time what Mr. Jefferson had actually bought with the Louisiana Purchase. An enticing vista opened before them.

As for the explorers, they were amply rewarded with 1,600 acres of land for the two Captains and 320 for the others, besides double pay for everybody, which in the case of the Captains amounted to $1,228. It was a fitting climax that Lewis should be made Governor of the new Territory early in 1807, while Clark became a Brigadier General of Louisiana Militia. Two years later Lewis was dead, on the Natchez Trace, a Tennessee wilderness trail, but whether he was murdered or a suicide was never fully determined. After an interim term by Congressman Benjamin Howard, of Kentucky, Clark succeeded his friend as both Governor and Superintendent of Indian Affairs in 1813. A year earlier Louisiana had become Missouri Territory.

While Lewis and Clark were struggling northwestward across the continent, Lieutenant Zebulon Pike, of the 1st Infantry, was leading two other expeditions, one northward and the other to the southwest.

Pike, a career officer, was five feet, eight inches tall, with blue eyes and light hair, "abstemious, temperate and unremitting in his duty," according to a contemporary description. He was a well-educated man, possessing some knowledge of astronomy, surveying, French and Spanish.

On his first expedition, setting out from St. Louis on August 9, 1805, Pike's intent was to explore the headwaters of the Mississippi. Like Lewis and Clark, he was conducting a military reconnaissance, instructed to look for likely places to build forts and to map routes up and down the Valley, as well as impress upon the Indians, the British and the French that the United States was in possession of this territory as a result of the Purchase. Pike's force hardly represented any such vast authority. It consisted, besides himself, of a sergeant, two corporals and seventeen privates.

Pike's first encounter with the Indians came in Sioux territory, at the meeting of the Mississippi and Minnesota rivers, where he met a war party of 150 savages. It was a peaceful meeting, however, in which Pike, after an exchange of presents, persuaded the Indians to give him a quit-claim deed to 100,000 acres of land, for the shameful price of $2,000. For the Indians, at least, it was better than being shot.

At the present site of Little Falls, Minnesota, Pike built a fort. Leaving most of his men to garrison it, he set off with a few others on a march through the winter wilderness to find the source of the Mississippi. It was characteristic of the new nation's sense of manifest destiny that Pike rewarded the hospitality of the British trading posts which gave him shelter along the way by informing them that their existence was now illegal, and that they would have to pay customs duties to stay in business.

Returning to his base without any significant incident, Pike found the fort demoralized by alcohol, in which the neighboring Indians had willingly joined. But he restored order and, traveling on short supplies, reached St. Louis again safely. In nine months he had covered 5,000 miles.

Little more than a year later he was off again, in the summer of 1807, with a force slightly augmented by two more soldiers, a civilian surgeon and an interpreter. His destination was the land around the Arkansas and Red Rivers, with the purpose of determining whether the Red River would be an adequate boundary between American and Spanish possessions, as well as to study the temper and disposition of Indian tribes, the resources of the land and the terrain and its trails. He also had secret instructions to find out, if he could, what the strength of the Spaniards might be in the Southwest.

Pike was not impressed by what he saw in the first part of his journey. He found the plains of what is now Kansas "incapable of cultivation" and therefore not appealing to "our citizens prone to rambling and extending themselves on the frontier."

There was another and more formidable barrier than the uncongenial soil of Kansas, however. The Pawnees, one of the wildest and most warlike of the tribes west of the Mississippi, had been encouraged by the Spaniards to resist any attempt by the Americans to take over their lands, and they were in an arrogant, angry mood when they came upon Pike's expedition at the Republican River, where Nebraska now has its southern boundary. It had to be admitted that the rough-and-ready frontiersman's appearance of the American troops was a sorry contrast to the armored splendor of the Spanish cavalry squadron which had already arrived in the Southwest to resist American invasion.

It was a belligerent confrontation. The Pawnee chief ordered the Americans to turn back, accompanying his furious harangue with the most emphatic gestures. Pike, with his interpreter, stood virtually nose to nose with the chief and defied him with these words: "My young warriors of your great American Father are not women to be turned back by words. We will sell our lives at a dear rate to your nation. If we are conquered we will be followed by others who will gather our bones and revenge our deaths on your people!"

The Pawnee chief, who had no reason to believe anything of the kind would happen, inexplicably yielded. Perhaps, like so many Indian leaders of the Eastern wars, he reasoned that if his white friends (the Spaniards, in his case) were so eager to eject the Americans they should do it themselves, since they were better equipped. That way the primary purpose would be accomplished without loss of Indian life.

Unhampered by further Pawnee opposition, the expedition moved onward and by November had reached the Rockies, where snow-clogged passes blocked their progress. They were now in the present state of Colorado, and within sight of the rugged peak which would one day be named after Pike. Desperately short of provisions and numbed by the icy winds swirling off the mountains, Pike and his men nevertheless struggled on across the Sangre de Cristo mountains until they reached the welcome warmth of the San Luis Valley, not far from the source of the Rio Grande del Norte. Pike mistakenly thought he was looking upon the Red River.

Meanwhile the Spaniards, warned by their Pawnee allies, had been searching for the invading Americans, and in February, 1807, happened upon them in a meeting which Pike himself induced, since he could not think of any other way to reconnoiter the Spanish stronghold of Sante Fé unless he got himself captured. The Spaniards obliged him. A hundred dragoons surrounded his little party, and the commanding officer informed him he was in the territory of Mexico. Pike replied with suitable meekness that he had lost his way in the mountains. The explanation was rejected by the Spanish commander, who marched his prisoners directly to Santa Fé.

But having captured the invaders, the Spanish officers did not know what to do with them. They were not entirely taken in by Pike's meek surrender, realizing that the Americans might well be spies, but on the other hand they did not dare keep them captive for long, much less execute them, for fear of precipitating a crisis between the two nations, which the Spaniards at the moment did not desire. The Spanish governor, therefore, decided to escort his unwanted prisoners back home again, but for reasons difficult to understand he sent them by the very route they had wanted to explore —into Mexico, up through Texas and at last over the Louisiana border, which they reached on July 1, 1807. It was the most valuable help the governor could have given his potential enemies. He had shown these spies the strategic routes to the Southwest, and in the process they had suffered not even a scratch.

Unlike Lewis and Clark, Pike did not go into government. He remained a career Army officer, became in due course a Brigadier General and died in Canada during the War of 1812. If he had lived, he would have had the satisfaction of knowing that his explorations, along with those of the others, had prepared the way for American conquest of the West. The door was now also ajar for the final campaign of annihilation against the Indians. To get through it, however, and cross the Mississippi, the Americans had to confront one more determined, last-ditch Indian stand in the old territories so bitterly fought over for so long. The Shawnee chief Tecumseh, one of the greatest of Indian leaders, was there to block momentarily the march of manifest destiny.

# 5 ★ ★ ★ ★ ★ ★

# Tecumseh and the War of 1812

As the last hope of the Eastern Indians, Tecumseh was admirably cast. His name in his own tongue (where it was spelled Tikamthi or Tecumtha) meant "Crouching Tiger." He may not have been "the greatest Indian who ever lived," as he has been called, since there are others who could justifiably lay claim to the title, but he was a most unusual man.

Like Pontiac and other leaders, his origins were obscure, and after he became famous, legends about him grew up like thickets, obscuring whatever could be definitely determined about his early life. In any case, it is unimportant whether he was born near Springfield, Ohio, or in Old Chillicothe, now Oldtown, in the same state; or whether he was partly white or all Shawnee. Pucksinwa, a Shawnee chief who died in the Revolution, was certainly his father, but it is not clear whether Tecumseh, as a young boy, also fought in that war.

It was not until after the Revolution that he came upon the stage firmly, in his own right. He found it easy to win renown as a warrior, but he essayed the more difficult role of Indian statesman. In this he made himself celebrated for a rock-ribbed integrity, so that both his own people and the white man learned to trust him implicitly.

That may have made it easier for him to live with the Indians when, following the pathway of other leaders, he found himself midway between the two cultures. Tecumseh was not a cruel man, for example. He would not torture prisoners himself, nor permit others to do so, if he could prevent it. Ordinarily other Indians would have regarded him with contempt for what they would have considered a sign of weakness, but Tecumseh somehow managed to hold their respect.

Moreover, he was critical of his people. He had been with Turkey Foot at Fallen Timbers, and considered the deposing of Little Turtle and the rejection of his advice to make peace as the prime reasons for the Indian disaster there. Meditating on other causes of the Indians' subsequent desperate position, it seemed to Tecumseh that matters might have been far different if Joseph Brant had been able to unite the Six Nations with the tribes of the Ohio Valley and thus form an army so powerful that it would have successfully resisted the white man's march westward. Pontiac had failed, too, he thought, because of the lack of cohesion in his conspiracy.

Tecumseh

Sometime during 1811 Tecumseh became convinced that he might succeed where Brant and Pontiac had failed, if he could unite all the tribes of the Mississippi Valley and push the white settlers back to the Hudson. From that moment he dedicated himself with a single-minded devotion to the fulfillment of this impossible dream.

He believed the time was right, because it was clear to him that the British were about to fight their recalcitrant former colonists again, and he could reasonably expect to gain their help.

The mystic in Tecumseh reached out to embrace as an ally his brother Elkswatawa, a half-crazy fanatic known as the Prophet. The Shawnees themselves did not believe that the Prophet talked with the Great Spirit, as he boasted, or really performed the miracles he proclaimed, but distorted stories of his powers were widely believed among other tribes. To Tecumseh, Elkswatawa represented something more practical. The Prophet was always preaching a kind of austere nationalism, an America-for-the-real-Americans philosophy, in which he exhorted his tribesmen to be true to their traditions, and if necessary to fight for them. That was the kind of talk Tecumseh liked to hear. The Prophet, for his part, apparently saw his brother's idea of a Confederacy in a somewhat different light as an invitation to a holy war.

While Tecumseh was not an evangelical figure, and no doubt thought some of Elkswatawa's ideas were nonsense, he had nonetheless joined forces with his brother. Their purpose was to establish a kind of utopian community on the Wabash River, not far from where it was joined by the Tippecanoe, which gave its name to the town, later called Prophet's Town for obvious reasons. By Indian standards it was a strange place. Alcohol was forbidden there, and in a manner somewhat like the divines of the early Bay Colony, Elkswatawa was forever giving impassioned sermons to the residents about the virtues of simplicity and tradition. He wanted them to work hard on their farms and never spend more than they earned.

Tecumseh did not do much exhorting, although he was a powerful speaker. He preferred to exercise his talents on the tribes of the Valley, whom he was trying to persuade to join his Confederacy. Spending little time in Tippecanoe, he ranged up and down the continent from Minnesota to the Gulf, expounding the idea of confederation. Whenever he encountered British or American officials, he seized the opportunity to argue the Indian case before them, in the hope that white men might see reason and war be averted. Needless to say, it was a vain hope. The officials listened to him with some respect, because Tecumseh's mere presence commanded that much from them, but they could not have halted westward expansion even if they had wished.

As he traveled from village to village, the chief found willing listeners among his own people. He made the same logical points with them that he used in arguing with the whites. It was his thesis that land was not owned by any single tribe but belonged to all of them in common, consequently it could not be sold or ceded unilaterally. He pointed to the Treaty of Greenville as a step in the proper direction, because the tribes had agreed there in concert to accept the government's guarantee of land to all of them.

Tecumseh was aware that this had not been an act of generosity and justice on the part of the government, but a mistake in the language of the treaty and the white men had no intention of adhering to it. The governor of the Northwest Territory had told him as much. General William Henry Harrison was determined, he said, "that the community of interests in the lands amongst the Indian tribes, which seemed to be recognized by the Treaty of Greenville, should be objected to." Object he did, and frequently, to Tecumseh, who argued the point with him.

As far as the Indian statesman was concerned, actual ownership of the land was not the important part of the argument. He saw clearly that if the Indians of the tribes up and down the Mississippi Valley could be persuaded that they had a common interest in the land, they would in effect be acting as a single great state to defend it, just as the American government was doing. In brief, he visualized nothing less than an Indian United States, running between the Lakes and the Gulf, acting as a buffer between the Americans and the British on the north and the Spanish on the west. It was a grand conception, already visualized by some American officials who saw in it a solution to what seemed like perpetual war with the Indians, but it had no possible chance of success. Experience had shown over and over that Indians could not unite as white men did, except for short periods, and in any event it was idle to dream of stopping the march of manifest destiny.

It is not unlikely that Tecumseh himself was realistic and intelligent enough to understand in his heart that he could not really carry out his dream. The most he could hope for was that he could save the Indians from being debauched by the white man—a fear he shared with his brother the Prophet—and perhaps prevent their destruction. Unity, even if it did not last for long, would pull them out of their old self-destructive ways.

Unlike previous leaders, Tecumseh made no particular secret of his hopes and plans. His chief antagonist, General Harrison, paid him the compliment of respect and admiration and wrote:

> The implicit obedience and respect which followers of Tecumseh pay him is really astonishing and more than any other circumstance bespeaks him one of those uncommon geniuses which spring up occasionally to produce revolutions and overturn the established order of things.

If it were not for the vicinity of the United States, he would perhaps be the founder of an Empire that would rival in glory Mexico and Peru. No difficulties deter him.

The British took a more sophisticated view of Tecumseh, and he in turn sadly misjudged them. The chief thought he could depend on them to help him, not only because it would serve their interest against the Americans but because their history of friendship with the Indians led him to think they would welcome the creation of an Indian state and would help guarantee its borders. He could not have been more wrong. The British permitted Tecumseh to believe he was correct in trusting them, but in reality they had not the least faith in his ideas. They were, in fact, doing what they had always done, as Tecumseh would have realized if he had applied his considerable intellect to a closer study of the history of British–Indian relations. They were using him and his great scheme to further their own design embodied in the grand strategy of the War of 1812. To embroil the Indians with the Americans would be useful.

So Tecumseh went about his labors of unity, with faith and determination to unite "all the red men." At Tippecanoe he had the nucleus of his new nation in a motley collection of a thousand Shawnees, Delawares, Wyandots, Ottawas, Ojibwas and Kickapoos. Traveling far and wide to recruit others, his voice, as one observer put it, "resounded over the multitude . . . hurling out his words like a succession of thunderbolts."

General Harrison watched all this with interest and apprehension. In Harrison, Tecumseh had a fit antagonist and the two men respected each other. The General was a tall, erect, lean soldier with a characteristic forelock hanging over the long upper slope of his forehead. On him, too, was the mark of greatness, which would later be realized in his election to the Presidency.

His strategy in combating Tecumseh was to split the tribes apart by negotiating separate land deals with them, in clear violation of the letter if not the spirit of the Treaty of Greenville. In a series of these treaties he succeeded in buying 3,000,000 acres of good Wabash River land for a total of a mere $10,550 in cash and annuities, since the Indians had no idea of the value of their land. Tecumseh was furious when he heard about these deals. For the first time he quarreled openly with Harrison, and told the General bluntly that he would either have to repudiate what he had done or fight to retain possession of the land.

Tecumseh was ready to fight. The British, acting their part faithfully, had been giving him arms and ammunition, as well as clothing, and he had told them gratefully: "You, Father, have nourished us, and raised us up from childhood. We are now men, and think ourselves capable of defending our country." With such support he could go to the tribes and proclaim: "Our fathers, from their tombs, reproach us as slaves and cowards. I hear them now in the wailing winds."

Yet the impasse with Harrison over the land sales was not clearcut enough to precipitate an immediate break. Tecumseh had ridden to their meeting with 300 armed braves, and Harrison had promptly answered this show of strength with a display of two militia companies. Tecumseh had been so violent in his first speech that Harrison had advised him to come back next day. The Governor himself took the lead in moderation at their subsequent meeting, promising to present Tecumseh's case to the President, and listening without dissent to the chief's offer of alliance with the Americans if the lands were returned. The Governor, of course, had no intention of doing so.

An uneasy peace prevailed, on these ambiguous terms, during the winter of 1810–11, but in the spring an outbreak of horse stealing and minor plundering in and around Vincennes prompted Harrison to warn Tecumseh that he would destroy Tippecanoe if these depredations were not stopped at once. The chief hurried to Vincennes and there was another inconclusive conference at which Tecumseh reiterated his demand that the land be returned. Harrison once more would not give him a direct answer.

It may have been the unsatisfactory result of this conference that sent Tecumseh away again when it was over, this time on a journey to the Southern tribes, whose support he had not yet secured. He would need these Creeks, Choctaws, Seminoles and Chickasaws in his alliance if it was to be successful. Harrison's spy system brought him word of Tecumseh's mission, and apparently he discussed it with other leaders at Vincennes, because they urged him at once to take advantage of the chief's absence and attack Tippecanoe. They argued that the time was ripe because the village's defenders would not have the benefit of Tecumseh's undoubted military talents, and the attack would offset any success the chief might achieve in the South.

Harrison permitted himself to be persuaded. Secretary of War William Eustis had given him rather ambiguous authority to act at his own discretion, which he now felt justified in exercising because of the danger to the frontier settlements from Tecumseh's growing strength. Consequently, history would have to record that it was the whites and not the Indians who broke the peace and struck first. It would be difficult to attach anything less than belligerent intentions to the size and strength of the force Harrison led out of Vincennes on

September 26, 1811. There were more than 1,000 men in it, including 250 regulars of the 4th United States Infantry, sixty Kentucky volunteers, 600 Indian militia and 170 mounted dragoons and riflemen. The infantrymen were resplendent in blue, brass-buttoned tailcoats, pantaloons worn skin-tight and stovepipe hats with red, white and blue cockades. They looked as though they were marching to a parade ground instead of a wilderness battle. By contrast the buckskin-clad militiamen looked drab, except for a single company known as the Yellow Jackets, whose coatees were of that color.

This colorful company swung along the trails of the Wabash Valley, pausing long enough to erect a fort where Terre Haute, Indiana, now stands; the general was immodest enough to name it after himself. The column came to a stop soon after at a place near Tippecanoe, where Harrison made camp on a strategic piece of high ground protected by the marshy prairies along Tippecanoe Creek. From this point he sent a message to the Prophet, who was in command during his brother's absence, making demands he was fairly confident would not be complied with, principally the return of stolen property and of two warriors who had murdered some settlers. The demands were not only ignored, as Harrison had expected, but the two messengers, a pair of friendly Miamis, failed to return.

At Tippecanoe, meanwhile, the Prophet was in a state of high excitement. Tecumseh had warned him not to attack the white men while he was gone, no doubt believing his brother incapable of leading an assault, but the Prophet now had an excuse to disobey since the white men were obviously about to attack him unless he did as they wished. Cannily, however, he did not at once reject Harrison's ultimatum, and did nothing more than to suggest blandly that negotiations take place. He implied that he himself sought peace. To his own people he told a far different story. They must fight to save their town, he warned them, and, resorting to his emotional mysticism, he assured them that he had cast a spell on the white men by which their gunpowder would be as sand and their bullets fall gently as rain. When the warriors were at a fighting pitch as the result of his harangues, he assembled a special war party of a hundred braves and charged them with the single mission of entering Harrison's camp and killing the general. With his death, the Prophet promised, the white man's army would fall apart.

Harrison had not anticipated any such suicide squad, but he had made the proper dispositions around his camp that a prudent officer could be expected to make. With the baggage and supplies piled up at the center, he had spread out his troops in a battle formation of two wings, slightly at an angle, and before them he laid down a screen of sentries.

These sentinels were ready in the dark pre-dawn hours of November 7 when the suicide squad, after "crawling half a mile on
their bellies like snakes," as a contemporary account put it, reached
Harrison's lines just as the drummer was about to beat reveille. There
was no time for more than a bare warning, a single shot from a sentry's musket, before the Indians struck at two places. The fury of
their first assault precipitated them through the lines in enough
strength so that they managed to kill several officers and men in their
tents before they could spring to arms, but they failed in their prime
objective. Harrison escaped from his tent, swung on his horse and
began riding about the camp setting up his defenses, disposing the
men where they seemed to be most needed. The Prophet, meanwhile,
directed Indian operations from a safe place on a high knoll, shriek-
ing incantations designed to doom the white men.

At first it seemed as though the gods might be listening to him.
Harrison's men were no more than able to withstand the first attack
before a second and a third were hurled at them. The Yellow Jackets
lost their captain, but they held their position nonetheless. Then for
two hours the Indians charged and charged again, driven by the
Prophet's exhortatory fury, while Harrison's militia and regulars
resisted with a desperate courage; wounded men fired until they died.
The Prophet had brought up the remainder of his forces as soon as
his picked squad had made its initial fruitless attempt to kill the
General, and the two armies were almost equal in number.

It was a tenacious, savage, fanatic attack, but its very emotion
carried it to a crest from which it began to ebb about daybreak after
two hours of heavy fighting. Sensing the change, Harrison ordered
a counterattack on the flanks, which was carried out by dragoons
and regulars with fixed bayonets, under covering fire from the militia.
This charge not only turned the tide but precipitated a rout among
the Indians, who broke ranks and ran for their lives. Harrison's men
did not pursue them immediately. They gathered about the General
and cheered. There was not so much to cheer about when the
casualties were counted. It had been an expensive victory—sixty-one
men killed or dying, and another 127 wounded.

To the Indians their loss in numbers was not significant, although
it was undoubtedly higher than that of the Americans, but their psychological defeat was overwhelming. The Prophet's magic had proved

to be false. Tecumseh was not there to rally or inspire them. They were utterly demoralized, fearing even to return to the village.

Harrison quickly followed up his advantage. His victorious army descended on Tippecanoe like a devastating tornado, burning everything in sight. Gone in the flames were the supplies Tecumseh had husbanded so carefully against the day when he would carry out his grand plan. Gone, too, were the British muskets he had stored. Gone in the indignity of death were the scalps of his warriors, flaunted on ramrods of Harrison's soldiers. It would have been no consolation to him to know that the General took so many wounded back to Vincennes that he had to burn some of his own provisions to make room in the wagons for them, making the return march a cold and hungry affair.

When Tecumseh came back from the South and found devastation awaiting him, he turned upon both his brother and Harrison in his fury. The Prophet had disobeyed his specific orders by attacking, he declared, and Harrison had used the disobedience as a pretext to make war in his, Tecumseh's, absence. "Had I been at home, there would have been no blood shed at that time," he declared.

Certainly not "at that time," but Tecumseh meant inevitably to shed the blood of his "white brothers" in large quantities. Now that the nucleus of his potentially mighty army had been destroyed he was compelled to abandon his master plan and turn in the only direction he could go, toward his British friends in Canada. The War of 1812 was about to break out, and Tecumseh nourished a forlorn hope that somehow the British would accomplish for him what he had been unable to do for himself. At least the British recognized his talents. They made him a Brigadier General at once, fitted him out with a handsome uniform and sent him into the field at the head of white as well as Indian troops, a remarkable honor indeed.

The American government was ill prepared for war. The Army could muster only seventeen regiments of infantry, four more of artillery and two of dragoons. This, at least, was its strength on paper. In reality, the ranks were not filled and would not be until men and officers to command them could be trained. Meanwhile, the nation would have to rely for its defense principally upon its Navy, leaving the Army to do what it could about defending the Northwest frontier.

Upon this ghost of an American Army, Tecumseh wrought a terrible revenge. He had in truth succeeded in accomplishing for the British what he had failed to do for himself; through the sheer magnetic force of his personality, he had drawn the tribes of the Lakes and the Ohio Valley to the British cause. With their help, the chief inflicted a series of devastating defeats on the Americans, to which they contributed in large measure by their own incompetence.

The first of these battles occurred late in the summer of 1812, when the bumbling Brigadier General William Hull marched out of his command post, Detroit, with a force of 3,000 men, seemingly enough to overcome any opposition extant. Tecumseh toyed with this army. Without ever attacking it directly, he first ambushed a scouting party of 200 men and cut it to pieces, after which he captured Hull's dispatches to the War Department, which proved of immense value to Tecumseh's superiors. Then he hovered about on the fringes of Hull's main force, cutting off its communications and pilfering its supplies until the demoralized General had to retreat in a panic to Detroit.

The captured dispatches by this time were in the hands of Isaac Brock, the able British General His Majesty had sent to the Northwest. For once there had been no mistake. Brock might be a stranger to the wilderness but he had no built-in contempt for Indians and in Tecumseh he recognized a military man of genius whom he treated as his equal. In fact, he ignored the counsel of his other officers and took Tecumseh's advice when the chief urged him to attack Detroit before the rattled Hull could reorganize his forces. Fort Malden lay just across the river from Detroit. Its cannon laid down a covering barrage which enabled Tecumseh to cross with his Indians and drive a wedge between American relief forces which were approaching and a party Hull had foolishly sent out to meet them. Tecumseh paralyzed the relief and pursued the others back to Detroit, which he immediately encircled. He then resorted to the stratagem George Rogers Clark had used so successfully at Vincennes, parading his men in and out of the woods until Hull thought he was besieged by three times the number of those who were actually there. Against the angry protests of his officers, Hull surrendered on the spot. The garrison was lucky they were dealing with Tecumseh and not another chief. He would not permit any torture of the captives, nor any harm to the 2,500 who were marched into Canada as prisoners of war.

With Detroit, the mainstay, in British hands, Tecumseh could turn his attention to other American outposts, which he captured one after another, at the head of an Indian army by this time numbering more than 1,500 warriors. No one can say how close Tecumseh came to reversing the eventual outcome of the war. Certainly he and Brock were winning it in the Northwest until a change in command on both sides once more set an evil tide in motion against the chief, who deserved better.

General Brock had been killed during the winter of 1812, and in the following spring he was replaced by Colonel Henry Proctor, described as "a fat, haughty man, disdainful of Indians." Tecumseh grew to hate and despise him, and in time quarreled with him violently. At the same time, the hard-pressed United States Army had turned in its extremity to the hero of Tippecanoe, General Harrison, and placed him in command in the Northwest. By a curious coincidence, his rank was now the same as that of Tecumseh, his old adversary.

Colonel Proctor's difficulty, aside from his general incompetence, was an excessive caution. Tecumseh learned about this early in April when he and the Colonel moved out of Fort Malden for an assault on Fort Meigs, which Harrison had built on the site of the Battle of Fallen Timbers, as an interim post on his way to recapture Detroit. Besides Tecumseh's 1,500 Indians, Proctor had in his command 522 British regulars and 461 Canadian militiamen. It should have been more than enough to overwhelm Harrison, who had 1,100 men at his disposal.

But Proctor preferred siege to storming, which permitted a relief force of 800 Kentuckians to arrive and drive back the British in a quick assault which seemed far more successful than it was, since it encouraged the Kentuckians to go whooping off in pursuit, in spite of a warning from Harrison. Tecumseh needed no more opportunity. His braves surrounded them, killed 500 and captured all but 150 of the remainder. Tecumseh then returned to the siege, leaving the prisoners to be taken to the rear, where their Indian escorts, without their chief's restraining hand, fell upon the helpless men and began a general massacre. Somehow Tecumseh heard of what was happening and galloped to the scene, where he struck down four of his own men. But it was Proctor he blamed for permitting the carnage to continue. He turned on the Colonel and cried: "You are unfit to command. Go and put on petticoats. I conquer to save and you to murder."

His anger was compounded when the Colonel refused to stay and renew the siege, although Tecumseh now was confident of victory, since Harrison could not expect further relief in time. To the chief's utter disgust, Proctor began a hasty march back to the safety of Fort Malden.

Back at the fort, however, there was a heartening reinforcement awaiting the returned besiegers. Indians had swarmed in from every part of the Northwest, responding to the magic of Tecumseh's name and his successes. They gave the British a total strength of 5,000 men, enough to undertake any kind of campaign they might desire. But Proctor cautiously refused to make any immediate move, in spite of Tecumseh's impatient, contemptuous prodding. The chief wanted to return to the siege of Fort Meigs, which Harrison had left in command of General Henry Clay while he pursued his march toward Detroit.

Tecumseh had evolved a brilliant plan for the capture of Meigs, which he pressed upon the reluctant Colonel. The British and the Indians would draw up to the fort, closely enough to be heard but not seen, and would then create a great noise of conflict. Tecumseh believed that Clay would hear the sham battle, conclude that an attacking British force had been set upon by an American relief column and would hurry out of the fort to help, whereupon the British could destroy the garrison at their leisure. Proctor agreed to try the plan, but his heart was obviously not in it.

As it happened, when it was carried out on July 20, the plot failed for a reason Tecumseh could not have anticipated. Those at the fort were taken in by the imaginary sound of battle with the single—and most important—exception of General Clay himself, who refused to believe that what he heard was authentic and would not give in to the importunities of his officers. Tecumseh was baffled and Proctor, for once, appeared to be right.

In an effort to salvage something from the expedition, the Colonel made one of his rare decisions to attack, picking as his potential victim nearby Fort Stephenson, on the Sandusky River, which he believed was so weak it would be an easy conquest. It was not hard to understand why he thought so. There were only 160 men in the garrison, under the command of a twenty-two-year-old Army regular, Major George Croghan, while Proctor had nearly 3,000 men, regulars and Indians, at his disposal.

But if Proctor thought the major would surrender when he saw the size of the force confronting him, he did not know young Croghan, who sent back a brisk defiance of the Colonel's ultimatum. Croghan knew he was hopelessly outnumbered but he had a surprise waiting for his enemy. It was a six-pounder carefully hidden at the fort's weakest point, where it could be expected the British attack would come. That was exactly what occurred. When Proctor's regulars charged, the cannon belched out a deadly supply of grape which cut a sickening swathe through the British. They charged again, and the result was even more horrifying. Dismayed and mangled, the regulars withdrew.

If it could not be done in the usual way, Proctor thought, at least the Indians could storm the fort with their overwhelming numbers. But Tecumseh's braves had watched the slaughter of the regulars with a terror greater than those who were taking the brunt of it. Cannon fire was a kind of warfare they wanted no part of, as Indians had often shown before, and nothing Proctor or Tecumseh could say would induce them to make an assault.

For the Colonel that was the last straw. His expedition had been a total failure, and he blamed it on the Indians—first because Tecumseh's strategy had not succeeded, and second because his red allies had refused to fight when he needed them most. All this had cost him more than a hundred men killed and wounded. Thoroughly disgusted, he ordered the march back to Canada. He would make no more attempts at conquering the Ohio Valley, he said; from now on the Americans would have to come to him at Fort Malden.

This was precisely what the Americans needed—to be given time for the organization of their forces. Proctor gave them all they needed, sulking in his fort while Tecumseh raged at him. He did not know, or did not care, that Commodore Oliver Hazard Perry, of the United States Navy, was busy during that hot summer building a fleet with which to secure Lake Erie as a necessary prelude to the invasion of Canada. By early September Perry was ready, and on the 10th won his celebrated victory at Put In Bay, routing the British fleet.

An anxious observer of that historic battle was Tecumseh himself, who heard the guns and paddled out on the lake in his canoe, trying to get near enough to see what was happening. But the distance was too great and he could discern the contending vessels only dimly. He had no idea how the battle ended. Proctor knew, through his dispatches, but he was afraid to tell Tecumseh for fear the Indian army would leave, and contemptuous of them though he might be, they constituted by far the largest part of his defenses.

He would soon have need of them. Colonel Robert N. Johnson, with a tough regiment of mounted riflemen from Kentucky, had joined Harrison in his camp on Lake Erie between Sandusky Bay and Port Clinton. There the General had gathered an army almost 10,000 men strong, including 260 friendly Indians.

As soon as the General received Perry's famous message—"We have met the enemy and they are ours"—he began to move on Proctor. Colonel Johnson's Kentuckians were dispatched on a long end run around the lake, while Perry's fleet transported Harrison's infantry to Amherstburg. Detroit was quickly taken, after which the General, joined now by the cavalry, began to push up the Thames River Valley. Perry, with three of his lightest vessels, kept pace with him for fifteen miles, then went ashore and joined Harrison as a volunteer aide, thus completing what was really an amphibious operation.

When Proctor's intelligence brought him news of impending assault, the Colonel's every instinct urged him to burn the fort and retreat into Canada while there was still time. He would have no trouble urging this course of action on his own officers, but Tecumseh was a different matter. Nevertheless, Proctor held a council with the chief and in his inept way tried to tell him what he intended to do. Tecumseh heard the decision with cold rage. In a voice heavy with contempt and bitterness he reminded Proctor:

You always told us that you would never draw your foot off British ground; but now, father, we see you are drawing back . . . We must compare our father's conduct to a fat animal, that carries its tail upon its back, but when afrighted, he drops it between his legs and runs off. . . . You have got the arms and ammunition . . . sent for his red children; if you have an idea of going away, give them to us . . . Our lives are in the hands of the Great Spirit. We are determined to defend our lands, and if it be his will, we wish to leave our bones upon them.

Unfortunately, Tecumseh spoke much more for himself than for his warriors, who were not ready to leave their bones on British land if the British were not prepared to join them. Seeing their temper, Tecumseh reluctantly gave in to Proctor's assurance that he would make a stand somewhere in Canada at a more advantageous place. With Harrison's advancing army only three days distant, Fort Malden was burned and the retreat began. Proctor kept the Indians between his regulars and the pursuing Americans, but it was an awkward situation because many of the Indians had their wives and children with them and they could not move rapidly. It was soon apparent that the Americans would catch up and surround both regulars and Indians unless the British moved faster, which meant they would either have to abandon the Indian allies or make a stand. Harassed and fearful of either alternative, Proctor chose what he considered the lesser evil and, acceding to Tecumseh's persistent pleas, announced he would make a stand at the Thames River, about eighty-five miles east of the burned fort.

It was the final mistake in a career of ineptitude. The terrain he chose, not far from the missionary village of Moravian Town, was flat land, protected only by a small piece of swamp. In a word, it was indefensible. Proctor posted the Indians in a swamp on his right and, at the left, on wooded ground between another small swamp and the river, he placed his regulars.

A bugle call on the morning of October 5, 1813, sounded the doom of Proctor's army. Changing his strategy at the last moment when he discovered how the Colonel's troops were deployed, and at the urging of Colonel Johnson, Harrison opened the attack with a cavalry charge by Johnson's Kentuckians. The dashing Colonel led one battalion himself, against the Indians, while his brother James, a Lieutenant Colonel, charged the British lines.

It took no more than ten minutes for James to destroy the British regulars, even though both he and his brother had to dismount their men because the horses could not advance in the swampy ground. Scores of prisoners were taken. Proctor barely escaped, with forty dragoons, and hid with them in the woods.

Robert Johnson did not have so easy a time with Tecumseh's army. The Kentuckians found themselves in a furious hand-to-hand combat, whose outcome for a time was in doubt. Savage hatred drove the men on both sides—the Kentuckians thirsting for revenge against

Indians in general who had terrorized their homeland for so long, and the Indians fighting with the passion Tecumseh inspired in them. The chief fought with an abandon so reckless that it seemed as though he was determined to immolate himself on this final altar of all his hopes. And so it was. Legend says it was Colonel Johnson, five times wounded, who fired a fatal bullet at the chief.

As Tecumseh fell, the will to resist appeared to flow out of the Indians. Without his inspired leadership they were lost, and in any case the American bayonets had weakened their resistance. In despair, they melted away into the forest, taking their chief's body with them. The savage Kentuckians, finding a body they mistook for Tecumseh's, skinned it in strips for souvenirs.

With this decisive defeat, Indian resistance in the Northwest was effectively broken, and the road to Canada was open. It had not been a cheap matter to shatter Tecumseh's magnificent dream. From beginning to end he had cost the American government some five million dollars and the mustering of twenty thousand soldiers.

Nor was the dream entirely ended with his death. His recruiting expeditions to the tribes of the South had not been ineffectual, although these people had not actively joined his Confederacy. He had inspired in them an unrest and a hatred which would not die; his name even in death was a symbol of revolt. They remained as the last pocket of resistance to white domination east of the Mississippi River, and it was to them, particularly the Creeks and the Seminoles, that the American government next turned its bloody attention.

# 6
★ ★ ★ ★ ★ ★

# The Revolt of the Creeks
# and Seminoles

**N**O TRIBE east of the Mississippi was in quite the same position as the Creeks. Although they had been subjected to the iniquities of the Spanish conquistadores and their colonizing successors, and had experienced some brushes with the French and English from time to time, they had come somewhat closer to assimilation than other Indians. There had been a good deal of intermarrying with the whites, and the Creeks, never a particularly warlike tribe, had appeared to be content with farming. Moreover, they had enjoyed the benevolent interest of an exceptionally intelligent and honest Indian agent, Colonel Benjamin Hawkins.

Nevertheless they listened with interest when Tecumseh came among them. The chief was under the mistaken impression that his mother had been a Creek, and the tribe was proud to be allied by blood with so great a leader. Beyond this they could not help being stirred by Tecumseh's dream. They also had some reason to be apprehensive about the white men. Settlers were beginning to flock to their lands, and what the invaders could not get by treaty or cession, they simply took. It had required all of Colonel Hawkins' persuasive talents to restrain the Indians from taking some kind of retaliatory action. They were a substantial people in their own right, about 24,000 of them inhabiting a hundred or so towns, many of which were well built even by white settlers' standards.

Revolt might have broken out sooner, without Tecumseh's inspiration, if it had not been for divided loyalties among those of mixed blood, who found it an uncomfortable necessity to choose sides. One of these was a remarkable young chief named William Weatherford, the descendant of a French great-grandfather and a Creek girl. Their beautiful daughter, Sehoy, had been the bride of a Creek chieftain but later the mistress of an English captain, who had in turn lost her to a Scottish soldier of fortune, Lachlan McGillivray. The Scot wearied of wilderness romance and deserted his family for Scotland, from which he never returned, but one of his sons, Alexander, became a notable figure in the New World. His mixture of French, Spanish, Scot and Creek blood did not persuade him to pass as a white man, which his father had desired, but led him instead to favor the wigwam and a career of sheer adventure, fighting for the British as a Colonel in the Revolution, living a life as civil servant under the Spaniards, eventually serving Andrew Jackson and finally becoming supreme chief of the Creeks. He died in 1793, a rich man with a fortune of $100,000, and with the rank of Brigadier General in the United States Army.

Alexander's half-sister had married a Scot trader named Charles Weatherford, who fathered two sons, John and the William who had listened so eagerly to the words of Tecumseh. William, like his brother, was only one-eighth Indian, and his father had given both of them a choice as to which world they wished to inhabit. John chose the white world, while William elected the Creeks and, as Red Eagle, soon became a chief in their councils. With the benefit of more education than his fellows, he probably was not swayed by the superstitious appeals of the Prophet, who came with his brother to persuade the Creeks to join the Confederacy, but he must have responded to Tecumseh's angry outburst when the older chiefs showed themselves reluctant to accept the war hatchet. "Your blood is white!" Tecumseh had accused them. "You have taken my talk, and the wampum and the hatchet, but you do not mean to fight. I know the reason. You do not believe the Great Spirit has sent me. But you *shall* know. From here I shall go straight to Canada. When I arrive there I shall stamp the ground with my foot and shake down every house in this village." Tecumseh meant only to make an oratorical effect. He would have been as astonished as anyone to know that an earthquake shook the country of the Creeks not long after he departed.

Eloquence and earthquakes, however, did not move the Creeks to revolt in any large numbers. Only a quarter of them answered Tecumseh's call to arms. They were poorly equipped and hardly a serious fighting force, but they frightened the settlers, who were further alarmed when a small party of their number tried to intercept a band of 350 Indians and were soundly beaten.

In this moment of tension, William Weatherford, the Red Eagle of his own people, took what seemed to be a natural position of leadership, and with the aid of 1,000 braves, perpetrated a massacre so horrible that it roused the United States government to action. Weatherford's objective was a place known as Fort Mims, just north of the Florida border on the Alabama River. It was not actually a fort, but rather the fortified house of a half-breed, Samuel Mims, who had given shelter to 500 refugees from the sporadic terror which had broken out here and there all over the territory of the Creeks. These refugees were planters and farmers, for the most part, with their families and Negro slaves. Many of them, like Weatherford, were half-breed Creeks, with mixtures of French and Negro and Spanish thrown in. They were protected, if protection it could be called, by seventy Louisiana militiamen under Major Daniel Beasley, another half-breed.

On August 29, 1813, Weatherford and the 1,000 warriors crept up on Fort Mims and hid in the tall grass overnight. Their presence was discovered by Negroes, but Major Beasley refused to believe what they had seen and rewarded their vigilance by having them whipped. In the blazingly hot morning of the following day, the garrison lay stupefied in the heat until noon, when a drum sounded the call to mess. At this signal the Creeks sprang from the grass and charged the stockade gate, carelessly left open. They swarmed through it, clubbing the Major to death in the process, and proceeded to annihilate the garrison and its terrified refugees.

It was not accomplished without a struggle, because the Creeks had only bows and arrows to oppose the militia's guns. In the end, after three hours of fighting, they had to resort to the oldest of devices, flaming arrows, which set the place afire. Those who were afraid to brave the Indians were roasted alive; those who were not

could expect no mercy. Stirred to a frenzy, the Creeks were out of Weatherford's control. He was enough of a white man in spirit as well as fact to be appalled by the mad savagery he had unloosed, but he could not stop it. No one was spared from the knife and the hatchet. By the time the hot sun went down, all but thirty-six of the inhabitants, including men, women and children, had been killed and scalped.

A wave of indignation ran through the United States when the news of this massacre reached the outside world. It rolled on to the Nashville sickbed of General Andrew Jackson, still ailing from wounds sustained in a duel with Colonel Thomas Hart Benton. Ill as he was, Jackson was summoned by an outraged government in Washington to exterminate the Creeks.

Sick or well, Jackson was unquestionably the man for the job. Of all the Generals who had marched against resisting Indians, he was the toughest and the one from whom the red men could expect least. He had no sympathy for them, no understanding of their prob-

lems and could not have cared less about the justice of their claims, or the persecutions which had led to their revolt. He was a hard-line military man who meant to do exactly as he had been ordered—exterminate, or at the least, suppress.

Jackson could not go in person at once because he was still too ill to sit on a horse, but he sent 500 dragoons on ahead into Alabama, under Colonel John Coffee, and a little later, on October 7, he was able to set out from Fayetteville with 3,000 men, infantry and cavalry. The general had his arm in a sling and he was still pale and drawn from his illness, but he spared neither himself nor his men, covering twenty to thirty miles a day and meanwhile cutting a supply road over Raccoon and Lookout Mountains. As he traveled, he made ambitious plans which far exceeded his orders. He intended to brush aside the Creeks, and if the government did not prevent him, he would go into Florida and eliminate the Spanish and British outposts there which were supplying the Creeks with arms and ammunition.

On the way he encountered a Cherokee chief named Pathkiller who complained that Weatherford had threatened him and every other Indian with death if he did not support the Creek cause. "Brother," Jackson answered, "the hostile Creeks will not attack you until they have had a brush with me; and that I think will put them out of the notion."

Jackson's army quickly penetrated deep into Alabama by virtue of its forced marches, and by November 3 had reached the town of Tallassahatchee, where Weatherford and the Creeks had holed up. Attacking it, the General employed a favorite formation, deploying his troops in a crescent which was intended to fold in upon the Indians. The Creeks fought back bravely from house to house, but the strategy was entirely successful. As Davy Crockett, one of Jackson's soldiers, put it: "We shot them like dogs." Fort Mims was at least partially avenged by the death of 186 Indians; only five Americans had been lost, with forty-one wounded.

Weatherford was not present at this bloodletting. He was busy at the town of Talladega, thirty miles away, where he was carrying out the threat he had made to Pathkiller by besieging a band of Indians who were friendly to the whites and had refused to join him. By dint of another series of quick marches, Jackson rushed his 1,200 infantrymen and 800 cavalry to the scene. Utilizing the same crescent formation, he was only slightly less successful. About 700 Creeks managed to break out and escape, but 290 others were killed. Again, Jackson's own losses were light; fifteen dead and eighty-five wounded.

Before he could resume the campaign, Jackson was confronted with a problem familiar to American commanders from the time of Washington. The enlistment terms of his militia were nearly up, and they were preparing to leave. They had had enough of hard marches and the General's harsh discipline, and they were seriously short of supplies in the bargain. Stricken with a dysentery so severe he could scarcely stand, the indomitable Jackson nevertheless answered the pleas of a hungry soldier by taking some acorns from his pocket and saying, "I will divide with you what I have."

When the moment of crisis came in late November, and the troops were about to leave, in spite of the fact that fresh supplies had arrived to relieve their hunger, Jackson did what no other general in a similar circumstance had ever had the raw courage to do. A grim, gaunt figure of a man, still not well, he sat his horse resolutely with one arm in a sling and, positioning his gun across the neck of his mount with the other, he warned the soldiers bluntly that he would shoot the first man who tried to leave. (He did not know until later that the musket was in as sorry a condition as he was and could not have been fired.) His action was, of course, illegal. The militia were not required to stay beyond the term of their enlistment. But it was effective nonetheless, and not a single soldier dared defy the man they called Old Hickory with good reason.

Jackson's troubles were far from over, however. Indeed, they began to increase at once. Indomitable as he was, he could not really prevent the men from leaving if they chose to do so as the time of their enlistment expired. Nor were they likely to stay out of loyalty. The General's bad health made him even more than normally irritable and impatient; tempers on both sides were wearing thin. Still Jackson was able to persuade the men to stay until their replacements arrived. He thought his difficulty had ended when these recruits marched in— 1,450 good men from Tennessee—but he exploded in renewed anger when he discovered that their enlistments would be up in ten days, at which time they intended to turn around and march home again. Another relief column, this one of volunteer cavalrymen, was also hurrying up, but when they encountered Jackson's original army straggling home they decided to go with them. When this news was brought to Jackson on his sickbed, the General could only groan, "Can it be true what I hear?"

By this time his forces had shrunk to only 500 effectives. Another man would have been glad to obey the order to retreat which came from his superior, Governor Blount of Tennessee, but Jackson shot back a scornful reply:

And are you my Dear friend sitting with yr. arms folded . . . recommending me to retrograde to please the whims of the populace . . . Let me tell you it imperiously lies upon both you and me to do our duty regardless of consequences or the opinion of these fireside patriots, those fawning sycophants of cowardly poltroons who after their boasted ardor would . . . let thousands fall victims to my retrograde . . . Arouse from yr. lethargy—despite fawning smiles or snarling frowns— with energy exercise yr. functions—the campaign must rapidly progress or . . . yr. country ruined. Call out the full quota—execute the orders of the Secy. of War, arrest the officer who omits his duty . . . and let popularity perish for the present . . . Save Mobile—save the Territory—save yr. Frontier from becoming drenched in blood . . . What retrograde under these circumstances? I will perish first.

This clarion challenge shamed Blount and the War Department into rescinding the retreat order and mustering a new relief army, but before it could arrive, most of Jackson's little force left him, with callous indifference to his condition, and for a few perilous hours the majesty of the United States Army in the South consisted of 130 men. When the relief came, 800 men, Jackson seized upon them like one drowning and threw them into action immediately while he could still count them in his service. As he had in the past, the General marched them seventy miles in three days to where Weatherford had encamped with his warriors, on the Horseshoe Bend of the Tallapoosa River.

Jackson was not optimistic about the impending battle. His recruits were raw, both officers and men; he expected little of them. Nevertheless, he was determined to strike while he had any strength. Weatherford, whose scouts had warned him of Jackson's approach, was resolved to strike first. But the General, experienced in these matters, anticipated that the chief would attack just before dawn, as the Indians so often did, and he kept his men under arms all night. If a battle began, he told them, they were to fire at the flashes from the attackers' guns until it was light enough to see. The attack went exactly as he had anticipated, and the Indians, failing in their surprise, soon retreated after a sharp skirmish.

Like two baseball managers in a close game, Weatherford and Jackson now tried to outguess each other. The chief pretended to retreat, hoping to draw out the white men's lines and make them vulnerable to flanking attack. But Jackson was too wise to fall into this ancient trap. He waited until he was confident that the Indians had given up that maneuver and were preparing to attack again, then he beat them to the charge. There was another skirmish and the Indians withdrew once more.

But Jackson decided it would not be safe to linger, seventy miles away from base and confronted by a superior force. He began a slow retreat, with the Creeks silently following him through the chill

January landscape, waiting to pounce if the opportunity offered. The General suspected that the Indians intended to fall upon him as he crossed Enotachopco Creek. That would be their best opportunity. Consequently Jackson laid an elaborate strategic trap for them at this crossing, but it failed when some of his raw militia colonels failed to stand firm and led their men in a panicky retreat. Jackson saved the day only by the sheer force of his personality. He rode about thundering at his men so fiercely that they feared him more than they did the Creeks. As one of the soldiers wrote later: "In showers of balls he was seen performing the duties of subordinate officers, rallying the alarmed . . . inspiriting them by his example . . . Cowards forgot their panic . . . and the brave would have formed round his body a rampart with their own."

By this act of courage Jackson saved his troops and completed the retreat successfully. Nevertheless he was wrathfully conscious that it *was* a retreat, and that after his initial successes he had little to show for his campaign. Weatherford was nearly as strong as ever, while he had only the green remnants of an army. It was no consolation that other generals by this time were also failing to exterminate the Creeks. True, General Claiborne had reached as far as Weatherford's own village of Econochaca and burned it. His militiamen had even surrounded the chief himself on a high cliff and might have ended the war then and there by capturing him, but Weatherford anticipated the motion picture thrillers of a later time by leaping his horse from the bluff into a river and escaping. No more than a month later Claiborne was in as serious danger as Weatherford had been, when his militia deserted him wholesale at the end of their enlistments and he found himself a long way from home with only sixty men.

The situation had improved somewhat by February, for all the American commanders in the field. Jackson had 5,000 new militia under his command whom he could expect to keep for a time, and this admittedly raw force was strengthened considerably by the arrival of the 39th United States Infantry. Now Jackson had one of the two things he knew he must have—a hard, disciplined corps of regulars. The other requirement was adequate supply.

Jackson whipped the green militiamen into line with a display of military savagery unusual even for him. Not even officers were exempt. He arrested a brigadier general and a major general and sent them home disgraced. For defying an officer, a seventeen-year-old boy was courtmartialed and executed. Jackson meant to have no more recalcitrance in his army. If the men feared him, so much the better.

Having prepared a force he thought he could depend upon, the General decided late in March to make a major move by attacking Weatherford at the strong point he was now occupying, a heavily fortified fort located at Horseshoe Bend, on the Tallapoosa River. It would be a difficult position to take, but Jackson believed that his superior force of 2,000 men would be more than a match for the 900 warriors Weatherford could command. The 300 women and children also in the fort could be counted on as a hindrance. As his first move, Jackson thoughtfully cut off the line of retreat Weatherford had prepared by taking away his fleet of canoes, a theft accomplished under fire by a detachment of scouts who swam the river to do it. Then Jackson issued a final order: "Any officer or soldier who flies before the enemy without being compelled to do so by superior force . . . shall suffer death."

With that uncompromising admonition the battle began with a bombardment of the fort's breastworks by Jackson's six-pounders. That proved to be ineffective. The cannon were too far away to send their balls against the solid logs with enough force to break them, and the cannoneers could not bring them closer because the Creek sharpshooters were picking them off.

Now with a flurry of drums the 39th Infantry charged. A young ensign named Sam Houston led the regulars when their major fell dead on the ramparts. Houston was twenty-two years away from his own glory at San Jacinto, but he fought well that day too as the battle swayed back and forth through the long afternoon. Obviously neither Jackson nor the Indians intended to give in this time. The General tightened his crescent slowly on the fort and the Creeks grimly dug in and fought back without quarter or respite.

If the defenders meant to fight to the last man, they nearly succeeded. Jackson must have been astonished to see that these Indians, contrary to usual behavior, did not flee when the battle was obviously lost. He did not know their medicine men had worked them up to a pitch of mystical confidence that the Great Spirit would save them. The sign was to be a cloud in the sky, and by strange coincidence a cloud did appear in the hitherto serene heavens just as Jackson sent in an offer to protect the survivors if they would surrender. Inspired by the sign, the Creeks cried out in triumph and fell to the battle with renewed fury.

Their cause was hopeless, however. They fought into the night, until Jackson roasted alive those who remained by using one of their own devices and setting the fort afire with flaming arrows. It had been a blood bath of the first magnitude. When daylight came and the dead could be counted, 557 of Weatherford's 900 warriors lay dead on the peninsula where the fort was situated, and another 200 were at the river's bottom. Most of those still alive were wounded. Jackson's losses were comparatively small—forty-nine dead, 157 wounded.

One important statistic was missing. Weatherford himself was not among the dead or wounded, and Jackson was beside himself with rage to think that the grand prize had escaped. In fact, Weatherford had escaped only by sheer accident. Apparently not expecting the attack so soon, he had been away that day inspecting another of his strong points and missed the battle entirely.

A few days later, for reasons that were never clear, he walked into Jackson's quarters calmly and surrendered himself. He must have made a deep impression. John Reid, Jackson's aide, who was present when the two men confronted each other, wrote of the meeting: "Weatherford was the greatest of the Barbarian world. He possessed all the manliness of sentiment—all the heroism of soul, all the comprehension of intellect calculated to make an able commander. You have seen his speech to Genl Jackson . . . but you could not see his looks and gestures—the modesty & yet the firmness that were in them."

The speech referred to by Reid was one full of dignity. Weatherford said: "I have come to give myself up. I can oppose you no longer. I have done you much injury. I should have done you more. . . . [but] my warriors were killed . . . I am in your power. Dispose of me as you please."

Jackson replied:

You are not in my power. I had ordered you brought to me in chains . . . But you have come of your own accord . . . You see my camp . . . You see my army . . . you know my object . . . I would gladly save you and your nation, but you do not even ask to be saved. If you think you can contend against me in battle, go and head your warriors.

Weatherford answered:

You can safely address me in such terms now. There was a time when I could have answered you; there was a time when I had a choice; I have none now. I have not even a hope. I could once animate my warriors to battle, but I cannot animate the dead. My warriors can no longer hear my voice. Their bones are at Talladega, Tallassahatchee, Emuckfau, and Tohopeka. I have not surrendered myself without thought. While there was a single chance of success I never left my post nor supplicated for peace. But my people are gone and I now ask it for my nation, not myself . . . But I beg you to send for the women and children of the war party, who have been driven to the woods without an ear of corn . . . they never did any harm. But kill me, if the white people want it done.

I look back with deep sorrow, and wish to avert still greater calamities. If I had been left to contend with the Georgia army, I would have raised my corn on one bank of the river, and fought them on the other. But your people have destroyed my nation. You are a brave man. I rely upon your generosity. You will exact no terms of a conquered people, but such as they should accede to. Whatever they may be, it would be madness and folly to oppose them. If they are opposed, you shall find me among the sternest enforcers of obedience. Those who would still hold out can be influenced only by a mean spirit of revenge. To this they must not and shall not sacrifice the last remnant of their country. You have told our nation where we might go and be safe. This is good talk, and they ought to listen to it. They *shall* listen to it.

To this magnificent speech, Jackson, as one brave soldier to another, could make only one reply. He drank a glass of brandy with Weatherford and agreed to help the women and children if the chief would keep the peace, after which Weatherford walked out of the camp under the noses of the astonished soldiers and disappeared. By late April, Jackson was back home in Tennessee and the Creek War was over.

For the Creeks who remained it would be a defeat worse than they feared. The American government was not inclined to be magnanimous in victory. Once more a treaty was signed—another shameful document in an increasingly long list—which took away most of the

Creek territory not only from the hostile Indians but those who had tried to help the government as well. Jackson later offered the lame explanation that the government had virtually expropriated this land in order to set up a barrier of white settlement against further encroachment from the Spaniards in Florida. If no one really believed this thesis, it could also be said that no one was left to care but the beaten, subdued remnants of the Creek nation.

Jackson, promoted to Major General, would soon be off to more historic glory at the Battle of New Orleans, ending the War of 1812 after it had already officially ended. But he was not through with the Indians. It was he who returned to Horseshoe Bend in July 1814 and negotiated, if it could be so dignified, the infamous treaty. The proud Creeks came to the council uncomplaining, but wretched and miserable and so hungry that, as Jackson wrote home to his wife, they were "picking up the grains of corn scattered from the mouths of horses." To these ragged, destitute people, Jackson had the sublime arrogance in summoning them to warn that "Destruction will attend a failure to comply." Then he had the gall to address them as "friends and brothers" and to suggest that since the war had been so expensive for the United States, these poverty-stricken survivors must help pay for it by giving up their land, 23,000,000 acres of it, comprising today about three-fifths of Alabama and one-fifth of Georgia. When the two principal chiefs, Big Warrior and Shelokta, tried to persuade him to mitigate the terms, Jackson refused adamantly. They must sign that night, or be considered enemies of the government and dealt with appropriately, he said, although, short of murder, it was difficult to imagine what more the government could do to them. Silently they signed and departed.

It was little wonder that many of the Cherokees chose to slip into Florida and there make common cause with the Seminoles, who were harassing the border while negotiations for the purchase of Florida from the Spaniards dragged on year after year. In a none too subtle effort to end these troubles and at the same time possibly seize Florida, without troubling to complete the negotiations, Secretary of War John C. Calhoun ordered Jackson on December 26, 1817, to take an army into Georgia and "adopt the necessary measures" against the Indians. President Monroe added a carefully worded, discreet but unmistakable permission for Jackson to take Florida if he could. Jackson later flouted the Constitution by enlisting volunteer troops (including a brigade of Creek Indians) and appointing officers without Congressional or Presidential sanction.

In his forthright way, Jackson lost no time. He took his army of 800 regulars and 900 Georgia militia, on the usual short rations and long marches, straight into Florida. There, although nothing official had been said about it, he had still another mission, which was to catch slaves. Negroes escaping from the Georgia and South Carolina plantations had made their way to Florida, where some of them intermarried with the Creeks and Seminoles, while others, ironically, were enslaved anew by Indian masters. After the importation of slaves from Africa was prohibited, the escapees had a much higher value to the plantation owners, who brought so much pressure on the government that, in some respects, the first Seminole War which brought Jackson to Florida was a military slave-catching expedition.

It had not been much easier for him to muster an army than on his first campaign. As always after a war, the aftermath of the War of 1812 found the regular army dwindled, from 33,000 to less than 7,500. At the time of Jackson's second foray into the South there were only eight infantry regiments, one of light artillery, eight artillery battalions which functioned primarily as infantry, a minimum staff corps and no cavalry whatever. These troops were fitted out in blue-and-gray woolen uniforms. On their heads they wore leather shakos trimmed with black cockades and brass eagles. Their high collars were uncomfortable, and their white crossbelts made them excellent targets for enemy sharpshooters. Unfortunately the government had not yet learned how to dress troops for fighting in their own country; they were still outfitted in a style befitting the open formations of Europe, where soldiers did not have to crawl through swamps or fight from behind trees and thickets or endure the doubtful pleasures of the wilderness.

These, nevertheless, were the troops Jackson led into Florida, along a trail well marked with blood during the previous two years. In the summer of 1816, American soldiers with naval support had attacked a Negro fort on the Appalachicola River, where 300 men, women, and children—ex-slaves or their descendants—were living. This action ended abruptly when a hot cannonball from one of the

supporting gun boats fell into the fort's powder magazine. Only fifty of the garrison survived. Two of the leaders were executed, and the others were sent back as slaves to their former owners.

Partly in retaliation, and partly as the result of encroachment and bad treatment by the whites, Seminole war parties had begun to appear soon afterward, and shortly before Jackson's march, a frontier war had flamed through Georgia, much as it had in the Ohio

Valley. This was the situation which had called out Old Hickory once more.

His campaign was entirely characteristic. He burned every Seminole village in his path, and at St. Marks, a fort on the west coast of Florida, he took his first prisoner of consequence, Alexander Arbuthnot. This Scot trader was known for his honest dealings with Indians and his distaste for the English and Americans who had cheated them. A dignified man more than seventy years old, Arbuthnot had long served the Seminoles well in trying to protect them in their various negotiations with white men. In the taking of St. Marks, Jackson also captured two Creek chieftains who were summarily hanged next day without a trial. Arbuthnot, because he was white, was given the privilege of a trial.

Moving off into the interior, Jackson next took the village of Chief Boleck, better known as Billy Bowlegs, but the Indians had fled from it. The General arrested two white men, Lieutenant Robert C. Ambrister, of the Royal Colonial Marines, a soldier of fortune, and his British friend, Peter B. Cook. Returning to St. Marks, Jackson had Arbuthnot and Ambrister tried in a proceeding that was a weird mockery of justice. When the courtmartial changed Ambrister's death sentence to a year and fifty lashes, Jackson promptly reversed the decision and the adventurer was shot. Nor did Arbuthnot's simple, eloquent plea that his judges "lean on the side of mercy" have any effect. This excellent old man had made the mistake of loving the Indians and helping them, and freely admitted as much. He was hanged. These two executions sent a wave of indignation over Britain when the news reached London, but nothing was done.

Meanwhile Jackson pursued his reckless course, reaching the Spanish fort at Pensacola on May 28. He captured it after a three-day siege, ran up the American flag, appointed a colonel as governor and further confounded international law by virtually annexing that quarter of Florida to the United States. Then he went on to capture every other Spanish fort within reach before he set off for home on May 30.

From a military standpoint, the General could hardly have been more successful, but he left behind him an international mess which precipitated a diplomatic war between Spain and the United States. Spain demanded return of the forts, indemnification and Jackson's punishment. President Monroe was ready to satisfy her on all three counts, but John Quincy Adams talked him out of it. Jackson was called to Washington to defend his actions, and the House conducted a furious debate on the Florida affair. But the General was able to bring enough political pressure to bear so that in the end the House refused to condemn the executions, or to approve a bill designed to prevent such arbitrary punishments in future, or to condemn the capture of Pensacola, or even to consider a bill barring invasion of foreign territory without authorization of Congress unless in pursuit of an enemy. A Senate committee later took a far different view of Jackson and his actions, but the General, a popular idol, prevailed.

The controversy died and Spain ceded Florida to the United States in 1821. Once more the old question arose. Would the acres of Florida, claimed by the Seminoles, be acquired by purchase, no matter how onesided the terms, or through brutal conquest? When it came time to decide this question, Jackson had reached the White House and the answer could not be doubted. The General had personally conducted the first Seminole War; he directed the second one as President.

Where the first war had been a farce as a military action, the second one was a different matter. The Seminoles by this time realized they were fighting for their lives as well as their property, and they were a tough, resourceful people who lived in a watery jungle, a kind of terrain previous Indian-hunting expeditions had never been compelled to penetrate. It took seven long years to subdue them, and even then the result was indecisive in a sense.

To fight over this different terrain, the Army had to produce new techniques, prototypes of some still in use today, notably collapsible rubber boats to replace the old wooden pontoons, and the development of guerrilla warfare.

As was so often the case, the second Seminole War began with a peace treaty. It was the Treaty of Payne's Landing in 1832, still another fraudulent affair. This fascinating document proposed to move the Seminoles from their home in Florida to Oklahoma, where they would be placed on a reservation in company with Creeks who had already been moved there. The price for this accommodation, by which a homeland was to be exchanged for exile and virtual slavery, was $15,400 in cash, and a blanket or a homespun frock for every man, woman and child.

In the finer print was a clause which was far worse, and it was the heart of the matter. The government was still under pressure from the Southern slaveholders to retrieve the Negroes who had escaped to Florida. In Jackson they had a President who listened sympathetically to their demands. Consequently the 1832 treaty first had the presumption to assess the Seminoles, who could hardly be held responsible, $7,000 if it was found that "slaves and other property" were indeed in Florida, for they would then be considered as stolen. How the government meant to sort out this human property was not set forth, and in fact it would have been impossible, since so much intermarriage and assimilation had taken place. When the slave-catchers came into Florida before and during the first Seminole War, the Indians had treated them as invaders and resisted their incursions. That had been understood by the Spaniards, who specified in ceding Florida that the United States must respect the rights of the Seminoles and treat them fairly. This clause, of course, was never taken seriously for a moment by the Jackson Administration, or any other for that matter. In fact, as soon as Florida passed into American hands, the government actually protected the slave-catchers as they went about their work, scooping up not only escaped slaves but Indians and half-breeds as well, to be sold in Georgia and Alabama. During this period the Seminoles withdrew deep in the swamps and became fugitives themselves.

Thus the Treaty of Payne's Landing was bad enough in itself, but the government added a verbal codicil which was worst of all. No Seminole who had Negro blood would be allowed to go to Oklahoma, but must stay and be sold into slavery. For hundreds of Seminole families, that meant dissolution and a living death.

Surprisingly, seven Seminole chiefs signed this infamous document, and several more added their names the following year. But the government wanted unanimous approval and urged the others to follow the example. One of the indignant and contemptuous holdouts was Osceola, little more than thirty years old, a leader among his people but not a chief, who had fought Jackson in the first war. He had something of Tecumseh's powerful personality, and was a natural leader of men.

On the third attempt by the government's negotiator to get unanimous approval of the treaty, in April, 1835, Osceola plunged his hunting knife into the document to express his contempt for it and, after an angry argument with the whites, was arrested and thrown into chains. At that juncture he employed some deception of his own.

Pretending to have changed his mind and offering to help bring about unanimity, he persuaded the whites to free him. Immediately he began to organize all those who hated the treaty for an all-out war against the government.

"You have guns and so have we," he told the Indian agent, General Wiley Thompson, in charge of the negotiations. "You have powder and lead, and so have we. Your men will fight, and so will ours, till the last drop of Seminole blood has moistened the dust of his hunting ground!"

To carry out this vow, Osceola introduced a kind of resistance the Indian Wars had not yet witnessed. Hiding the women and children deep in the swamps, he deployed his small forces into guerrilla units. Much like the Viet Cong more than a century later, these hardy fighters slipped in and out of the swamp, striking whatever they could and disappearing again.

This warfare brought inevitable retaliation. Brevet Major Francis L. Dade set out from Fort King on Christmas Eve, 1835, with 112 men from the 4th Infantry and 2nd and 3rd Artillery. Also in the train was a six-pounder with an accompanying ammunition cart, a ration wagon and, unfortunately, a spy in the person of a Negro guide named Luis, who had informed the Seminoles of the party's route.

Osceola and 180 braves waited in a palmetto grove beside the trail. On the morning of the 28th, the Indians caught the advancing column woefully unprepared, with only a small advance guard and no flankers. Worse, because the day was cold Dade had permitted the men to button their overcoats, thus making it difficult for them to get at their cartridge belts in a hurry.

At a signal from Osceola, a withering blast burst from the palmettos, mowing down the advance guard in the first volley, Dade and his staff and nearly half the troops, who had been caught at a range of thirty-five yards. Those who survived managed to fire the round in their muskets, but then they were fatally delayed getting at the cartridges beneath their overcoats. The artillerymen, however, were in a better position and fired a round or two of canister before the Seminoles picked off the crews. When it was over, only three men of the expedition had escaped, all of them seriously wounded. They crawled into the tall grass and feigned death. Two of them finally made their way to Fort King.

The whole affair was over so quickly that Osceola had time to settle a score elsewhere. Taking a small party of braves with him, he hurried to Fort King and crawled through the grass to a house about 150 yards from the fort, where General Thompson, the man who had negotiated the treaty and thrown him into irons, was having dinner with nine other men. Although the day was cool, it was clear and the doors and windows had been left open to let in the warm sun. Through these openings Osceola poured a volley which killed Thompson and four of his friends. The Payne's Landing Treaty was avenged. Osceola was content to let the others escape to the fort.

Now there began a grim game of pursuit and retreat as one expedition after another tried to trap the elusive Osceola. The Seminole risked only one open battle, a skirmish at Ouithlacoochee River ford, in which he himself was wounded and lost many men, although he inflicted a loss of sixty-three Americans killed and wounded. After this near disaster, Osceola returned to guerrilla tactics.

More men were poured into the field by an irritated President Jackson, who no doubt wished he could undertake the job himself. General Gaines led an expedition of 1,100 men out of New Orleans, arriving in Tampa on February 9, 1836, and sailing grandly up the Alafia River in three steamboats. Basing his army on Fort King, he fought several indecisive skirmishes with Osceola's warriors, with little to show for it, since the Seminoles refused to make a second mistake and avoided any kind of orthodox conflict.

Other and even more distinguished generals joined the pursuit as the frustrating war dragged on through the summer. General Winfield Scott, a War of 1812 hero who would go on to greater deeds in Mexico, took command but he accomplished nothing of a military nature, although his tact and forbearance did much to prevent a more destructive conflict. His only accomplishment was to ship off to Oklahoma some 400 Seminoles, most of them women and children from friendly villages which had signed the treaty. Scott's failure was not entirely his fault. He was an extremely able commander who had unfortunately incurred Jackson's dislike. It was no accident that Scott was always short of arms, ammunition and equipment during his Florida campaign. The President, however, had nothing to do with the epidemics of mumps and measles which reduced the American forces, along with the perennial militia losses. Nevertheless, Jackson was vindictive enough to have Scott recalled and brought before a board of inquiry, which exonerated him.

The failure to eliminate Osceola and the Seminoles was beginning to be a political embarrassment in Washington. It was a public joke, although anything but a laughing matter to Jackson, when general followed general southward and with each one statements were issued from the White House announcing Osceola's imminent downfall. The President's harsh treatment of those career officers who failed soon made Florida the most feared assignment in the Army.

At last, in his extremity, Jackson turned to the Quartermaster General, Thomas Sidney Jesup, who was instructed to do what no one else had been able to do. Jesup had a somewhat better understanding of the problem than his predecessors. He insisted that he be given enough men and supplies to do the job, which Jackson readily granted. He was also given exceptionally able subordinates in such men as Colonels William S. Harney and Zachary Taylor.

Jesup reached Florida in January 1837, and for a time it seemed as though he would have no better luck than the others. Once more there were skirmishes but never a decisive meeting, and the dispatches from Washington soon began to take on an ominous note of complaint. Jesup concluded that he would have to take some other tactic to save himself and conceived the idea of acting as peacemaker. Somewhat to his surprise, the Seminoles responded. In May he found himself host to 3,000 men, women and children, including Osceola and several prominent chiefs of the tribe, at Fort Mellon, on Lake Monroe. It was Jesup's intention to persuade them to accept Thompson's original plan and ship them to Oklahoma. For that purpose he had thoughtfully assembled twenty-four transports off Tampa to begin the journey, so confident was he of success. When Osceola saw these ships, he understood what the real purpose of the peace council was to be. Overnight all 3,000 Seminoles disappeared.

That was a blow so crushing, combined with sickness and desertions among his troops, that Jesup asked to be recalled. Jackson would readily have obliged anyone else, but there was no one to turn to for the moment, so in reply the General got only a torrent of abuse from Congress and the Secretary of War's promise to send him 700 Indians from the Ohio Valley to help in the guerrilla warfare. The news did not cheer Jesup. If there was one thing he did not need it was more Indians. In fact, about 1,000 of them arrived in September, but Jesup could see that they had no enthusiasm for hunting down their countrymen.

Jesup by this time was a thoroughly frustrated man, feeling himself sinking slowly into a morass large enough to accommodate his entire career. With growing desperation came a plan. It was clear that the second Seminole War would never be ended until its leader, Osceola, was captured, and if he could not be captured by the fair means of traditional warfare, Jesup was prepared to use foul.

The method he chose was as simple as it was unconscionable. He asked Osceola to meet him for a council under a flag of truce, and when the Seminole appeared with seventy-five of his men, Jesup simply arrested them all. He was astounded by the instant reaction in Washington and the nation. Instead of being applauded for succeeding in so inexpensive a ruse, he was denounced for violating the rules of warfare and displaying what was considered a shameful example of treachery, although it was no worse than a thousand other things the government had done in its treatment of the Indians.

Osceola was a prisoner, nevertheless, and rules of the game or not, Jesup did not intend to jeopardize whatever remained of his career by letting his captive go. If he could now achieve the end, the means might be forgotten.

In captivity Osceola was a pitiful figure. This brave man to whom the outdoors was home could not stand his confinement in the dank Federal prisons at St. Augustine and Charleston. Three months after his capture, he was dead, having wasted away to a mere remembrance of what he had been. Osceola was not a leader of Tecumseh's caliber, but he might have become a constructive force in the tribe if they had been left in peace. As it was, his name became a legend among his people and lives in history today.

Ironically, Jesup achieved nothing by his treachery, either militarily or for himself. The war went on as before, with the Seminoles now in a more violent mood than ever and thirsting for revenge. Jesup had his earlier request granted summarily and was recalled. Only the intervention of his friend, Senator Thomas Hart Benton, saved him from losing his job as Quartermaster.

A new commander came upon the scene, one of lesser rank but more talent. Colonel Zachary Taylor was experienced in fighting Indians. His nickname, "Old Rough and Ready," suggested that he was cast in the same mold as Jackson, and that was true. Like Jackson, he was tall and lean, rugged and profane, a born fighting man. Curiously enough he was following substantially the same path Jackson had taken to the White House.

Taylor inherited a dangerous situation. The Seminoles were now in full revolt. Not only were they intent on avenging Osceola, but quite naturally they would not listen to anything the white men said, and had no intention of moving to Oklahoma. They were hidden away in central Florida and, as far as Taylor could see, they would almost literally have to be blasted out if the war was to be won.

Never a man to be daunted by impossible tasks, Taylor set out boldly to do it. Late in November, 1837, he assembled nearly 1,000 men, including 727 regulars from the 1st, 4th and 6th Infantry and 4th Artillery, along with Missouri volunteers serving as mounted infantry. Supported by a baggage train of eighty wagons and pack mules, he marched inland from Tampa Bay on December 19, and soon reached Lake Okeechobee, only twenty-five miles from Lake Kissimmee, where the main body of Seminoles were encamped.

On Christmas morning Taylor appeared before the camp, and for the second time in the war the Seminoles permitted themselves to fight an orthodox action. They were well protected by a dense hummock, which Taylor's men charged time and again for an hour against a skillful defense conducted by Chief Alligator, who had accounted for the destruction of Major Dade's command. The chief had departed from Osceola's practice and allowed the battle to occur because he thought his position impregnable. It was flanked by thick groves of palmetto and cypress, and before it lay an oozing swamp from which grew sharp sawgrass five feet or more high.

Against this formidable position, Taylor soon saw that the frontal assault with which he had begun would not work. Nor could his cavalry outflank the position because the horses could not get through a deep creek and, in any case, were sinking into the muck. But the cavalry dismounted and, holding their rifles high, began to wade forward. A solid volley from the Seminoles caught them flush, and their leader, Colonel Gentry, fell mortally wounded. The first wave broke as men fell headfirst into the slime and the others staggered back.

Taylor then sent in his regulars, who were also hard hit but they closed ranks, held steady and poured in a heavy return fire. The 4th Infantry, closing on the left, made better progress and established a position on a piece of higher ground. The reserves were poured in and the 1st Infantry charged. It was too much strength for the Seminoles. They gave ground, and fled. Taylor had a victory at last, but he had lost twenty-eight men killed and 111 wounded. As usual, no one knew what the Seminoles suffered.

As the winter wore on, Taylor appeared to be making some progress, although he had nothing further to show for his efforts except a few brisk skirmishes, but Jackson was too impatient to wait for what the spring might bring. Taylor was recalled, remarking as he left that the other commanders had been right and it was impossible to conquer the Seminoles. At least he had not resorted to Jesup's treachery, nor to that General's other desperate resort of importing bloodhounds, which brought further indignation on his head. The dogs, as it turned out, had only added to Jesup's history of frustration. They were trained to hunt Negroes, and Seminoles did not smell the same to them. Not only did they refuse to chase Indians, but if they found any, they deserted and made friends with them. By a choice irony, the Seminoles trained them to hunt white men.

Taylor was succeeded by General McComb, who was instructed to employ neither dogs nor men but to see what he could do about making peace. Two years of earnest effort on his part came to nothing. The Seminoles would not stop harassing him at every possible point, nor would they talk about peace. Consequently McComb was supplanted by General W. R. Armistead, who was instructed to be even more conciliatory. Armistead conceived the brilliant device of bringing in fourteen Seminole chiefs from the Oklahoma reservation, men who had opposed the migration at one time but were now reconciled to it. The General sent them among the tribes as salesmen in his behalf. They held a conference with the resisting chiefs, deep in the swamp, and when it was over they went back to Oklahoma. The war went on.

Armistead was dismayed, but he was willing to go back to military measures. The government, however, was disappointed in him and set about looking for a successor. It was still firmly believed that the war would be won if only the right general could be found. This time the Secretary of War appointed, in the spring of 1841, an officer who had been on the scene in Florida since 1838. He was General William J. Worth, the son of Quaker parents, who had served with distinction in the War of 1812, acted as Commandant at West Point and won his general's commission in an earlier victorious skirmish against the Seminoles.

Worth's theory of the war was that the Indians would not be defeated by force of arms, nor would they be lured to the peace table; therefore they must be conquered by the only other means remaining —that is, by attrition. During the summer of 1841 he began such a campaign, systematically destroying crops, shelters and every source of supply on which they might depend. In this shadow war, he never came to grips with the enemy. They always fled before him, but they left behind the means of war, which he forthwith removed from them. Once he was lucky enough to capture a chief and some other resistance leaders whom he held, in effect, as hostages. He sentenced them to be hanged, but he sent word to the Seminoles still in hiding that he would spare the lives of these captives if the others surrendered.

In the fall, as winter drew on, Worth's policy of attrition bore its bitter fruit. Slowly the Seminoles began to drift in from the swamps, hungry and homeless, proud but driven to the outer limits of their endurance and bravery. Looking upon this thin, ragged, barefoot, starving army, it was hard to understand why the United States Army and a dozen eminent generals had been unable to subdue them in six years of earnest effort. They were a wretched lot, and their weaponry had been reduced to little more than knives and clubs. Upon this defiant tribe the government had spent $20,000,000 and employed more than 30,000 troops, including nearly all the regular Army, more than half the Marines and a quantity of Navy ships and transports. The American casualties had been 1,466 killed, including 215 officers.

Even at that the victory was not complete. More than 4,000 Seminoles were finally removed to Oklahoma, but there were some who withstood even Worth's campaign of attrition and refused to come out of the swamps. They were not enough to start a new war, but they never signed a peace treaty with the government. Their continued defiance came to light a century later when, in the Second World War, many of them would not register for the draft because they did not consider themselves American citizens, but members of the Seminole nation, a sovereign country.

The generals had been right. These were the only Indians who could not be defeated. All they could do was to demonstrate what a high price, both moral and material, the government was willing to pay for total dominance of the Indians.

# 7

# Black Hawk's War, and the Trail of Tears

Two EPISODES of high drama and deep tragedy closed the white man's conquest of all America lying east of the Mississippi River. They were, in a sense, preludes to that greatest emotional experience of our people, the Civil War. Because of these episodes the battle lines drawn in that conflict in the major theaters of operation did not have to take into account the temper and disposition of Indian tribes. By that time those that were hostile lived entirely beyond the Mississippi and their participation in the war was little more than a sideshow well away from the big tent.

To accomplish this suppression, the government needed only to defeat one more Indian revolutionary leader, and to remove by force an entire, unresisting Indian nation, in what can only be called one of the most shameful acts in our history.

The last leader of the Eastern tribes was a Sauk (or Sac) chief whose Indian name was Ma-ka-tai-me-she-kia-kiak, that is, Black Sparrow Hawk. To the white men he was known as Black Hawk, and this name was given to the war he fought. It was not a grand conspiracy like Pontiac's or Tecumseh's. By comparison it was little more than a rear-guard action against the advancing invaders, but like the Seminoles, Black Hawk compelled the Federal government to put an army in the field. In that army, serving with widely varying distinction, were such future great men as Abraham Lincoln, Jefferson Davis and Zachary Taylor; the sons of great men like Alexander

Hamilton and Daniel Boone; and career Army officers who would soon win distinction in the Civil War, men like Albert Sidney Johnston and Winfield Scott.

Against this array of leaders, and the troops who fought with them, was pitted the intelligence of one Indian, Black Hawk, whose motivation was his passionate hatred of all white men. As a boy growing up in the great Sauk village on the Rock River, in Illinois, near its junction with the Mississippi, he had known what it was to live under the refined cruelties of the Spaniards, who were the masters of his country from 1769 to 1804. But if he hated the Spaniards, he learned from them to hate the Americans more when, on trading trips to the post at St. Louis, the Spanish entrepreneurs told him tales, no doubt well embroidered, of what the Americans had done to them.

Thus Black Hawk grew up to be a white-hating Indian leader. George Catlin's splendid portrait shows him as a man with a high forehead under a shaven skull, his roached scalp lock jutting up from it, and a great beak of a nose projecting boldly. His wide-set eyes are somber and cold, his sullen mouth drawn in a melancholy line above a deeply dimpled chin.

This was the man who, at thirty-seven, came to a turning point in his life when the Americans came to take over St. Louis from the Spaniards. The government sent Tecumseh's conqueror, General Harrison, to negotiate with the Sauk and Fox nations for land that lay in northwestern Illinois. It was fertile land, carefully tended by the Sauks, who had 700 acres of it under cultivation. Harrison negotiated a typical treaty, in which thousands of acres were ceded for a pittance and a promise the government had no intention of keeping —that the Sauks could hunt and plant on their former acres until they were opened up to settlement.

Sauk & Foxes
1904

When he heard that three chiefs of the two nations had signed this treaty, a flame was lit in Black Hawk that never went out while he lived. Not only was it an evil treaty, Black Hawk said, but these chiefs were not even empowered to negotiate it. They had come down to St. Louis on other business, the General had hailed them as emissaries sent to fashion a treaty and then had proceeded to get them drunk before he sat down with them. For years it was believed that this story was the imaginative product of Black Hawk's hatred, but there has since been some scholarly evidence that it might be true, at least in part.

Like so many of the noted chiefs before him, Black Hawk was a highly articulate Indian. In his autobiography, which later became a classic of Americana, he stated the whole land controversy in the clearest terms, from the Indian standpoint. He wrote: "My reason teaches me that land cannot be sold. The Great Spirit gave it to his children to live upon. So long as they occupy and cultivate it they have the right to the soil. Nothing can be sold but such things as can be carried away."

Nonetheless most of the Sauks obediently carried out that part of the treaty which called for them to move their villages across the Mississippi to the prairies. Only Black Hawk and those who sympathized with him refused to go. When the incoming settlers complained to the government, troops were sent to enforce the treaty, and Black Hawk had to retreat across the river. But this forcible move lighted the fuse laid down by the Treaty of 1804. Black Hawk repudiated that treaty on the spot, and determined to fight for his native land.

As the others had dreamed before him, Black Hawk also had his dream—a confederation of Indian tribes from the Rock River to Mexico, barring the way to further western migration by the white man. It was a dream that had even less chance of fulfillment than those of Tecumseh and Pontiac. By this time the temper of most Indians in the Mississippi River Valley was pacific and, it must be admitted, commercial. Why fight for freedom against such overwhelming odds when the fur trade could make them comfortable? This was the prevailing sentiment in Black Hawk's own tribe. It had led them to follow his rival chief, Keokuk, over the river and submit meekly to the white man's rule.

Black Hawk had also the vain dream of his predecessors that he could get help from the British. He had helped *them,* after all, in the War of 1812 when, as a young chief, he had joined Tecumseh's forces and fought at Frenchtown, Fort Meigs, Fort Stephenson and probably at the final Battle of the Thames as well. Since the War, his followers had done so much trading with the British post at old Fort Malden, in Ontario, that they had come to be known as the British Band.

There was no question of Black Hawk's ability to lead a resistance movement. He had grown up on the legends of Pontiac, had taken his first scalp when he was only fifteen, and in truth had devoted his life

and his remarkable talents to war. But in his travels about the Northwest, trying to stir up the tribes, he found little support. An apathy had
settled over nearly all the once-fierce warriors of the territory. They
were convinced resistance was no longer possible.

Possibly Black Hawk's dream would have remained no more than
that if it had not been for the manner of his removal from the ancestral lands. The Treaty of 1804 had promised that the Sauks could
hunt and plant their corn on these acres, but the British Band, returning from winter quarters in the spring of 1830, found that white
squatters had moved in, although the land had not yet been officially
opened for settlement, and appropriated the cultivated acres for
themselves. Worse, they had broken new ground and in doing so
had ruthlessly plowed up an Indian graveyard.

The chief was furious. He consulted his British friends at Fort
Malden and they encouraged him to fight, but offered him no practical help. Both he and they believed the treaty had been violated. A
tense accommodation existed through the summer and fall, after
which the Indians went away again on their long winter hunt. Returning in the spring, they discovered a much increased white occu-
pation of the land and Black Hawk peremptorily ordered the white
men to leave, emphasizing his demand by burning down a few cabins
and permitting his braves to shake their tomahawks at the settlers.

Naturally frightened by this development, the settlers appealed to
the Governor of Illinois, John Reynolds, who in turn sent the Western
Department's military commander, General Edmund P. Gaines, with
700 militiamen, to see what was going on. The General sailed down
the Rock River on a steamboat until he was in a position to destroy
the Sauk Village with his artillery and then summarily demanded
that Black Hawk remove his people. About a third of the Indians
deserted their chief and went peaceably across the Mississippi to join
the others. The rest refused to go.

Gaines made a last attempt at persuasion in a council with Black
Hawk. But the proud chief told him imperiously: "I am a Sauk. I
am a warrior and so was my father. Ask those young men who have
followed me to battle, and they will tell you who Black Hawk is.
Provoke our people to war and you will learn who Black Hawk is."

The General was not inclined toward war. He still hoped to reach
an accommodation of some kind, and besides, his militia had not yet

come up. When they did appear they were so formidable that Black Hawk could not restrain his braves from fleeing across the river. The chief returned under a truce flag two days later and General Gaines agreed, on behalf of the settlers, that the Sauks should have some of their own corn, at least, and he made other minor concessions. But as soon as he and his soldiers were gone, the settlers proved so niggardly in carrying out their promise that the Indians were compelled, as Black Hawk put it, "to steal corn from their own fields." As a result, they spent a miserable, hungry winter, having already been driven from their corn crops for the past two years and therefore prevented from laying up the usual supply.

Infuriated anew by the suffering of his people, Black Hawk resolved that as soon as the winter was over he would descend on the settlers and drive them from Sauk land. He hoped to patch together some kind of alliance with other tribes to supplement his own small numbers, particularly with the Winnebagoes, Potawatomies, Mascoutens, Foxes, Sioux and Kickapoos. It would have been an unlikely alliance in any case. Most of these tribes had little in common with the Sauks, and the Sioux, in fact, were their active enemies because they resented the thrust of the refugee tribe into their territory. When it came time for the grand assault in April, 1832, only the Foxes came to help Black Hawk, who wrote of his abandonment with civilized irony: "I discovered that the Winnebagoes and Potawatomi were not disposed to render us any assistance."

Even without allies, Black Hawk could muster more than 500 of his own Sauk warriors, so that with 100 or so Fox braves added, he made a frightening enough display of strength when he came over the river again in April, 1832. It was enough to send a stream of refugees into the rough frontier town of Chicago, whose inhabitants were so terrified by the stories they heard of Black Hawk's imaginary grand alliance that they considered abandoning their muddy little community.

When word of the outbreak reached Washington, greatly exaggerating the strength of Black Hawk's threat to the frontier, it elicited a hurried call to the militia, along with a mustering of a few regiments of regulars. Brigadier General Henry Atkinson was to be in command of this army summoned to put down the uprising, with Colonel Zachary Taylor his second in command. Atkinson was not an ideal choice for the assignment. He was able enough, but slow and cautious in temperament and therefore not well able to control his motley militia. This consisted of war veterans interested in keeping their pensioned land tracts, frontiersmen and settlers who hoped to end the necessity of plowing with their rifles strapped to the beam, and the usual collection of frontier rabble out for a bit of excitement and possible plunder, with the expiration date of their short-term enlistment as a handy escape hatch. Their inexperienced commanders would be no help to Atkinson.

Illinois, naturally, produced the largest militia contingent, since its own territory was immediately threatened. Many of its 1,800 men were mounted. Six hundred of them were assigned with 400 regulars of the 1st and 6th Infantry, as a probing force aimed at Black Hawk's village. Perhaps because he was so badly outnumbered, the chief appeared reluctant to begin the hostilities he had provoked. There undoubtedly was also a persistent belief in simple justice in the messages Black Hawk kept sending to the advancing American General, informing him that the Sauks wanted only to plant and harvest their corn, and that if the white men wanted war, they would be compelled to attack him first.

Black Hawk's hope for fair treatment was blasted, however, when the advance force of 270 under Major Isaiah Stillman finally confronted the Indians. The chief sent three of his men under a truce flag to negotiate, and Stillman gave them the same treatment that had been given the Seminoles, except that he made them prisoners and did not kill them. But when five other warriors were sent to look for the emissaries, they were attacked and two were killed. Unaware or uncaring of the mortal blow he had given to any hope of peace, Stillman blundered ahead and marched his troops straight into a bloody ambush. They retired in a panicky flight, leaving the dead and dying behind them.

This retreat momentarily discouraged the militia, and Atkinson was left with so little strength that he had to return to his base. In Washington and the nation there was an indignant reaction as Black Hawk turned on the frontier settlements and ravaged them. There were demands for a new army and a new commander. The response was an outpouring of troops from forts in the East, South and Great Lakes, to be placed under the command of General Winfield Scott.

But this new army was hardly formed before it was attacked by an enemy against which it had no defense—Asiatic cholera. One unit alone, the 4th Artillery, lost thirty per cent of its men. Another, the 2nd Infantry, stationed at Detroit, suffered 200 deaths among its 1,500 men, and many others were stricken by the disease. When Scott assembled his army at last, he saw that it was too weak to take the field and, worse, the diseased units were communicating the cholera to those not yet infected. The new effort collapsed, for the moment.

It was reorganized by June, and the command turned over once again to General Atkinson, who now had the added inducement of restoring his reputation. He was given reinforcements—a contingent of regulars and 1,000 or more militia—and with these he set out after Black Hawk again.

In his *Abraham Lincoln,* Carl Sandburg has described poetically what the ensuing conflict was like:

> And now over the rolling prairie and the slopes of timber bottoms along the Rock River, with a measureless blue sky arching over them, the red man and the white man hunted each other, trying to hand crimson death to each other. As they hunted they measured small and were hard to see, each trying to hide from the other till the instant of clash, combat, and death—bipeds stalking each other; only keen eyes could spot the pieces of the action and put together the collective human movement that swerved, struck, faded, came again, and struck, in the reaches of rolling prairie and slopes of timber bottom where the green, rain-washed bushes and trees stood so far, so deep under the arch of a measureless, blue sky.

Captain Abraham Lincoln's company of the 1st Regiment of the Brigade of Mounted Volunteers took part in the campaign, although it had no horses to mount at first. It was part of Colonel Taylor's army of 1,600 men, which never fought an action. Another of its officers was Lieutenant Jefferson Davis, who would one day marry Taylor's daughter, without her father's permission.

Although the nation's newspapers depicted the war as a vast struggle between good and evil, an epic of the midwestern wilderness, it was in reality little more than a masterfully conducted retreat whose outcome was never in doubt. The government's policy was once more extermination, and Black Hawk could do little but avoid it as long as he could. He did so with skill and courage, withdrawing slowly into southern Wisconsin, inflicting as much damage as he could. But he knew he could not run forever. The river was at his back, and beyond it waited the hostile Sioux.

The climax came on August 1 and 2 when Black Hawk and what remained of his army came to the Mississippi at last, near where it is joined by the Bad Axe River. He could not cross because Scott had blocked his retreat with the river steamer *Warrior,* Captain Throckmorton commanding, which was equipped with both cannon and riflemen. Realizing that his plight was hopeless, Black Hawk once more tried negotiation. He sent 150 of his men under a flag of truce down to the river bank. But Throckmorton considered this no more than a decoy. He fired on them with his six-pounder, loaded with canister, and followed that barrage with a volley from his riflemen. There was nothing for Black Hawk to do but attack the steamer, and a savage skirmish of more than an hour followed.

Meanwhile, Atkinson was bringing up 1,600 men by forced marches, leaving his baggage behind. He was only ten miles away while Black Hawk was attacking the *Warrior,* which nearly ran out of wood for its fires at nightfall and had to leave the scene for re-fueling down the river. Atkinson gave his weary men only a few hours' rest that night, and on the morning of the next day he fell upon Black Hawk's trapped, exhausted army, which had already lost twenty-three men to the *Warrior's* guns. What followed was nothing less than a massacre. One of its most shameful aspects was the deliberate killing of Indian women and children, who rushed into the river in a futile effort to escape, and were picked off by white marksmen. At least 200 Indians were killed before the day was over, while Atkinson lost only twenty men.

The aftermath of Black Hawk's war was at once tragic and bizarre, filled with irony and a summary in essence of the long conflict between white men and red in the territory lying between the Mississippi and the Atlantic Ocean—a territory now completely conquered.

Black Hawk was the principal figure in this afterpiece, as he had been in the war itself. He had escaped to the Winnebago village of Prairie la Cross, where the squaws made a handsome dress of white deerskins for him. Resplendent in this outfit, he surrendered himself to General Street at Prairie du Chien, and was at once placed in chains and taken aboard the steamer *Winnebago* by Lieutenant Jefferson Davis. He was to be returned to his own country, but this time to Fort Armstrong, located on Rock Island, where General Scott awaited him.

It must have been a melancholy journey down the river and a bitter homecoming, to be followed by months of imprisonment in the fort while the government tried to decide what to do with him. At last he was summoned to Washington by President Jackson, and as Jackson had once confronted another Indian leader, Weatherford, he now found Black Hawk before him, straight and tall. As Sandburg writes of this meeting, "They faced each other, a white chief and a red chief; both had killed men and known terrible dangers, hard griefs, high dangers, and scars; each was nearly seventy years old; and Black Hawk said to Jackson, 'I—am—a man—and you—are—another.' " Then Black Hawk went on:

> We did not expect to conquer the whites. They had too many houses, too many men. I took up the hatchet, for my part, to revenge injuries which my people could no longer endure. Had I borne them longer without striking, my people would have said, "Black Hawk is a woman; he is too old to be a chief; he is no Sauk." These reflections caused me to raise the war-whoop. I say no more of it; it is known to you. Keokuk once was here; you took him by the hand, and when he wished to return to his home, you were willing. Black Hawk expects that, like Keokuk, we shall be permitted to return, too.

Jackson did not yet know what he wanted to do with Black Hawk, but there was no doubt whatever about his intentions toward the disputed territory. It was to be the subject of another of the government's Indian treaties. This time the white negotiators got 10,600,000 acres of land belonging to the Winnebagoes, Sauks and Foxes for a mere $20,000 a year, for thirty years, along with some fringe benefits and the beneficent grant of a forty-square-mile reservation on the Iowa River.

Meanwhile, Black Hawk was kept in prison, in Fort Monroe. Nearly a year later, it was decided to release him, and apparently the government hoped to accrue some political capital by displaying the chief on a grand tour, responding to the great public interest in him, as an example of the government's efficiency in putting down Indian rebellion. The journey, however, turned into something of a triumphal tour. The public, which only a year or so before had demanded Black Hawk's head, now saw in this proud, splendid figure a romantic symbol of the frontier, which was comfortably removed from the eastern seaboard by this time. They cheered his appearances and cities held formal banquets for him.

Black Hawk would have been less than human if he had not thawed under such attention. For the moment he forgot his hatred of the white man, forgot what had been done to him and his people. After a virtual eulogy at a banquet in the Exchange Hotel in New York City, he told his guests: "Brother: We like your talk. We will be friends. We like the white people; they are very kind to us. We shall not forget it. Your counsel is good; we shall attend to it. Your valuable present shall go to my squaw [he had been given a pair of topaz earrings, set in gold], it pleases me very much. We shall always be friends."

The tour went on, into upper New York State, where Black Hawk was entertained by an ancient Seneca chief, known as Captain Pollard. This representative of a tribe which had given the white man so hard a struggle was long since resigned to conquest. He made a speech advising Black Hawk to remove himself peaceably to the West and never fight again. In his new and strange mood of amiability, Black Hawk answered him:

> Our aged brother of the Senecas, who has spoken to us, has spoken the words of a good and wise man. We are strangers to each other, though we have the same color, and the same Great Spirit made us all, and gave us this country together. Brothers, we have seen how great a people the whites are. They are very rich and very strong. It is folly for us to fight with them. We shall go home with much knowledge. For myself, I shall advise my people to be quiet, and live like good men. The advice which you gave us, brother, is very good, and we tell you now we mean to walk the straight path in future, and to content ourselves with what we have and with cultivating our lands.

After he left the Senecas, Black Hawk continued his tour of old battlefields along the Mohawk Valley, into the country of the Great Lakes, where the bloodshed of the past was too near to be forgotten by citizens and he was burned in effigy in Detroit. His journey ended at Green Bay, in the heart of the country of the Sauks' enemies, where white troops had to protect him on his progress to Chicago, and from there back once more to Fort Armstrong. On this last stage of the journey, the resigned, forgiving, even hopeful mood which had possessed the chief from the beginning slowly receded as he passed through his home country and he realized that it would never be his again, and that the conquerors were already raising their corn on his ancestral lands. He became silent and withdrawn, sunk in a depression which was hardly relieved by the government's calculated humiliation which awaited him at Fort Armstrong: he was told Jackson had ordered specifically that the Sauk nation was thereafter to be only one tribe, under the rule of Black Hawk's old rival, Keokuk. There was precious little remaining to rule, but nevertheless it was a final crushing blow to the chief's pride.

He lived quietly on the Iowa reservation until 1837, when he went once more to Washington with a party of thirty-five chiefs, who had just signed over another 26,500,000 acres of Indian land for three cents an acre, and an aromatic bouquet of worthless guarantees. On this second trip, Black Hawk's wife and son were with him, and the government once more sent him on the grand tour. It ended at Madison, Wisconsin, on July 4, 1838, where he was given a fine banquet, ending with this toast: "Our illustrious guest. May his declining years be as calm as his previous life has been boisterous from warlike events. His present friendship to the whites fully entitles him to a seat at our board."

It is inconceivable that Black Hawk, rising to reply, was not conscious of all that the white men had done to him. He looked down at the bland white faces turned up to him, this humiliated and broken old man confined to a reservation, and he responded with one of his most memorable speeches, in which resignation and pathos were sadly mingled.

It has pleased the Great Spirit that I am here today [he said]. The earth is our mother and we are now permitted to look upon it. A few snows ago, I was fighting against the white people; perhaps I was wrong; let it be forgotten. I love my towns and corn fields on the Rock River, it was a beautiful country. I fought for it, but now it is yours. Keep it as the Sauks did. I was once a warrior, but now I am poor. Keokuk has been the cause of what I am, but I do not blame him. I love to look upon the Mississippi. I have looked upon it from a child. I love that beautiful river. My home has always been upon its banks. I thank you for your friendship. I will say no more.

Three months later he was dead, on October 3, 1837, and a year later even his rest was violated by white vandals who beheaded him and tried to display that grisly relic, along with other parts of his remains, in a tent show.

Less than a year after Black Hawk's death, in May, 1838, the final act of the eastern Indians' tragedy took place. It was no longer war, but a land grab of the most appalling brutality, in which a whole Indian nation was sacrificed ruthlessly. The victims were the Cherokees, who lived in the Valley of the Tennessee, occupying about 40,000 square miles of this rich land. They rivaled the Iroquois in culture, and in some ways even surpassed them. They had done nothing to merit the enmity of white men since 1792. Like all the tribes, they had resisted the first westward push, and some of them had fought for the British in the Revolution. One of their leaders, Dragging Canoe, had even tried to form an alliance with the Creeks to resist white invasion, but it was never accomplished, and after the chief's death in 1792, the Cherokees resisted no more. More than any other tribes, they assimilated with the white men and learned to live like them. In the War of 1812, they rallied behind Jackson and fought with him against the Creeks at Horseshoe Bend.

The Cherokees were a strong, unified nation in the early nineteenth century, dealing with the government almost like a separate state. They were extremely prosperous. By 1826 they had accumulated 22,000 cattle, 7,600 horses, 46,000 swine, 2,500 sheep, 762 looms, 2,488 spinning wheels, 172 wagons, 2,942 plows, ten sawmills, thirty-one grist mills, sixty-two blacksmith shops, eight cotton machines, eighteen schools, eighteen ferries and numerous public roads. Only the poor lived in log cabins. The others had houses as good as many white men's in the city, and their chief lived in a $10,000 two-story brick house designed by a Philadelphia architect, situated on an 800-acre plantation. These highly civilized tribesmen read books and American and British newspapers, and they sent their daughters to boarding schools. Their own newspaper, the *Phoenix,* was printed in both English and Cherokee; it advocated culture, prosperity and peace with everyone. To insure all these, the Cherokees had drafted and adopted a written constitution in 1826—the only Indian nation ever to do so.

This was the nation and these the people upon which the state of Georgia cast covetous eyes. Its claim was based on an agreement signed with the Federal government in 1802, which had promised that these lands the Georgians claimed would be given to them as soon as the Indians could be removed peaceably. In 1822, it was obvious that this had not been done, and Georgia brought heavy pressure to bear on Congress, as a result of which the House voted $30,000 to end the land titles of the Cherokees.

The Cherokees answered with a vote in their own legislative body, the Council, forbidding the making of any land treaties with the government. Two commissioners were sent out from Washington to negotiate the question, but the Cherokees would not be persuaded and were indifferent to threats. Then the commissioners tried bribery, but John Ross, Principal Chief of the Council, exposed this attempt publicly and indignantly rejected it.

The beginnings of the controversy had occurred during the administration of John Quincy Adams, who might have found a way to settle it with some justice to the Indians. But unfortunately for the Cherokees, Andrew Jackson's arrival in office coincided with renewed, arrogant pressure from Georgia's governor and legislature, who advised Jackson that if the Federal government did not remove the Indians, their own sovereign state would do it. To Governor John Forsyth, the Cherokees' constitution was "presumptuous," although in fact the state of culture and political sophistication in the Cherokee nation was considerably higher than it was in the state of Georgia at the time.

No further pressure was necessary, however, once Jackson was in office. The new President had already demonstrated that he had no understanding of Indians, nor sympathy for them, nor any intention of treating them justly. He had a removal bill introduced in Congress during 1829. Beginning in the next year, a succession of laws were enacted by the Georgia legislature, all of them illegal, first extending state laws to the Cherokee territory, and then dividing it up into lots, after which further laws were passed depriving Cherokees of their civil rights. These provisions, and others even worse, were vicious and fraudulent enough in themselves, but the Georgians, who would not wait for the laws to take effect, began burning, killing and stealing in Cherokee territory, as Indians had done years before in the supposedly uncivilized past.

The Cherokees replied to this treatment in a way no Indian tribe had ever done. They took their case to the Supreme Court of the United States where, in a historic decision in 1832, the Court ruled that Georgia had no right to extend its laws to the Cherokee nation, and were not entitled to seize it as they wished. To this verdict, President Jackson made an equally historic reply: "John Marshall has made his decision, now let him enforce it." Thus in effect the President nullified the Court's decision and Georgia was given tacit permission to do whatever it wanted. John Ross was arrested, although later released, and his house confiscated, along with those of other leaders. The *Phoenix* was suppressed. The Georgia militia ran riot. John Howard Payne, the composer of "Home, Sweet Home," was with Ross when he was arrested, and later wrote an account of what was going on in the Cherokee territory which aroused the nation, particularly the northeastern states, but there was no stopping a government whose President was intent on destroying the Indians.

At least a seemingly better complexion could be put on the affair by the usual device of a treaty, and this was done on December 29, 1835. Of 17,000 Cherokees, only 500 witnessed the signing of this document, and not one was an elected official of the nation, although the government declared brazenly that the treaty had been concluded with "chiefs, head men and people . . ." This statement was as fraudulent as the treaty itself, by which the Cherokees gave up everything they owned for $5,000,000, a gross undervaluation. In return they were to get 7,000,000 western acres, with an option to purchase another 8,000,000 for $500,000.

But the heartbreaking clause in the treaty was the stipulation that they must move themselves over the Mississippi to their new home within two years. It was that clause, more than anything else, which made many Cherokees refuse to accept the treaty. They petitioned Congress, with 16,000 of them signing the petition, but the President ignored it and the Congress, when it was called upon to approve the treaty, turned the debate into a shabby political farce in which the Whigs tried to discredit Jackson. It is noteworthy, nonetheless, that there was enough decency remaining in that body to resist Jackson's Senatorial steamroller. The treaty was ratified by a single vote.

In the two-year interval granted for removal, more than 2,000 Cherokees went quietly. The others continued to hope that Ross would find some way to nullify the treaty. Meanwhile the grace period ran out and the government realized that the Indians would have to be removed forcibly. This thankless task was given to General Winfield Scott, who commanded an army of 7,000 men to carry it out. They were to load the Indians into wagons and take them to a stockade, from which they would be transported across the Mississippi.

A young man named William Cotter, who drove one of the wagons that lovely May morning, left us this melancholy description of what befell the Cherokees:

After all the warning and with soldiers in their midst, the inevitable day appointed found the Indians at work in their houses and in their fields. It is remembered as well as if it had been seen yesterday, that two or three dropped their hoes and ran as fast as they could when they saw the soldiers coming into the fields. After that, they made no effort to get out of the way. The men handled them gently, but picked them up in the road, in the field, anywhere they found them, part of a family at a time, and carried them to the post. Everything in their homes was left alone for a day or two and then hauled to the post. When a hundred or more families had been collected, they were marched to Ross' Landing. It was a mournful sight to all who witnessed it—old men and women with gray hairs, walking with the sad company. Provisions were made for those to ride who could not walk. . . .

In hauling the stuff from the cabins a file of six or more men went with me as a guard. They forced open the doors and put the poor, meager household effects into the wagons, sometimes the stuff of two or three families at one load. After following me a mile or two the guards galloped away, leaving me in worse danger than anyone else, for if there had been an Indian hiding out, I would have been the one to suffer.

But few of the Indians even went back to their homes. We turned the cows and calves together, as they had been apart for a day or two. Chickens, cats and dogs all ran away when they saw us. Ponies under the shade trees fighting the flies with the noise of their bells; the cows and calves lowing to each other; the poor dogs howling for their owners; the open doors of the cabins as we left them—to have seen it all would have melted to tenderness a heart of stone. And in contrast there was a beautiful growing crop of corn and beans.

It was not quite as peaceful a removal as Cotter described. Some of the soldiers were brutal and there were acts of unnecessary and despicable cruelty. Later the frontier rabble came in to plunder what remained.

Nor was the misery of the Cherokees ended with that long day's desolation. Taken to a stockade inadequately provided with sanitary facilities, they were stricken wholesale with dysentery and fevers of various kinds. White vultures hovered around the stockade trying to get what little money they possessed in exchange for liquor. Then they were put on flatboats and ferried down the Tennessee River. They feared that western journey for a special reason. Their mythology told them that the Wind of Death itself blew from that region. And Death, indeed, appeared among them. They began to die by dozens in the terrible summer heat.

Over the objection of Jackson and the Georgians, General Scott waited for cooler autumn weather to continue the removal. Even so, 4,000 Cherokees died on the way to the West, including Chief Ross's wife, before the terrible episode came to its end. In their new home the Cherokees gave a name to the hard road over which they had come. In their tongue it was Nuna-da-ut-sun'y—"The Trail Where They Cried."

The trail of the eastern Indians had ended at the Mississippi. A half-century of struggle lay ahead for the tribes remaining to be conquered.

# Part Two:

# The Conquest of the West

# 8

★ ★ ★ ★ ★ ★

# The Army Takes Over

IN THE TROUBLED DECADES before the Civil War, the United States Army for the first time began the task of policing a 6,000-mile frontier along a line stretching from Canada to Mexico. After Black Hawk's war, the line lay entirely west of the Mississippi. Into this immense territory the Army's forts thrust like spearheads toward Indian lands which were being subjected for the first time to the ever flowing tide of westward migration.

These Plains Indians were not like the eastern tribes in some respects. They were accomplished horsemen, for one thing. They had grown up in treeless spaces where the horse was not simply useful but an absolute necessity. Their cultures were somewhat different, too, and as warriors they were regarded as fiercer and more intractable than their eastern brethren, although such a generalization would have been difficult to prove. Certainly they had enough to irritate them. The white men who were now streaming into their hunting grounds were hardbitten trappers and miners, traders with scant respect for any law, peddlers of bad whiskey and squatters in search of land. None of these invaders had the slightest respect for treaties.

As a kind of buffer state between the Indians and these white men and other hardy emigrants who were simply seeking to settle a new place, or were on their way to the promised land of California, the Army manned its string of forts with only a few thousand men. The troops in the forts were as varied a collection as those they intended to defend. Some were veteran soldiers, others were adventurous young men learning about the military life in the hardest possible way. For the first time there were a good many immigrants, German and Irish for the most part, in the ranks of the regulars. Along with all these was the customary quota of derelicts and drunks, the failures in life who had chosen the Army as a means of escape, and criminals seeking to avoid jail sentences.

There were not a few experts in using the Army for shelter or gain. The "Snow Birds," for example, enlisted in the fall to secure warm quarters for the winter and deserted in the spring. The bounty jumpers, whose slogan was "Enlist today, desert tomorrow," stayed only long enough to get the premium for recruitment. In eight years they swindled the government out of a half-million dollars. The frequent financial panics and depressions of those days also produced a ready flow of recruits. The perils of the frontier at five dollars a month for privates, with allowances bringing it to almost fifteen dollars, was far better to most men than destitution in a city.

Fighting was not the only function of these soldiers in their lonely outposts. They too, in their own way, were helping to develop the West. Settlers had refused to believe that wheat would grow on the prairies until the soldiers grew it in their garrisons. The Army was first to set up and operate sawmills for the purpose of cutting lumber to build forts, and these mills were the beginnings of the lumber industry in the West. It was the Army, too, that laid out a network of military roads, later the nucleus of a modern highway system, and launched the first steamboats on the western rivers. Armies had to eat, and so cattle were brought out to the plains as a meat supply for the forts, forecasting one of the West's principal industries in later years.

The Army contributed something to the nation's culture by protecting and helping writers and artists—men like Francis Parkman, George Catlin and Frederic Remington—who came to record the life of the region. It offered similar aid to the smaller army of military and civilian scientists who were eager to explore the ornithology, geology, anthropology and other scientific aspects of a land few except explorers and traders had ever seen.

As military units, the men in the forts had to be entirely self-sufficient, depending on their own labor for everything, since it would have been impossible to hire any civilian help even if the money for it had been available. It was possible to find almost every skill among the ranks of the recruits. For example, 203 men reporting to Fort Gibson, Arkansas, in 1837 numbered among them blacksmiths, carpenters, clerks, mill hands, farmers, hatters, machinists, harness makers, masons, tailors, wheelwrights, bookbinders, bakers, druggists, gardeners, jewelers, printers and teachers. It even included five sailors, whose experience was not immediately useful.

western Block house

A discipline as harsh as the terrain was imposed on the troops. If a cavalryman lost his carbine, he had to dismount and lead his horse, sometimes for as much as twenty-three miles, and had to pay for the weapon in the bargain. At some forts punishment for infractions meant walking post for a week with a heavy bag of round shot on the shoulders, or perhaps a large log. Again it might mean standing for hours locked in stocks like those of Puritan days, beside the parade ground. Army records disclose the case of a chronic drunkard who was sentenced to be immersed in an icy river for fifteen minutes each morning for ten days.

Army justice was derived from the traditions of the British military service, with its tendency toward the cruel and unusual. Deserters might be branded with the letter "D," and floggings were so common as to be the order of the day. If Army justice was attacked for its brutality, as it was occasionally in the press by some returning soldier, the commanders argued that there was no other way to control such a body of men and, in any case, discipline in these dangerous outposts, in hostile territory, could well mean the difference between life and death. Drunkenness, alone, was a formidable problem, whose perils were obvious. The daily ration was one gill per man in 1830, when the Army drank up 72,537 gallons that year at a cost to the government of $22,132. A soldier could scarcely get drunk on so little, but it was not difficult to find traders or sutlers from whom to buy additional supplies. Curiously, it never occurred to the white men, so well aware of how demoralizing liquor was to Indians, that they, too, could be ruined by alcohol. On payday, there were always drunken sprees and post commanders had to put on guard duty all those guaranteed to remain sober.

It was not hard to understand why so many men drank, beset as they were by the grinding monotony of garrison life in a country where they could not relax, enjoy the company of women or expect any kind of amusement except what they themselves could provide. As time went on, however, the posts improved somewhat. Living conditions were better, as were medical care and sanitation; hospitals were built; and, best of all, the base pay was raised to eight dollars a month. Even such rough posts as Fort Gibson saw the death rate lowered as a result of these improvements. This Arkansas hellhole was no longer known as the "Graveyard of the Army," a title earned when six officers and 293 enlisted men died there within two years.

Some primitive forts rose so rapidly in the scale of civilization that they became pleasant places to live. One was Fort Leavenworth, on the west bank of the Missouri River. George Catlin lived there for a time, with the six or seven companies of infantry and ten to fifteen officers, some with their wives and daughters. He found it

"a very pleasant little community, who are almost continually together in social enjoyment of the peculiar amusements and pleasures
of this wild country. Of these pastimes they have many, such as riding on horseback or in carriages over the beautiful green fields of the
prairies, picking strawberries and wild plums, deer chasing, grouse
shooting, horse racing."

Slowly the attributes of Army life taken for granted today came to
these frontier posts. The Corps of Chaplains, abolished after the War
of 1812, was reconstituted in 1838, and churches and chapels arose
at the garrisons. Schools and libraries appeared here and there, and
sometimes even a theater where the soldiers put on original plays
and minstrel shows. Music, as always, was a great help to morale. The
conventional field music of fife, drum and bugle was disappearing,
and in its place came the modern military band. The 6th Infantry had
an excellent one of fifteen musicians, which played not only for marching but for cotillions and square dances, whenever girls from nearby
settlements could be brought in as partners.

There was, of course, a chronic scarcity of women. Laundresses
were the only females given official recognition; all others, even wives
and daughters, were listed as "camp followers." There were always
camp followers—in the civilian sense—available, usually Indian girls,
some of whom married white men. Duels were fought over these girls
on occasion. After the Cherokee removal, there was an increase in
marriages between Indian girls and the soldiers and settlers, because
the girls of this tribe were of unusual beauty and their eastern back-
grounds made them much more like the white girls back home. Some,
indeed, had gone to the same boarding schools. The descendants of
these unions still populate Oklahoma, and have produced some of
the nation's beauties.

As for the white women, they were the families of officers, wives
of enlisted men and laundresses, who were often the wives of non-
commissioned officers. They were not an unmixed blessing. One
soldier wrote that he thought waiting on an officer's lady and her
maids was more than he should be asked to do, besides his other
duties. A commander whose column was late in starting on an assignment because of an officer's wife wrote in a somewhat classic vein:
"Hang all women in camp! If Love wants to mount the warrior's

steed, let her wait until the steed is brought home from the war again!"

More and more families came to the posts as time went on. Some were the brides of young West Point officers, and friends from the East who visited them later on had no difficulty finding a husband. The Army wife was becoming an institution.

On the military side, the primary difference in this western army was its mobile character. Most of the eastern wars had been fought

largely by foot soldiers, as we have seen, but now cavalry was essential to meet the swift-riding Plains Indians, who were superb horsemen. This situation transformed what had been a moribund arm of the service. Until 1833, the United States Cavalry had been no more than a few irregular units with a nondescript battle record. In that year, however, Congress authorized the establishment of the 1st U. S. Dragoons, and these were followed shortly by the 2nd and then the Regiment of Mounted Riflemen (later 3rd Cavalry). Dragoons meant, in a tactical sense, that the Army now had mounted men who had been trained to fight on foot as well as horseback. This form of combat proved so successful that during the Civil War the word "dragoons," a European import, was dropped and all mounted units were known as cavalry.

The early days of the dragoons were anything but easy. To enlist men to fight on foot or in the saddle, recruiting officers had to depict dragoons as the élite of the Army, not subject to such mundane assignments as fatigue details. It was considered disgraceful for dragoons to speak to infantrymen, some recruiting officers declared. There was, of course, no truth in these advertisements. One of the first drafts for the dragoons, in fact, was assigned immediately to build stables, precipitating a mass desertion of more than a hundred men. At another post a shortage of horses compelled the disgruntled cavaliers to train on foot.

At every post the dragoons had to endure the amusement of the infantry, who were well aware these enlistees had been told they were to be the élite. These infantrymen had been compelled to take a good deal of derision from the Indians, who looked down from their horses and called them "walk-a-heaps," because they had to plod along on foot like squaws.

After these early difficulties, however, the dragoons quickly became something near the élite they had been promised. Their new uniforms were dashing, they learned to walk with a horseman's swagger and many of them sported sweeping mustaches, which were not permitted anywhere else in the service. Their uniforms alone made them enchanting to the ladies—blue jackets, pantaloons of lighter blue or white, flared foragé caps with orange bands. If "something soldierly and colorful was needed to impress the Indians," as one colonel observed, the Army needed to look no further than its dragoons. Even their horses were of matched colors—blacks, bays or chestnuts. Trumpeters and bandsmen rode grays or creams. When the dragoons lined up for duty with their carbines slung, Harper's

Ferry pistols in their holsters and their heavy spurs sounding, they were truly resplendent. In every respect they presented a façade of spit-and-polish, and the Indians soon came to fear and respect these colorful columns as they wound across the prairie, followed by their supply wagons and often a pair of brass howitzers, which were especially frightening to the tribesmen. This highly mobile column, with artillery and supply train attached, was the forerunner of today's armored force.

Dragoon regiments in time acquired their own personalities. The 1st was a conservative outfit, while the 2nd was known as the Dandy Regiment, "the epitome of military impudence whether in the parlor, the tavern, or on the battlefield," as one writer put it. A verse of their regimental song declared:

> Oh! the dragoon bold! he scorns all care,
> As he goes the rounds with uncropped hair:
> He spends no thought on the evil star
> That sent him away to the border war.

As vital as dragoons were to the frontier, they could not replace the foot soldier. Infantry officers and men made historic occasions even out of military reconnaissance. On leave from the Army, Captain Benjamin L. E. Bonneville, with 107 volunteers, made the most remarkable expedition since Lewis and Clark, between 1832 and 1835, when they visited the Blackfoot, Crow, Nez Percé, Bannock and Shoshone Indians, made friends with Jim Bridger and other mountain men, and contributed greatly to the Army's understanding of terrain and the tribes they must deal with.

Then there was John C. Frémont, of the Topographical Engineers, who first made a place for himself in history with his exploration and mapping of the Platte River country, and his pioneer crossing of the Rockies to the mouth of the Columbia River and thence to Sacramento. Frémont traveled more than 10,000 miles during the two years he was in the field.

Other officers made their names celebrated. The Pawnees would not forget the expedition Colonel Henry Dodge led against them on the Red River in 1834. Nor would the exploits of that hardbitten disciplinarian, Colonel Stephen Watts Kearny, be forgotten by anyone, soldier or Indian, who crossed his path. In May, 1845, he led five companies of cavalry out of Fort Leavenworth and in ninety-nine days traveled 2,200 miles with them. Kearny was to be the conqueror of Santa Fé and California in the war with Mexico.

Such marches as Kearny's were not wildly unusual in the history of the western frontier, where men traveled great distances through fierce heat, dust, cloudbursts, floods, mud and the danger of stamped-ing herds of buffalo, who could easily overrun a column of men. These perils, along with cold and snow in the mountainous regions, did not even include the primary danger they had come to confront—the Indians themselves.

Skirmishes were usually hot and desperate. The Indians fought the white cavalry on relatively equal terms until it came to firearms, in which they were still inferior. Even so, carbines and pistols were sometimes not enough to hold off a barrage of arrows released at full gallop by massed mounted Indians. Horses joined the battle, but it was often decided on foot, with the carbine. The cavalry charge itself was never effective against Indian forces, and it was not long after the Civil War that the saber was relegated to dress parades along the frontier.

It was not the mission of the Western garrisons to make spectacular cavalry charges, in any case, or to follow the conventional military patterns of the war in the East. Their job was primarily to protect the routes of the emigrants and the tradesmen. Along the Santa Fé Trail, for example, the Kiowas, Comanches, Pawnees and Apaches were an expensive and perilous nuisance. Every year the toll they exacted was high in scalps and loot from the wagon trains. Their depredations, and the subsequent howls of outrage from the traders, inspired what may have been the first escort force—a battalion of the 6th Infantry, under Major Bennett Riley, which marched out of Fort Leavenworth in 1829 to meet a wagon train bound homeward from Santa Fé. They had no more than joined it before a war party of 400 braves rode swiftly down upon the train's beef herd and cut it off from the caravan. With imminent starvation facing them, Major Riley's men counterattacked, but the Indians split up and surrounded the camp, in the classic manner.

After Riley discovered that his long-range volleys were not

preventing the Indians from making quick sorties and driving off the herd a little at a time, he succeeded in dropping a round shot from the detachment's only cannon squarely into the middle of a large body of the Indians, sitting their horses a mile away. He then reloaded with grapeshot and broke up a charge from another direction. That was enough for the Indians, who retreated forthwith, leaving only one man dead among the defenders, a private who died from thirteen arrow wounds.

That was typical of day-to-day fighting in the West—mean, uncomfortable, miserable, often cruel and full of every imaginable ordeal. Sometimes in the mountains, the dragoons' hands would be so numb they could not reload their carbines, and they would have to attack with sabers.

The Mexican War of 1846 brought with it the first real clash between this new American army of the West and its Indian adversaries. One of the incidents in that war was unique because it confronted the army for the first time with a fortification utterly new in its experience, the pueblo. These familiar Indian homes of the Southwest were a far cry from the log huts and palisaded forts of the East. Their adobe walls were thick and stout and high enough —from three to eight stories—to make assault extremely difficult, especially since the only access was by ladders which could be drawn up under threat of attack. Narrow windows gave bowmen and musketeers excellent defensive positions, as the well-armed and armored Spaniards had discovered in their conquest of the Southwest.

Lieutenant Colonel Sterling Price was the officer who was probably first confronted with the problem of taking a pueblo, when in 1847 he was called upon to capture the Pueblo of Taos, in New Mexico. The task of wresting that territory and Arizona from the Mexicans had been the mission of General Stephen Kearny and his Army of the West, which had seized Santa Fé and marched on to California, leaving behind it sufficient strength, so it was believed, under Colonel Alexander W. Doniphan and others to finish the job. The mopping-up process was complicated at once by a sudden uprising of the Pueblo Indians, the first warning of which came when they murdered Charles Bent, the first American governor of New Mexico, and other officials in the village of San Fernando de Taos. Five other settlers were killed when the Indians attacked a mill.

Until this time, the tribes of the Southwest had remained more or less under American control while the war with Mexico went on, but the government believed it could not look the other way from the Pueblo rebellion because it would encourage neighboring tribes to do likewise. Consequently, within three days after the affair at San Fernando, Colonel Price was on his way to Taos, the pueblo stronghold, with 400 men, both cavalry and infantry; four twelve-pound mountain howitzers; and a six-pounder. His path led seventy dangerous miles up the Rio Grande, a trail infested with Mexican irregulars and Indians who, so his intelligence reports said, outnumbered him three to one.

Price was not a man easily intimidated, but he had not gone far before he found himself in difficulties. The way was barred near the small settlement of Cañada by a force of 800 Mexicans and Indians who lay along the rim of a canyon. Price brought up his howitzers (commanded by Lieutenant Alexander B. Dyer, future Chief of Ordnance in the Union Army) and tried to blast his way through. His ammunition and supply train were a mile to the rear, however, and the enemy moved at once to cut them off, detaching part of its force to do the job while the others pinned down the howitzer crews with heavy fire from their small arms. But Price saved his supplies, and Dyer moved his battery onto a hill nearby which gave him a much better position—good enough to drive his adversaries off the canyon rim.

After that it was an unequal contest. The Indians and Mexicans were no match for the howitzers. Price had taken the town of Cañada by nightfall, losing only two killed and eight wounded in the process, while the other side suffered losses of thirty-six killed and fifty wounded. Price did not pursue his advantage immediately. He wanted to wait for another six-pounder and more ammunition to arrive from Santa Fé. When this armament arrived, on January 28, 1847, Price resumed his march into the mountains, where the enemy was waiting for him. Another sharp skirmish occurred, again with success for the Americans, but now the Colonel found himself pitted against a more intractable enemy, the winter weather of the Taos

mountains. His men had to struggle through an eight-inch snowfall, and for three nights had to camp without tents, water or forage for the animals. The cold was intense and, on the march, men had to break roads for the wagons to follow. It was an exhausted, numbed fighting band that finally reached Taos on February 3, but it marched directly to the pueblo fortress it had come to besiege.

There were two pueblos, in fact, rising from inside a walled rectangle 250 by 220 yards. A stream flowed through it, ensuring the defenders a supply of fresh water in a siege, and it was equipped with storerooms, corrals and a church. Franciscan friars had long since Christianized most of these Indians. The inhabitants of the Pueblo de Taos evidently felt themselves to be secure, because they greeted Price's advancing troops with cheers and yells of defiance from the walls and windows, daring them to attack.

Methodically Price unlimbered his howitzers and for two and a half hours the guns pounded against the walls of the twin pueblos with no visible effect. The colonel realized it would take heavier artillery than he possessed to breach these solid walls, which appeared simply to absorb the shot from the lighter guns. There was no alternative but to retreat into the town momentarily and devise a different plan of attack.

Next morning Price returned, ringed the fort with his dragoons and riflemen and, after another ineffective barrage from the cannon, he directed Dyer to lay down still another one to provide cover for a charge. His infantrymen got as far as the church before heavy fire pinned them to the walls and they could advance no farther. Two volunteers, a captain and a lieutenant, leaped over the corral before the church and attempted to break open the door, but both fell, mortally wounded. Indian sharpshooters had meanwhile picked off five dragoons and wounded several others.

Under constant fire from the artillery, the troops made another attempt to axe their way through the church walls but these were too thick and the Indians' fire too heavy. Dyer succeeded in getting one of his six-pounders up to within sixty yards of the wall and, taking advantage of the dent already made in it by the axes, he breached it wide enough so that five or six men could enter. Then he moved his cannon closer, no more than thirty feet from the breach, and poured a round of grapeshot through it, after which Price gave the order to storm the church. It was a completely successful charge. The Indians were routed out and fled from the fort, where the dragoons cut down most of them before they could reach the hills.

That left only the Indians remaining in the other pueblo, and they begged for mercy. Price was merciful enough, but he singled out the leaders who had perpetrated the Bent massacre and had them executed after a perfunctory trial. Certainly the tribe itself had suffered a severe punishment. At least 150 of the pueblos' defenders lay dead, out of a garrison of 650, and many others were wounded. The Pueblo uprising ended quickly with this blood bath.

There remained a further danger, however, this one from the Navajos. These Indians were raisers of sheep and cattle, and farmers who scratched a meager living from the canyon bottoms. They were also accomplished thieves, raiding other tribes and white settlements almost as a business. Between 1847 and 1867, according to territorial records, they made off with 3,559 horses, 13,473 cattle and 294,740 sheep. These activities and their whole economy were threatened by the Mexican War, so quite naturally they turned against the white soldiers who threatened to deprive them of their always precarious existence.

Colonel Doniphan concluded in the winter of 1846 that he would have to institute a campaign against the Navajos. His decision was a masterpiece of bad timing. His troops did not have enough heavy clothing, and the winter weather made forage for the animals in equally short supply. There would not be enough fuel for campfires. Moreover, in the rough terrain where the Navajos lived it would be impossible to move wagons and it would be necessary to carry everything by pack mules and horses, whose loads would have to be limited to rations and ammunition. The soldiers could not expect tents and extra blankets in the bitter mountain weather.

Nevertheless, Doniphan sent three columns to the field, in the hope that he could put down the Navajos before the worst of the winter weather defeated him. The colonel himself started out with two of the columns, planning to meet the third at a rendezvous. This third column, under Major William Gilpin, consisted of 180 men, augmented by sixty-five Mexican and Pueblo allies. The Major had begun his march in late November, covering the first hundred miles in six days, but then he plunged into the Cordillera Mountains and was soon bogged down in heavy drifts through which his little force struggled with the greatest difficulty.

They conquered the mountains, nonetheless, and came down out of them into a barren plain without wood or grass, whose scanty water supply was undrinkable. Out of this hell they moved up again on a trail that led over Tunicha Ridge, another snowy barrier, where they lost some of the pack horses, who died of exhaustion or disappeared over the brinks of precipices. To make matters worse, the cold suddenly became intense and biting winds tore at the column. There was a night of severe hardship on the summit, and then the battered troops moved down again and came to a sheltered cleft at the base of the mountain, where they were revived by water and forage and the warmth of campfires. They had survived the incredible journey and soon they were at the rendezvous, Bear Spring, where they were to meet Doniphan.

The Colonel had meanwhile made nearly as heroic a march with his two columns, traversing the mountains in snow three feet deep; it was at least thirteen inches deep in the valleys. They had done so with little attrition, so that the three columns numbered 330 effectives, now that they were combined—more than enough to hurt the Navajos where they were most vulnerable—their herds and flocks, without which they could not exist.

The Indians possessed one advantage. It was a natural fortress, the Canyon de Chelly, a formidable chasm in the northwest corner of Arizona, a little west of the New Mexico line. It had seldom been approached, much less explored, by white men. Not only was it virtually impregnable from attack, but it was a place made for ambush. "No command should ever enter it," was the verdict of one officer who had done so.

Fortunately for Doniphan, he was not required to make a penetration of the canyon at that moment. He sent word to the chiefs that he wished to make a treaty with them, and the Navajo leaders,

Navajo hut

reluctant to fight against the United States Army, even though they stood an excellent chance of defeating that part of it, came out and concluded a treaty. That it was as worthless as most of the others negotiated by the government was evident later. When the Navajos realized what they had virtually given away, they declared the agreement void. Nor were they pleased by subsequent treaties. Like nearly all the other tribes, they had to be removed by force, which Colonel Kit Carson accomplished in his notable campaign of 1864.

The West was, in fact, proving more difficult to conquer than the East, because of the immense distances. After the Mexican War, the United States found itself with a territory of 1,200,000 square miles, whose inhabitants were mostly hostile Indians. To complicate the nearly impossible problem of protecting such an area, the customary postwar diminishing of military strength had taken place; there were no more than 8,000 men in the Army. With the discovery of California gold in 1849, it was difficult to hold together even this inadequate force. The desertions were wholesale, and not unnatural when the

Army's low pay was taken into consideration. The poor sanitation and scarce medical aid of the western territories also cut heavily into Army strength. Cholera sweeping through westward-bound wagon trains killed escorting soldiers as well as pioneers. Yellow fever struck troops moving across the Isthmus of Panama to California; this scourge alone killed 107 men of the 4th Infantry in 1852. The Army learned to evade this peril by transporting its men around Cape Horn, but the stormy waters off that promontory wrecked more than one ship. In one disaster, a ship carrying the 3rd Artillery cost 300 lives by drowning and exposure.

At the lowest ebb of Army strength and morale, Congress took its usual belated action and raised pay by means of a re-enlistment bonus and allowances for "foreign service," including California and Oregon. While this was calculated to aid recruiting, Congress sabotaged its own intentions by increasing the term of enlistment from five years to ten.

Thus it was a still weakened Army that was compelled to undertake the perilous task of policing the West in the days before the Civil War. Recruiting was steady but slow, and in any case Congress had authorized a total of only 8,000 men. These soldiers were called upon to face Navajos, Yumas, Mojaves and Apaches in the Southwest; the Comanches, Kiowas, Arapahoes and Sioux (tribes totaling a quarter of a million Indians) on the Great Plains; and in the Northwest, the Nez Percés, Modocs and Shoshones.

If the Army was short of men and supplies, at least it was better equipped than before. A French officer, Captain Claude Minie, had invented a hollow-based, conical bullet for which Army muskets had been altered after it was officially adopted in 1855. These reconditioned muskets, equipped with the new "Minie ball," as it came to be known in its Civil War fame, now had an effective range of 400 to 600 yards and a maximum range of 1,000 yards. Moreover, this .69 caliber bullet  could be shot with powerful impact from the rebuilt weapons. The Indians had nothing as good to oppose it, but they were better armed than they had been, as the result of assiduous trade, capture and purchase. Their armament was various and plentiful, if not always up-to-date. A certain traffic in weapons had developed between Indian agents and braves who declared they needed modern weapons for the hunt.

Besides fresh weapons, the Army also had a supply of veterans to use them, men who had learned to like the life during the Mexican War and had never returned to the mundane routines of civilian life. They were men like Lieutenant Thomas W. Sweeny, a New York volunteer. Sweeny was known as "Fighting Tom," with reason. A mad Irishman from Cork, he did not leave the wars after losing his right arm at the Battle of Churubusco, but went into later conflicts with his left arm swinging, undaunted. Many of the other veterans had lost eyes, arms, legs, fingers, toes, even parts of their scalps; some were prosaically but painfully lamed by rheumatism, which was common.

Sweeny, a splendid example of these indomitable men, was assigned to the 2nd Infantry, and went with them in November, 1848, to southern California, at Fort Yuma, the junction of the Colorado and Gila Rivers. It was not enviable duty. The heat was overpowering, water was scarce, and the only abundance of anything was rattlesnakes and scorpions. The assignment of the Fort Yuma garrison was to subdue the Indians for whom their outpost was named—a mean, vicious war of small skirmishes and constant danger. The Yumas had few guns but they were superb archers who knew how to use their six-foot willow bows with deadly effect. When the arrows failed, they were also adept with spears, two-foot warclubs and long knives.

Against this foe Sweeny once led twenty-five men on a quick raid into Lower California, where he burned villages and destroyed crops in the standard manner, but on a more heroic plane compelled 150 warriors to surrender. Crippled though he was, Sweeny turned into one of the Army's best young leaders, serving with distinction in the Sioux campaign of 1855-56, and leading a Union brigade in the West during the Civil War. Wounded severely at Wilson's Creek and again at Shiloh, he survived all his perils and retired relatively intact in 1869.

In the pre-Civil War decades, the pattern of conquest spread past the Plains and the Southwest and southern California into the Northwest, where the same dismal story of seizure of land and betrayal through treaties and broken agreements was repeated over and over, with the all too familiar results. There were Indian raids, reprisals by the settlers, burnings of villages on both sides and assorted massacres. The white men produced a few refinements of their old iniquities. A particularly atrocious one was the poisoned feast to which a volunteer captain invited a troop of trusting Modocs. As a poisoner, however, the captain proved to be less expert than the Borgias. Annoyed by the failure of his potions, he ordered his men to shoot the guests.

To the Northwest came officers whose names would shortly be famous. A freshly minted captain named Ulysses S. Grant arrived at Fort Humboldt, in northern California, and in that bleak post overlooking Humboldt Bay, a backwater used mostly as a base for expeditions, he found so much more of boredom than of the action he desired that he sought desperately for some distraction. Riding, hunting and planting crops were not enough, even though his work in the fields produced a grateful improvement in Army rations. With neither action nor promotion in sight, Grant turned to alcohol, the solace which was later to get him into so much trouble, and soon was threatened with a court-martial by his commanding officer. Disgusted, he resigned his commission and went back to his Illinois home.

Major Phil Kearny was another officer who was restless in the boredom of these northwestern posts, missing the excitement of the Mexican War action in which, like Sweeny, he had lost an arm. Kearny fought briefly against the Klamath Indians, but he resigned soon after. His service was only a prelude to his brilliant Civil War career.

One officer who stayed with it in the Northwest was Lieutenant George Crook, who came there fresh from West Point to join the 4th Infantry. Crook was a man of broader interests, who could supplement hunting with a scientific study of the region's flora and fauna. He was also a man who made an effort to understand the Indians, a pursuit which seldom occupied the attention of his fellow officers. This is not to say that he was any less eager to hunt them down. On his first skirmish, he was so zealous in following a fleeing brave whom he wounded with a rifle shot and later killed with his pistol that he found himself separated from his party and without ammunition. In this plight, he was attacked by another Indian whose arrows, he wrote later, flashed past him "with such velocity that they did not appear over a couple of inches long." Jumping on his horse, Crook dashed for safety and escaped. On the next sortie, however, he was not as lucky and took an arrow in his right hip, which he jerked out leaving the head in his body.

Crook thus came to respect Indian archery, especially that of the Rogue River Indians, and often said these tribes were more effective with their bows than with the muzzle-loading guns they acquired. It was not until they possessed breech-loading guns, he said, that the Indians became a real threat. An accomplished sharpshooter himself, Crook knew what he was talking about. He also showed promise as a strategist even as a young Lieutenant in Indian country, daring in the charges he led and skillful in keeping the enemy off balance and in disposing his men. His command suffered few casualties.

Elsewhere on the Northwest frontier, less talented but no less courageous officers dealt with the inevitable outbreaks which occurred as the white traders and settlers began to move into the territory both from overland and by ship, after the long journey around Cape Horn. Peaceful tribes like the Spokane, Coeur d'Alene and Pelouse nations were stirred to the warpath by the seemingly unavoidable sequence of injustice and abuse that invariably followed in the wake of the white man's coming.

Early in May, 1856, the Pelouse dispatched two miners over some now unrecorded quarrel, and an expedition went out from Fort Walla Walla, under command of Colonel E. J. Steptoe, to punish them. Steptoe had 157 infantry and dragoons, backed up by two howitzers and some friendly Nez Percé scouts. This force was inadequate for the task, and in addition it was suffering from a serious shortage of ammunition. Each man had only forty rounds.

As for the Pelouse, they had marshaled allies from the Spokane, Coeur d'Alene and Yakima tribes, until they were able to confront Steptoe with at least 1,200 men, who worked their way around to the rear of the Colonel's column and fell upon it. These soldiers were well-trained, however. They did not panic at the unexpected onslaught. The dragoons galloped to a nearby hill, where they turned and poured down a hot fire into the Indians until the infantry could reach this superior vantage point. Meanwhile the howitzers were brought into position, and against these the Indians had no defense.

After he had secured the hill, Steptoe discovered that he had inadvertently cut himself off from the water supply of a nearby stream. Knowing that if the battle were to be a long one, this deficiency could be disastrous, the Colonel decided he must hack his way through the besiegers to the river. It was a bloody path, cut with sabers and clubbed rifles; it took a half-hour of savage fighting to cover a mile, even with the aid of the howitzers to keep the Indians from overwhelming them. A heavy price was paid for this initial mistake. By the time the troops reached the precious water, three officers were dead and many of the men were wounded. At least they could refill their canteens, and once this was done, they cut their way through wave after wave of red attackers to another hill, where they stood off the Indians until nightfall, after which the enemy withdrew. It was not a moment too soon. Only three rounds of ammunition remained to each soldier.

Steptoe took advantage of the darkness to retreat, the only way out of his desperate situation. The dead and the howitzers were buried together, since both would have hampered the retreat, and the column fumbled on its way through the night to safety.

This withdrawal was not only considered a blow to the Army's prestige, but an invitation to potential disaster, since all the tribes in the region would now believe that the white man was too weak to defend himself. In a move to correct this impression, Colonel George Wright set out from Fort Walla Walla in September, 1858, with two squadrons of the 1st Dragoons, an artillery company equipped with two twelve-pounder mountain howitzers and two six-pounders, a battalion of the 3rd Artillery serving as infantry, a 9th Infantry battalion, plus the customary pack train and a few Nez Percé scouts. This force was equipped with the new "Minie balls" and the muskets to fire them, and in Colonel Wright it had a commander who was not likely to take the unnecessary risks which had caused Steptoe so much trouble.

Crossing the Snake and Pelouse Rivers, Colonel Wright came into a broad plain known as Four Lakes, shadowed by rolling hills. From one of these summits the Colonel saw a spectacle that would later be reproduced in a thousand motion picture and television shows—more than 500 Indians on their horses, silhouetted against the deep blue of the sky, raising their plumed lances in defiance. It was, apparently, to be an open battle.

Wright ordered a charge and his army swept over the hill, considerably aided by the howitzers, and the Indians fell back before this assault onto the plain below. The Colonel followed them with another rolling attack, using the sabers of his dragoons to good effect. The Indians were demoralized now, and a grass fire started by the cannon inadvertently caused them a further disaster because it provided a screen for the dragoons, who burst through it and cut down many of those who were fleeing. It was a complete victory for Wright. He had not lost a single man.

Following the doctrine of hot pursuit, Wright's army rode after the Indians, who rallied and turned to face their pursuers at a place called Spokane Plain. There Wright's men completed the rout they had begun, capturing most of the Indians' horses in the process. He provided his men with their pick of this herd, and killed the remainder, after which he burned the lodges and storehouses of the Indian village. Those Indians who were unlucky enough to be captured were tried and convicted summarily for the sins of those who had brought on the war, whoever they might be.

This defeat was so staggering that it virtually put an end to resistance in the Northwest for years to come. The core of revolt, however, was not in this far part of the nation but on the Plains. Sensing that this was the case, the government made a determined effort to negotiate with these tribes in 1851, at a council held in Fort Laramie, Wyoming. To this conference came Cheyennes, Arapahos, Crows, Assiniboins, Hidatsas, Mandans and Arikaras. It was, on the whole, a peaceful affair. Surprisingly, the tribes agreed to the government's proposition that they divide themselves up and be assigned to territories for each tribe, territory being in reality a synonym for reservation. Of course the territories were large—too large, if the negotiators had known it. The Cheyennes and Arapahoes got most of what is today Colorado and Western Kansas, and that would be a later cause of trouble.

Like all the other treaties, this one too had its heavy price for the

Indians. In exchange for permitting the white men to build roads and military posts on their lands, the tribes were to get $5,000 a year for fifty years, but when the treaty reached the United States Senate its members were appalled by such generosity and cut the figure to ten years, a change the Indians were not told about. It was a worthless treaty in any case, like the others, because the government never meant to enforce it. Nothing was said in 1859 when the onrushing settlers attracted by the second gold rush ruthlessly violated the treaty, brutally drove out the Cheyennes and Arapahoes and took whatever land they wanted for settlements and farms.

It was not surprising that the Indians were provoked to war by this seizure, which was so raw and with so little justification that the white commissioners sent out seven years later to investigate the causes of the war were appalled by what they discovered and issued a report which declared, in part:

> Before 1861 the Cheyennes and Arapahoes had been driven from the mountain regions down upon the waters of the Arkansas and were becoming sullen and discontented because of this violation of their rights . . . If the lands of the white man are taken, civilization justifies him

in resisting the invader. Civilization does more than this: it brands him as a coward and a slave if he submits to the wrong. Here civilization made its contract and guaranteed the rights of the weaker party. It did not stand by the guarantee. The treaty was broken, but not by the savage. If the savage resists, civilization, with the Ten Commandments in one hand and the sword in the other, demands his immediate extermination. . . . These Indians saw their former homes and hunting grounds overrun by a greedy population, thirsting for gold. They saw their game driven east to the plains, and soon found themselves the object of jealousy and hatred. They must go.

No more cogent a statement of the Indians' plight could have been made, but the commission's report was ignored.

It is surprising, under the circumstances, that the patience of the Indians did not end sooner. In the country of the Sioux, for example, these irascible tribesmen were restless and apprehensive but had not been inclined to make war until a foolish Army Lieutenant provoked it. This young man was 2nd Lieutenant John L. Grattan, who came out of West Point to Laramie in 1854, convinced that Indians were cowards. He boasted that he could demolish the whole Cheyenne nation with a force of ten men, and with twice that many would sweep the remaining Indians off the Plains.

A trivial incident gave Grattan the opportunity to prove himself the idiot he was. A Sioux had killed an emigrant's sick cow for its hide, and although the owner had originally left it to die, he came to the fort and demanded angrily that the Indian agent see that he was paid for his loss. The Lieutenant in command was willing to handle the matter in the usual way by negotiation, but Grattan insisted that he could do better and inexplicably his superior agreed to let him try. With thirty volunteers and two howitzers, he marched forth, grandiloquently announcing that he would "conquer or die."

With this pitiful force he approached the camp of three Sioux bands and astonished the peaceable chiefs by abusing them roundly. Even so, they would have pledged payment for the cow if some nervous soldier in the company had not fired a shot, for what reason was never known. It set off a furious chain reaction. One of the howitzer crew, thinking hostilities had begun, fired a round from his gun and a chief fell to the ground, mortally wounded.

Sioux warrior

At this the Indians seized their guns and opened fire. Grattan tried to retreat to the fort but he was cut off, and in a few minutes he and every one of his men lay dead.

Back home the newspapers trumpeted "Massacre!" and the War Department, ignoring the facts of the matter which the commander at Laramie quickly forwarded, ordered a punitive expedition sent out under the command of Colonel William L. Harney, an officer noted for his hatred of Indians. He had never forgiven them for compelling him to run for his life in his underwear during the Seminole War.

Harney set out from Fort Leavenworth with a substantial little force, consisting of six companies of the 6th and 10th Infantry, a battery of the 4th Artillery and four companies of dragoons. At Ash Hollow, on the North Platte River, he encountered a camp of the Brulé Sioux and issued an ultimatum to them, demanding that they give up those responsible for Grattan's massacre.

Scarcely waiting for a reply, he encircled the camp with his cavalry and ordered an infantry charge. The Sioux were caught by surprise, not anticipating so precipitous an attack, and with no more than a token resistance to cover their retreat, they fled before they, in turn, were massacred. At that they left eighty-six dead behind, along with five wounded braves, most of their squaws and children and all their ponies. Harney had lost only five killed and seven wounded.

The Army had marked the Sioux as troublemakers and continued to harass them whether they made trouble or not. Through the decade of the 1850s, they fought no less than twenty-two small wars with them and with other tribes, on terrain ranging all the way from Florida to Arizona, and from the Missouri River to Oregon. In one year alone, 1857, there were thirty-seven engagements, and during the following year every regiment in the West was on the march, an average of 1,234 miles per regiment.

These were the desultory conflicts between the end of Black Hawk's rebellion and the Civil War. They were cruel and harsh enough for the men who had to fight them, but they had no major significance except as symptoms of the inevitable westward movement which would one day end all Indian resistance.

With the coming of the Civil War, however, a new period in the melancholy history of the Indian Wars began. As before when the white men fought each other, the Indians were expected to choose sides and, as before, no matter which side they were on it could be guaranteed that in the end they would be losers. This time the divided loyalties were overshadowed by the increasingly fierce resistance of all the tribes west of the Mississippi to any further white encroachment on their territories. The accumulated grievances of more than two decades were stirred to open revolt in a dozen places as the larger war overflowed its main eastern theaters into the West. The United States found itself, in effect, fighting a war on two fronts, one against the seceding states and the other against the Indians.

For the Indians, as for the southern slaveholders, it was the beginning of the end. /

# 9 ★ ★ ★ ★ ★ ★

# The Indians' Civil War

On the eve of the Civil War the Army could look at its chain of posts guarding the West and justly declare that it had fulfilled its mission beyond what could be expected from an outnumbered and often badly supplied force. Within reason the garrisons had protected emigrants and settlers and had kept the tribes west of the Mississippi under control, from Texas to Oregon, from Kansas to California and Minnesota. It had been an astonishing military accomplishment.

But with the outbreak of the great conflict which overshadowed everything else, the power and control so carefully built up over two decades was quickly diminished as Federal troops had to be withdrawn from their frontier posts for the Union army. Nor could Washington be expected to send out armies to quell uprisings.

The Indians saw in this situation an opportunity for revenge, and possibly for pushing back the invaders. They began to attack here and there, the fever spread, and soon matters were out of hand. On August 10, 1861, a territorial newspaper, the *Arizonian,* reported, "Since the withdrawal of the Overland Mail and the garrison troops the chances against life have reached the maximum height. Within but six months nine-tenths of the whole male population have been killed off, and every ranch, farm and mine in the country have been abandoned in consequence . . ."

Thus, in new violence, began the last chapter of Indian resistance in America. It had taken three centuries to conquer the eastern tribes, but from the date of the *Arizonian*'s cry of despair it took only thirty years to end every semblance of revolt, kill the leaders and pen up the tribes on reservations. Yet those three decades, the so-called "winning of the West," are far better known to Americans than the previous three centuries of warfare. It is a period with its own voluminous literature—historical, biographical and fictional—and its depiction in radio, motion pictures and television has made it probably the best-known period in the life of the nation, although in a highly exaggerated and romanticized way.

The records of this era have also touched off endless controversy among scholars and a coterie of Americana specialists who regard it as "their" period. Versions of what really happened are fiercely disputed; sources are both discredited and defended. These specialists are still carrying on the Battle of the Little Big Horn, and there is no more than general agreement about what truly happened to George Custer and his men on that disastrous day. The Custer literature alone would fill a good many library shelves, if it were brought together in one place.

About one thing there is no dispute. The Indian Wars of the West were fought with a peculiar ferocity, as though every stand were a last stand. Certainly the wisest of the Indian leaders must have realized that this was nearly the case, that they were all that stood in the way of complete domination of the continent by the white man. Sometimes the resistance was intense simply because the tribes themselves were violent and intractable people. The Apaches, for example, fought with a blind fury that could only have come from temperament, since their plight was no worse than any other tribe's.

The Apaches had excellent leadership in two chiefs, Mangas Coloradas and Cochise. They had made their tribe so feared in northern Mexico that the provinces there stood ready to pay $100 for an Apache warrior's scalp, fifty dollars for a woman's and twenty-five dollars for a child's. Apaches had been Mexico's problem until New Mexico and Arizona were ceded to the Union, after which it was all both countries could do to keep them under some kind of control. The Apaches fought without quarter or mercy, and for the first time there was little argument from humanitarians when the Army ordered its commanders to exterminate every member of the tribe they could find.

As a fighter, the Apache was ideally adapted to the terrain which he sought to protect. As elusive as he was vindictive and a master of ambush, he possessed endless endurance to withstand the heat and lack of water in his homeland. He was also a skilled torturer. Soldiers fighting the Apaches soon learned to prefer death to capture.

Both sides made an effort to win the Apaches as allies at the beginning of the Civil War, but these tribesmen made it plain they wanted no part of either side. The Confederates took the hint and withdrew to Texas. They were content to leave to the Union Army the job of coping with the Apaches, as indeed it had been trying to

apache warrior

do since the 1850s. An assistant surgeon, Bernard J. Irwin, had won the nation's first Medal of Honor in the course of this attempt. The action which won him the award took place in 1856, but since the Medal had not yet been created, Dr. Irwin had to wait until 1894, when it was bestowed retroactively. By that time he was a Brigadier General and ready to retire as Chief Medical Officer of the Army.

The incident which won Irwin the award was typical of the kind of war the Army had to fight against the Apaches. In 1856 this Irish-born doctor was only a 1st Lieutenant when the Indians abducted a settler's boy from his home. Lieutenant George N. Bascom led a detachment of sixty 7th Infantry men into the mountains in pursuit of the kidnapers, who were led by Cochise himself. Bascom overtook the band, but Cochise refused to give up his prisoner, and after narrowly escaping capture himself, attacked Bascom's force.

Fearing himself trapped, Bascom sent a messenger for help. When he heard that there were wounded men in the trap, Irwin volunteered to lead the rescue party, and at the head of fourteen men mounted on mules, he hurried through a driving snowstorm to the canyon beyond which Bascom was at bay on somewhat wider ground. The doctor's tiny force burst out of the canyon, took the Apaches by surprise and routed them, after which Irwin got out his medical bag and began to take care of the wounded. When he had bound up their wounds he went on with Bascom's men to destroy Cochise's village.

A more extraordinary feat, unrewarded by medals, was recorded by a Dutch officer, Captain Albert H. Pfeiffer, of the New Mexico Volunteers, stationed at Fort McRae. On a picnic one day with his Spanish wife, her two maids and a detachment of six soldiers, he was interrupted during a peaceful swim in the river by a commotion on the bank. The Apaches had swooped down, killed the soldier escort and seized the three women. They meant to kill Pfeiffer too, but, naked and wet as he was, he had time to pick up his rifle and cartridge belt and get behind a pile of rocks. From that vantage point he held off the Indians singlehanded for hours, until his skin was so raw from the sun it was difficult for him to move. The fort was nine miles away, but Pfeiffer managed incredibly to withdraw slowly the whole way, with an arrow through his back and jutting out from his stomach. His fire was so accurate that the Indians did not dare close in.

Having given the alarm, he collapsed and troops rode out at once after the Indians. They did not catch them, but were in such close pursuit that the Apaches abandoned their hostages. Two of them, Mrs. Pfeiffer and one maid, were dead. The other girl was wounded but survived.

After this frightful experience, Pfeiffer became one of those men occasionally seen on the frontier obsessed with a hatred of Indians and devoting his life to killing them. These were usually men who, like Pfeiffer, had seen some loved one killed or tortured. Although he continued to command troops and eventually became a Colonel, Pfeiffer went out alone whenever he could to hunt Indians. He claimed that a wolf pack always followed him, knowing that eventually they would get Indian meat.

Men like Pfeiffer and Irwin were not uncommon in the rough, tough outfit known as the California Column, which fought Indians up and down the landscape of Arizona and New Mexico during the Civil War. Brigadier General James H. Carleton commanded the Column, which had been put together from volunteer regiments of westerners. During the war it was this unit—part of the Army of the Southwest—that prevented the Apaches from making a disaster area of the whole broad territory. As it was, the Indians succeeded in amassing an impressive amount of horses, cattle, arms, ammunition and other booty. In a single massacre of thirteen miners, the Apaches got away with $50,000 in gold dust.

When it encountered the Apaches for the first time in July, 1862, the California Column was on another mission—to clear out what Confederate forces might remain in Arizona and New Mexico. Appropriately enough the meeting occurred at a place called Apache Pass, in southeastern Arizona, whose high walls and fresh springs providing the only water within a day's march made it an ideal place for an ambush.

Into this deadly trap marched Captain Thomas F. Roberts, of the 1st California Infantry, leading an advance guard of the column. He did not know that nearly 700 Indians were lying in wait for him, but he was well aware of the dangers such a piece of terrain presented and he took every precaution. But his three infantry companies and detachment of cavalry were hot and thirsty from a long desert march and he was anxious to reach the water he knew was in the pass. It was worth the chance, because Roberts had two mountain howitzers with him. These raised a blinding cloud of dust in the desert, but they could throw a 6.9 pound shell a thousand yards, and burst shrapnel at 800 yards and canister at 250 yards.

Moving cautiously, Roberts entered the pass and was within sight of the springs when the Apaches opened up with a barrage of arrows and bullets from both sides. They had made a mistake, however. Their attack was too soon, and the troops were able to pull back to the entrance of the pass.

Roberts realized he was outnumbered, perhaps by as much as seven to one, but he had to have the water for his men. He deployed them as skirmishers and they began to fight their way back. After hours of combat they reached an old stone stage station near the springs, but still short of the precious water. At that point Roberts brought up his most potent weapons, the howitzers, and put them into action. That dispersed the Apaches. They retreated, leaving sixty-three braves dead from the artillery fire and three others dead of musket wounds—a striking testimony to the advantage the white men possessed with these guns. Roberts had lost two killed and two wounded.

Although he had won the battle, the Captain had no delusions about his victory. He was certain the Apaches would return next day and he would have to do it all over again. Meanwhile, he thought it essential to send a warning message back to the first section of his supply train, under the veteran Captain John C. Cremony, and for this purpose he dispatched a Sergeant Mitchell and four of his cavalry-men. But the watching Apaches saw and guessed what he was up to. Mitchell was scarcely on his way when Chief Mangas Coloradas and fifty of his warriors rode hotly after them. Like a western movie, the white men rode for their lives, firing at their pursuers over their shoulders and trying to dodge bullets and arrows. One man was hit but continued to cling to his saddle. Three horses were shot down, throwing their riders, but two of these men were picked up.

The man left behind was Private John Teal. On the ground, facing what seemed certain annihilation, he sheltered himself behind his dead horse and began to fire with his carbine at the Indians who were circling about him in the classic manner. "They knew I also had a revolver and a saber," he wrote later in his report, "and seemed unwilling to try close quarters . . . I got a good chance at a prominent Indian and slipped a carbine bullet into his breast. He must have been a man of some note because soon after they seemed to get away from me . . . I thought; this is a good time to make tracks . . . and started for camp. I have walked eight miles since then."

Mangas Coloradas was the "prominent Indian" Teal had hit, a chief next only to Cochise. He could not fight again for months as a result of the chest wound Teal had given him, and it was not long after his recovery when he was lured to his death. Considering the notorious cruelty of the Apaches, it would have been too much to expect any sort of mercy or fair dealing from their white pursuers. Nonetheless, the manner of Mangas Coloradas' capture and death was neither just nor humane. He was enticed into the Army camp on the promise of a parley and then arrested. That night Colonel J. R. West told two of his night sentries: "Men, that old murderer has got away from every soldier command and left a trail of blood 500 miles along the stage line. I want him dead or alive tomorrow morning. Do you understand? I want him dead!"

After the Colonel departed, one of the guards thrust his bayonet in the campfire, heated it red hot and plunged it into the chief's leg. When he leaped up with an agonized cry, one of the guards shot and killed him. The official report said that he died "while attempting to escape" after his capture.

Two months after Teal's exploit, General James Henry Carleton put three detachments in the field in a major effort to hunt down the Apaches. His orders were explicit: "The men are to be slain whenever and wherever they can be found. The women and children may be taken prisoners, but, of course, they are not to be killed." This war of extermination, like so many others, failed. Retreating into the mountains, the Apaches carried on a guerrilla campaign during the remainder of the Civil War, and it was not until after the conflict was over that they were finally subdued. Even then it took an over-whelming army of thousands of troops to do it.

As the struggle between North and South developed, Indian out-breaks in the West increased in direct proportion to the weakened garrisons until the Federal government had no choice but to divert men from the eastern battlefields to reinforce the forts. Confederate prisoners were urged to volunteer. They were dressed in the hated Union blue, promised that they would never have to fight against southerners and shipped out to the western posts. The Army regulars referred to these recruits as "galvanized Yankees."

Another odd development in the war was the fate of those southern tribes which had been transplanted from the Southeast to the West —Creeks, Seminoles, Cherokees, Choctaws and Chickasaws. To which side, one might ask, could these tribes be expected to give their loyalty? To the Federal government, which had moved them out of their homes and hunting grounds, or to the South, where they had been born and reared? The answer appeared to be that it depended on the tribe, and sometimes on the individual Indian. Some fought with one side, some the other, and there were those who fought with both at different times. Their leaders were taken into the ranks of the regulars as they demonstrated their merit. Two chiefs became brigadier generals, one in each of the contending armies.

In the Southwest, the Indians had a direct stake in the war because it was their grain and cattle which represented a valuable source of supply to both North and South. Both sides wooed them, but they leaned strongly toward the Confederacy, since they themselves were slaveholders, who had brought their Negroes with them when they were displaced from their Alabama, Georgia and Florida homes. Southern Indian agents took advantage of that fact. They were tellingly persuasive in their arguments with the Indians, convincing them that the Southern cause was also theirs and promising to protect their property rights in the slaves they owned, as well as grandly assuring them that the South would restore all the rights and privileges for which they had been contending against the Federal government.

The North had no great expectation of winning the Indians' allegiance. They could hope for little more than neutrality, if that. When it became obvious that they would have to make some attempt to enlist Indian help, they had nothing to promise them except to maintain conditions as they were, a small consolation to the restless tribesmen. At that, strangely enough, a few did come over to the Union side, as a gesture of respect for the Army—Indians always wanted to be on whichever side was likely to win—or out of simple loyalty to the government, in spite of everything Washington had done to them.

On the Confederate side, the man who did most to ally the tribes to the southern cause was undoubtedly Albert Pike, the Indian Commissioner, who used money, gifts and soft talk to stir up the Kiowas and Comanches particularly. These tribes were a scourge to Union wagon trains on the Santa Fé Trail. Pike also persuaded the Choctaws and Chickasaws and most of the Seminoles. The Cherokees, always more civilized, actually voted formally to secede from the Union, in August, 1861. It was not a unanimous decision. The Upper Creeks and a faction led by Chief John Ross eventually seceded from the secceders.

This was no minor split. When Chief Opothleyhola, of the Upper Creeks, took his people over to the Union side, the eighty-year-old sachem brought with him 4,000 Indians, including 1,700 fighting warriors, and a store of treasure. The chief was pursued by a hard-fisted, hard-drinking Confederate colonel, Douglas H. Cooper, and an army of 1,400 Chickasaws and Choctaws, and Texas cavalry. After beating off two attacks, a third was in progress when the Cherokees suddenly refused to fight the Creeks, and Cooper was compelled to withdraw and wait for reinforcements. These proved to be a strong force of 1,380 men, including another Cherokee unit and white veterans of Wilson's Creek. It was too much for the Creeks. They fled in headlong retreat, leaving 700 dead behind them before they reached the Union safety of Kansas, where they endured a winter of horror and suffering in this alien land. Nor could the Union Army help them a great deal. Between winters they would somehow have to get back to their own lands, but meanwhile that territory would have to be taken from the Confederate troops who occupied it.

This attempt was made early in March, 1862, at a place in Arkansas called Pea Ridge, a height above Little Sugar Creek. Nearby was Elkhorn Tavern, which gave its name to the battle. General Samuel R. Curtis commanded the Union Army of four divisions, totaling about 10,500 men. General Earl Van Dorn was in command of the Confederate forces, of nearly 16,000 men. An able officer, a veteran with experience in the Indian Wars, Van Dorn had a low opinion of red men, whether they were allies or not. No doubt he looked with some disgust on the spectacle of the Cherokee chief John Ross—he had not yet defected to the Union side—riding to battle in an open carriage. Ross wore a stovepipe hat and frock coat, while General Pike sat incongruously beside him in an Indian outfit. Ross had always dressed as the white men did, but Pike's gesture was intended somehow to convince any doubting Indians that the Confederates were their brothers.

There were some in the line of march who were not convinced. One of the Cherokee regiments, led by Colonel John Drew, meant to desert at the first opportunity, and they were watched warily by the other Cherokees, who knew all about it.

Van Dorn himself came to the battle in an ambulance, ill and in a bad humor. He was poorly supplied, and the rations were particularly short. The weather, too, was against him. There had been a heavy, wet snow to hamper his progress, and it had taken three days of forced marching to travel fifty-five miles.

The Confederate strategy Van Dorn had devised was an enveloping movement around Pea Ridge, since the Union force was smaller, and he went about it at once. General Curtis, however, was not so easily trapped. He was an officer with an excellent record in the Mexican War, noted for his quick, intelligent moves in battle. Anticipating Van Dorn's movement, he placed two divisions on the bluffs overlooking Sugar Creek, and sent messengers to General Franz Sigel, who was coming up with support, urging him to hurry before he was cut off. In the race between Van Dorn and Sigel, the Union General got to the ridge first, except for the rear units, which were under his direct charge. These were attacked by the Confederates, but Curtis sent back sufficient strength to rescue the German-American regiments Sigel headed. The Union force was now intact and in command of the high ground.

During the night, Van Dorn tried another piece of strategy. While presenting a posture of peaceful bivouac, with the red campfires flaring against the snow, he dispatched a force of Indians and cavalry under Pike to his extreme right, and then before dawn pulled back his center leaving the campfires going, in the hope that Curtis would be sucked into an envelopment.

As he had anticipated, the Union troops began to march during the early morning. The advance unit, under General Peter J. Osterhaus, a Prussian-trained officer, was first to make contact, coming suddenly upon a large part of the Confederate Indian troops, who charged him before he could get his artillery unlimbered. Even when he got them into action, the Indians came on in spite of the big guns, for the first time, and broke his line. Behind them came the Texas cavalry, sweeping against their opposite Union numbers so hard that the Federal horsemen fell back into their supporting infantry. Simultaneously, the Union center was assaulted by another Confederate force, under General Ben McCulloch, and the right was also in trouble.

For a time it seemed as though Van Dorn's plan would succeed, but the Union generals held stubbornly, and the Confederates meanwhile found themselves in difficulties with their Indian allies. General Pike might have arrayed himself to look like the red men he commanded, but he did not have their temperament. After their first furious charge, the tribesmen had no inclination to try another, in spite of all the General's exhortations. Federal artillery was now in action and that reduced their enthusiasm still more. At this point Colonel Drew's Cherokees decided the moment for defection had come, the other Cherokee unit moved in to block them, and Van Dorn was scandalized to witness the spectacle of two of his regiments fighting each other.

All this had given Osterhaus' forces time to recover, regroup and launch a counterattack. Confederate and Union troops met head-on. Both McCulloch and his second-in-command were killed. Union artillery backed up the countercharge, and soon the battle was moving in the other direction. By nightfall the two armies had broken apart, both suffering heavy casualties, and a clearcut decision not yet reached. Curtis concluded to rest his men overnight and attack again at dawn.

When the battle was resumed, Van Dorn's gloomy predictions about his Indians came true, but in truth there was little enthusiasm for the conflict among the Indians on either side. Drew's Cherokees pulled away and prepared to go home. All the other Indian units except the second Cherokee regiment were of a similar mind. That left the white men to fight it out between themselves. At the end of the day, Curtis emerged the victor.

One of the Confederate officers who fought with great distinction that day was a grim-visaged chief named Stand Watie, in command of the loyal Cherokee regiment. Colonel Watie deserved his elevation to Brigadier General for his services then and later. Among other feats, he captured the Cherokee capital of Tahlequah and burned down John Ross's splendid home there, invaded Kansas with some success until he was driven off by a brigade of Indian and Negro troops and conducted numerous destructive raids until the end of the war. Watie was nearly the last of the Confederate officers to surrender, on June 23, 1865.

The defection of Drew's Cherokees during the battle at Pea Ridge, resulting in their Union reorganization as the 3rd Cherokee Mounted Rifles, led to John Ross's removal from the Confederacy, bringing most of the Cherokee nation with him.

Perhaps the most unusual of the Union Army's Indian recruits was Ely Samuel Parker, a Seneca who had studied law in an effort to help his people until the Supreme Court, in a decision which passes belief, ruled that Indians could not be admitted to the bar because they were not citizens! Parker graduated from Rensselaer Polytechnic Institute nonetheless, and as an engineer went out to Galena, Illinois, to work on a construction project. There he met Ulysses S. Grant, just returned from his tour of duty in the Northwest and for the moment discouraged with Army life. They became close friends.

When the war came, Parker tried to join up with Grant but Secretary of War Seward curtly refused to commission him. The white men did not need the help of Indians to win the war, he said, but Seward was glad to accept the help of 3,000 of them before the war was over. Parker, undiscouraged, finally persuaded the Corps of Engineers to grant him a Captain's commission, and thereupon recruited 628 Iroquois as volunteers.

Parker found Grant again at Vicksburg and began serving with him on his staff, following him afterward through the Chattanooga campaign and the fateful maneuvers of the Army of the Potomac. He rose to be Lieutenant Colonel in 1864, and eventually, as Grant's military secretary, a Brigadier General. He was with his friend at Appomattox, where Lee observed him transcribing the surrender terms, put out his hand and remarked, "I am glad to see one real American here." Parker shook Lee's hand and answered with dignity: "We are all Americans, sir."

Thus the feelings of combatants on both sides were mixed when it came to considering the role of Indians in the war. On the one hand there were men like Parker and tribes like the Cherokees to cheer about on the Northern side, but on the other hand there were the fierce tribes of the Southwest who were a valuable aid to the Confederacy simply by pinning down so many Federal troops. Moreover, the pot of trouble in the Plains was constantly boiling, as it had been for a long time, and it boiled over for the first time before the war had barely started.

The great Sioux uprising which began in Minnesota in 1862 has been one of the most written about episodes in Indian history. Occurring as it did in the midst of the larger struggle, it had more than the ordinary significance because it was a diversion too large to ignore. A Federal government in danger of its existence had to divert men and money from the larger arena to fight a smaller war.

Of course it could be argued that the white men had brought this disaster on themselves. The Santee Sioux who lived in southwestern Minnesota on a reservation were the least warlike of that belligerent tribe. Many were Christian converts. Yet the traders who dealt with them cheated everyone impartially, godly or ungodly alike. Often the rations sent by the government to supplement Indian crops were spoiled or of a quality not fit for human consumption. The government agents were a callous lot, by and large, and the proprietors of the agency stores were an inhuman collection who would not feed a starving man without payment. In the spring of 1862 the cutworms had ruined the Indians' corn crop, their annuities from the government were late in arriving and what supplies they had on hand were either inadequate or inedible. Their situation was desperate—and maddening, because they knew there was food in the government warehouses ready to be parceled out as soon as the belated annuity money from Washington arrived. According to the treaty, provisions could only be given with the money, and since a Washington preoccupied with war had neglected to send it, the commander at Yellow Medicine, where the agency was situated, said he could do nothing.

This was an urgent grievance but there was another one. The hard-nosed traders had a good many claims against the Indians, not a few of them fraudulent. Some of the Indians feared that when the annuity money did come it would all be taken from them by the grasping traders. A few of the young men, led by a fiery brave named Red Middle Voice, visited Captain John Marsh, at Fort Ridgely, and asked him pointblank if the soldiers were going to help the traders collect. The captain was reassuring. "My boys are soldiers, not collection agents for the traders," he said.

The traders had counted on such help, and when they heard they were not going to get it, they immediately put up signs in their stores advising the Indians that they would get no more credit until the money came and the claims were paid. When an interpreter pointed out that the Indians might starve meanwhile, one trader remarked heartlessly, "If they're hungry, let them eat grass."

These words, widely circulated, infuriated the Sioux as nothing else might have done. It seemed to sum up for them all of the white man's iniquity and cruelty. On a Sunday afternoon, August 17, some of them sat down to discuss the situation, but it was already too late for reason and negotiation. That morning four braves had murdered five settlers in Meeker County.

After an uneasy, ominous Sunday night, the morning light disclosed, although not to the settlers, one of the most dangerous aggregations of Indians the Plains had seen for many years. They had been holding a secret council all night, arguing whether to turn on their white oppressors. The young braves were, quite naturally, for war. The older ones, and particularly the leading chief, Little Crow, were more cautious, but at last gave in to what obviously could not be avoided.

Little Crow was another extraordinary Indian leader. In the Kapoja band of Medewkanton Sioux from which he came, his name (Chetawakan-mani, "the sacred pigeon-hawk that comes walking," in his own tongue) was not uncommon; four other chiefs had borne it. It was unlikely that any of them had the curious mixture of good and bad qualities that were blended in Little Crow. Of the good, there was substantially less to be said. He had always appeared friendly to the whites, and indeed was liked more by them than by his own people. Little Crow had been useful to the government in getting approval for treaties. In Washington, where he wore a plug hat for such state occasions, he was a familiar figure for a time. On the reservation he lived the life of a fairly prosperous farmer, in a white man's house. Little Crow, in a word, appeared to be assimilated.

But this hawk-faced Indian was, at heart, something of an opportunist. He was, moreover, arrogant in his manner and not inclined to let a principle stand in his way. A lover of alcohol, Little Crow had been a quarrelsome, roistering young man with a decided penchant for stealing other men's wives. Husbands had suggested that he leave his native village of Pig's Eye, where St. Paul now stands, and he had drifted on to other tribes, acquiring six wives along the way. His father's observation that he "had very little good sense" seemed a masterpiece of understatement—that is, until he became chief of his tribe. Then he abruptly changed his habits, astounded everyone by coming out against alcohol and adultery, and encouraged morality among the young.

This was the man who emerged on a hot August morning as a monster whose deeds shocked the nation. One of his braves began that day's work by shooting in cold blood a young clerk in a Redwood, Minnesota, store. Ironically, this victim had an Indian wife. After that the terror spread like a forest fire. Houses and stores at Redwood were attacked and burned. A relief column from Fort Ridgely was ambushed and decimated. Less than half the men escaped alive. Then the Indians fanned out over the settlements in one of the most gruesome slaughters ever seen on the frontier. More than 400 settlers had been killed by nightfall, and at midnight the Indians were still at it, looting the stores in Yellow Medicine.

Next day there was a hurried marshaling of troops from nearby forts, but the roads and trails were choked with terrified refugees, nearly 40,000 of them, seeking the shelter of the garrisons. Little Crow was already planning their downfall, and on Wednesday, he moved his considerable force of braves up to Fort Ridgely, failed in an assault on it and then laid siege. Detachments of Indians pursued the fleeing settlers and annihilated them wherever they were found. At Lake Shetek, for example, an entire group of them was massacred without a single survivor.

After two ineffectual attempts at assaulting Ridgely, Little Crow had withdrawn, and by Friday the place was packed with 300 refugees who joined the soldiers in feverish preparations for the further attacks they were certain were coming. Everyone prayed that help would come from Fort Snelling before Little Crow returned to the assault. A heroic private, William Sturgis, had carried the alarm to Snelling, riding the 125 miles in eighteen hours.

If men could not save Ridgely, however, the garrison and refugees hoped that guns would do it. The fort had been an ordnance depot at one time, and it still held a formidable collection of artillery—a six-pounder and two twelve-pounders, both mountain howitzers, and several large twenty-four-pounders. An ordnance Sergeant, John Jones, had faithfully kept these pieces in good condition, and had trained crews to fire them.

Still the hope lay with Colonel Henry Hastings Sibley, who had set out from Fort Snelling with a rescue party, which he realized was inadequate as details of the uprising began to reach him during his progress. The settlement of New Ulm sent a desperate appeal to Sibley while he paused at the village of St. Peter, but the General believed he did not dare heed the appeal because his force was too small. He had sent back for reinforcements. Meanwhile, New Ulm lived through a day of attack, suffered the loss of a third of its buildings, but repulsed the Indians. By the time Sibley's fresh support reached him, he concluded that it would be best to march on to Ridgely, which he reached with 1,500 troops.

He found it full of dead, wounded and the sick. It was necessary first to bury the dead, for reasons of sanitation, but the burial detail he sent out from the fort was attacked by Little Crow's braves, and after a day's heavy fighting, all but one of the ninety-six horses drawing the wagons were dead, forming a barricade over which the soldiers continued to fire. A relief column drove off the Indians, but twenty-three of the burial party were dead.

Sibley continued to build up his force until he had 1,600 men in it, with enough equipment and supplies to make a new march possible. He started for Yellow Medicine and, five days later, with the goal in sight, he was set upon by 700 Sioux, the cream of Little Crow's army. The chief had prepared his assault carefully, but had timed it badly. Sibley had been able to get his cannon into action before the artillerymen could be overwhelmed, and they were the decisive element in the battle, which ended with the Indians routed.

That was the turning point in the uprising. Little Crow had been with the white men long enough to know when his situation was hopeless. He and all the other chiefs and leaders of the Sioux banded themselves together and began to leave the territory, taking dozens of captives with them. The chief was in the blackest of moods. He saw his entire career lost. Everything he had done as the white man's friend was lost, and with it everything he had hoped to do as the leader of the revolt. Out of sheer revenge he wanted to torture and kill his prisoners, but another chief, Red Iron, argued against it and prevailed.

As the Indians prepared to depart and the council broke up, Little Crow made a final eloquent speech. "I am ashamed," he said, "to call myself a Dakota. Seven hundred of our best warriors were whipped yesterday by the whites. Now we had better all run away and scatter out over the plains like buffalo and wolves. To be sure, the whites had wagon-guns and better arms than we, and there were many more of them. But that is no reason why we should not have whipped them, for we are brave Dakotas and whites are cowardly women. I cannot account for this disgraceful defeat. It must be the work of traitors in our midst."

Whatever the cause, Little Crow and the leaders who had been most responsible knew they could not stay for an accounting. The revolt had not only failed, but the wrath of the white men would be terrible. Little Crow could not know, but he guessed, how the horror he created had been received by a people already appalled by the news from the Second Battle of Bull Run, and from Antietam, where the casualties had been 23,000. By comparison the Minnesota casualties were much smaller, but the North was nevertheless outraged when they heard that hundreds of settlers had been killed in the first week of the revolt. Piled on top of the battlefield casualty reports, it seemed to them an indignity they ought not to bear, and they wanted its perpetrators punished.

On this point the Indians divided. Little Crow and many others continued their flight. But the majority stayed behind to guard the prisoners and wait for Colonel Sibley (he would shortly be made a Brigadier for his labors) to come up and arrange their release. Inexplicably the Sioux compounded their crimes by raping some of the women prisoners, a most unusual occurrence in itself, one almost unheard of in the Indian Wars.

By the time Sibley reached the prison camp he had sufficient reason to be angry. "The woe written on the faces of the half-starved and nearly naked women and children," wrote one eyewitness, "would have melted the hardest heart." But when the colonel cast about for someone to arrest and hold responsible, the Indian leaders who had remained swore that it had been others who had committed the crimes, which in a sense was true, since nearly all the real perpetrators of the uprising had vanished with Little Crow.

After a month of inquisition, Sibley solved his problem by ordering the arrest of every Indian in sight, and soon he had 400 braves in irons, with sixty or seventy others under close surveillance. Setting up a military court on the spot, he began to dispense mass justice right and left, often at the rate of forty defendants a day.

In no time he had sentenced 306 men to be hanged. Their names were sent to President Lincoln, since the executions could not take place without Presidential permission. Lincoln answered: "Your dispatch giving the names of Indians condemned to death is received. Please forward as soon as possible the full and complete record of the convictions; if the record does not fully indicate the more guilty and influential of the culprits, please have a careful statement made on these points and forward to me. Send by mail." It would have cost more than $400 to telegraph the names.

It took no great perspicacity to see, when the records reached

Washington, that they were not full and complete. Lincoln appointed two Administration officials to sort out the evidence and try to decide degrees of guilt, a virtually impossible task. While they were engaged on it, the Indian prisoners were taken to Fort Snelling and placed temporarily in a wooden stockade. Then they were moved to another on the Mankato River. On both marches the settlers who lined the routes in the villages exacted savage revenge. Babies were snatched from the arms of squaws and dashed to death on the ground. People tried to get at the Indians with every imaginable kind of weapon, even their garden hoes, and succeeded in wounding fifteen of them.

Away from this scene, however, in the parts of the country where Indian war was becoming no more than a memory, the Indians had their defenders. There were those who defended them because of the obvious wrongs done to them. Others were opposed to capital punishment for anyone. Still others believed the captives should be treated as prisoners of war. But in Minnesota there was unanimous opinion that the Indians ought to be executed as speedily as possible.

By the time Lincoln's committee had finished its work, there were only thirty-nine names on the list of the condemned. Then there was a new problem. It was no easy task to find out which Indians fitted the names. Many had the same name, and there was a further confusion between the numbers on the commission's list and the numbers of the men in Sibley's original letter. Consequently some of the innocent were punished with the guilty and, in any event, the real culprits were by this time in Canada or the Far West, and were never caught.

On the day after Christmas, the execution took place. They stood together on a huge scaffold; the cutting of a single rope would release all the traps simultaneously. While they waited, the Indians wailed the death cry of the Dakotas, a weird cadence blending with the ominous roll of the military drums. William Duley, the executioner, took pleasure in his work. He had seen two of his children killed and scalped by the Indians. Duley did his work cleanly and well. In a moment thirty-eight bodies (one had been reprieved) twisted and squirmed in the cold winter air.

Later that night doctors took the bodies from their mass grave to be used in laboratory experiments. As for Little Crow, he could not stay away from his homeland and that proved his final undoing. Returning with his son in July, 1864, he was killed by a settler who found him prowling about his farm. Sibley pursued the other leaders far into the Dakota Badlands and, only a month after Little Crow's death, he finally cornered most of the remaining refugees and slaughtered 500 of them in a battle that lasted all day. Those who escaped went farther West and joined the Cheyennes, to fight another day in one of the final battles of the Wars.

For the Sioux, however, the Minnesota uprising was not a final defeat. They no longer threatened for the duration of the Civil War, but in its aftermath they fought one of the bloodiest last stands before Indian freedom was ended in America.

# 10 ★ ★ ★ ★ ★ ★

# The Revolt in the Southwest

As THE CIVIL WAR moved toward its climax, action in its Indian phase swung once more to the Southwest. There, after three years, hostilities had reached such a peak by 1864 that the Union commanders were compelled to withdraw enough troops from the major battlefields to launch one expedition after another into mountain and desert in pursuit of the fiercely resisting tribes.

Now, however, it was not a case of any vain hope on the part of the Indians that they might drive the white man back to the East. Their battle was one of desperation as they saw their hunting grounds taken over, and their cattle and crops appropriated for the contending armies. The Arapahoes were starving in Colorado Territory, and as a result they raided ranches up and down the valley of the South Platte, burning and killing. They made the trails so hazardous that supply trains could not make their trips, and for a while Denver was nearly without food as scarce provisions like flour sold for forty-five dollars a sack. Even the mail was cut off.

These conditions could only invite severe reprisals. Some idea of the military's response can be gained from the matter-of-fact report written by a Major Downing after an 1864 expedition:

> We started about eleven o'clock in the day, traveled all day and all that night; about daylight I succeeded in surprising the Cheyenne village of Cedar Bluffs, a small cañon about sixty miles north of the South Platte River. We commenced shooting. I ordered the men to com-

Kit Carson

mence killing them. They lost, as I am informed, some twenty-six killed and sixty wounded. My own loss was one killed and one wounded. I burnt up their lodges and everything I could get hold of. I took no prisoners. We got out of ammunition and could not pursue them.

One of the most effective Indian fighters in the Army was a man whose name became much better known in American history for other reasons. Colonel Christopher Carson, of the 1st New Mexico Cavalry, has been a familiar figure to generations of boys as a hunter, trapper and scout. Comparatively little, however, has been written about his exploits as a cavalry commander.

Carson was not like many of his fellow officers. He had no particular affinity for spit-and-polish, nor was he a commander who fought by the book. He knew nothing of the orthodox tactics taught at West Point, relying instead on his intuition and natural abilities. A quiet man, Carson left orthodoxy to others and pursued his own way. Perhaps that was why, in some desperation, the Army turned to him in 1863 and asked him to do what had hitherto proved impossible—to rout the Navajos from the Canyon de Chelly, where Colonel Doniphan had been unable to penetrate nearly two decades before.

The Navajos were confronted with an enemy entirely different from Doniphan and his men, who were volunteers enlisted for the Mexican War, with plenty of courage but little knowledge of Indian warfare. Doniphan himself had been a lawyer before he volunteered, but he was a born soldier. Carson was a volunteer and a seasoned wilderness fighter; most of the men under him were frontiersmen of similar background. The Colonel did not underestimate his assignment, but he was confident he could carry out his instructions to round up the Navajos and turn them in to the government, which intended to resettle them on the Bosque Redondo Reservation.

The Navajos were no strangers to Carson. For two years, as General Carleton's second in command, he had hunted them with so little success that these elusive Indians were attacking everything in sight with a careless confidence they would not be caught. They even found time to quarrel with their old enemies, the Apaches, Utes and Pueblos. The Army's campaign of attrition eventually had taken its toll, but it could never be wholly successful as long as the Canyon de Chelly remained as the last stronghold. The Navajos simply holed up in it and dared anyone to enter the canyon and root them out.

In January, 1864, Carson took the dare. He marched into the field with 650 infantry and cavalry, supported by two mountain howitzers, a few Ute and Apache scouts and a supply train drawn by oxen. His depleted enemy still numbered a dangerous 10,000, and in addition, there were the familiar other enemies: terrain and weather. The oxen could haul the heavy supply wagons no more than five miles a day through the snow, and even less as they began to suffer from a short supply of grain, as did the horses. Carson had to shoot one after another of his animals, meanwhile fighting brief skirmishes with the Navajos, who hovered about his column harassing it as they retreated slowly toward the canyon.

Short of supply though he was, Carson intended to leave nothing for the Indians. He cut down their orchards, ruined their fields and commandeered their flocks and herds. Eventually he drove the Navajos into their canyon and penned them there, compelling them to subsist on whatever sustenance it offered. Then he set about methodically to assault it. Every exit was blocked, and he made sure that the trails leading down from the rims were similarly covered.

With his plans laid, Carson began a several-pronged assault. One detachment plunged straight down toward the canyon floor from the rim, along a perilous trail. It took four frightful hours to descend 800 feet. Two mules fell and were killed; others were saved by their loads.

Carson, meanwhile, drove into the canyon from the west. Falling back, the Navajos tried to get out by a side entrance, but there, thanks to the Colonel's careful planning, they fell headlong into a detachment of fifty men. Retreating hastily, they tried again to get out at the rear entrance of the canyon, since they could see troops along the rim and knew they would not be able to escape by scaling the cliffs.

As they streamed toward the canyon's eastern exit, their only remaining hope, the Indians could not know that lying in wait for them was the redoubtable Indian hater, Captain Pfeiffer, whose exploits have been recounted earlier. The Captain had reached this exit only after a hard, forced march in bitter cold, with an advance guard cutting a path for him through the snowdrifts with pick and shovel.

This hardbitten unit got into the canyon before the Navajos could get out. The Indians found themselves engaged in a desperate, last-ditch defense, in which they employed rocks plunging down the canyon walls along with their arrows and guns.

Carson's column and Pfeiffer's slowly came toward each other, squeezing the Indians between them until they had a clear choice between annihilation and surrender. It was probably the largest mass surrender ever accomplished in the Indian Wars. Eight thousand Navajos could do nothing but give up now that their impregnable canyon had been breached and captured. Like the Cherokees, they marched into exile on their reservation in eastern New Mexico. For the Cherokees it had been "The Trail of Tears." For the Navajos it was "The Long Walk," as they always called it, a solemn, mournful, pitiful procession of twos and threes—men, women and children mingled indiscriminately, along with what horses, sheep and wagons remained to them. In spite of their long record of warfare against the white man, even the soldiers who had hunted them down at last could not help feeling pity for them. General Carleton wrote of them in his report that they were brave men who had fought with gallantry in defense of their fatherland, and so deserved the government's magnanimity and an opportunity for rehabilitation.

Pity and kind words were not enough to save the Navajo. From that day to this, their story has been one of unbelievable oppression and neglect. They were pastoral people, and they were taken to a dry country. They were subject to diseases like smallpox and tuberculosis. They were often hungry. Carleton did what he could at the beginning, even putting his own troops on half-rations to save the Indians from starvation. The Department of Indian Affairs returned the Navajos to their own country in 1867, and they made some progress, but the plight of the Navajos even now remains a disgrace to the richest nation in the world.

Ending the resistance of the Navajos in 1864 did not by any means complete the white man's conquest of the Southwest. It only removed one troublesome enemy. Out on the trail, in the desert and the mountains, there was a daily record of murder and massacre, but those who lived in the larger communities were relatively complacent until one summer day in 1864 the authorities put on public display in Denver the scalped and mutilated bodies of a settler, his wife and their two children. That brought an instant demand for punishment.

It was not so easily done. So widespread had been the Indians' revolt in the West that all the troops that could be mustered were not nearly enough to handle them. Stories of their brave but futile efforts came from every quarter. In western Kansas, a hundred troopers of the 1st Colorado Cavalry had beaten off an overwhelming force of 400 Cheyennes, with the aid of two howitzers. Not far from Fort Laramie, Wyoming, another detachment in pursuit of a marauding band of Sioux had suffered the indignity of having their horses run off after a pursuit of 120 miles. They had to burn their saddles and walk all the way back to the fort.

The Indians controlled every line of communication east of Denver except for the Santa Fé trail by the summer of 1864. Colorado had to get its mail by way of Panama and California. In each community which had managed to preserve itself, every man who could fire a gun was armed, drilled and ready. It was widely believed that the war with the Indians had reached a point where it was a question of which side was going to be exterminated.

Into this situation came a new military leader, Colonel John Milton Chivington, who would soon become both a hero and a villain. He was an extraordinary officer. Beginning his career as a minister, he had once been a missionary to the Indians until the coming of the Civil War, when he joined the Union Army and fought against Southern troops in New Mexico. It was there he achieved his initial fame as a military genius who feared nothing. He had been the architect of victory in the Battle of Santa Fé, on March 27, 1862. Although it was little recognized in the East at the time, this "Gettysburg of the Southwest," as it later came to be called, was in reality one of the decisive battles of the war. The Confederates had an important supply base in Santa Fé, and from it they meant to acquire the gold fields of Colorado, Arizona, California and Nevada. By ending this plan with his victory, Chivington may well have influenced the outcome of the war.

After Sante Fé, he devoted his time to hunting down the Indian devastators of the Colorado District, where he was now commanding, and it was to Chivington that the citizens turned after the gruesome exhibit of atrocities in the summer of 1864. Neither he nor his men were of the regular Army; they were militiamen, of whom a few were veterans.

The Colonel set out from Denver in November, 1864. His force included 750 cavalry, mostly new recruits, a contingent of infantry and some artillery. On the 29th, they found themselves suddenly at a large camp of Cheyennes, under the redoubtable chief, Black Kettle. This Cheyenne sachem was a novelty among the Indian leaders of the Southwest. He had done his share of scalping and had perpetrated atrocities, but at this moment he was not driven by vengeance or a desire to eliminate the white man. He sought peace because he had become convinced that his tribesmen could expect nothing but disaster if they continued to fight.

Controversy surrounds what happened to Black Kettle in his camp of 130 lodges on the south bend of Sand Creek, a tributary of the Arkansas River, but it appears that he had already sent word to nearby Fort Lyon that he wished to negotiate, and was even willing to exchange prisoners. It is also said that he had raised an American flag over the white flag of surrender at his camp.

Whether Chivington was ignorant of the message, and simply disregarded or did not see the flags, is still not entirely clear, but there is no doubt about what he did. His troops attacked the camp from three directions, cut off the pony herd and drove the Indians back into the sand hills at frightful cost. For two hours Chivington's men poured a merciless fire into the Indians, finishing up the job with artillery. Emulating the Cheyennes, and no doubt in revenge for those mutilated bodies exhibited in Denver, the soldiers scalped more than a hundred braves. When the Indians finally broke and ran, Chivington pursued them for five miles, leaving a trail of bodies along the prairie. Only darkness ended the slaughter.

Three hundred Cheyenne died that day. Most were women and children. Only about twenty-six were warriors. Chivington's losses were seven killed and forty-seven wounded, seven of whom died later. It was no victory but an outrage, and was so considered by all but a few local desperadoes.

When the story of Sand Creek reached the public, there was first a cry of victory in the nation, and then, as more of the details seeped out, a revulsion against the scalping and the apparent violation of the rules of warfare—if war was to have any rules. There was a Congressional investigation of the Sand Creek Massacre, as it soon came to be known. The reports of eyewitnesses and other testimony filled

700 pages, and about some matters there was no agreement. Some saw the American flag and the white flag flying, others saw no flags at all. It had also been said that Black Kettle had assured his people that they were under the protection of the government, but this could not be proved either.

Some of the eyewitnesses' stories were horrifying. Only two squaws and five children had been taken prisoner. Everyone else who was caught had been killed, whether man, woman or child, and one witness told of a naked three-year-old child shot down by a soldier. Howitzers were used, it was testified, to make the end of the battle a wholesale slaughter.

In the midst of the controversy, Chivington was summoned to appear before a court-martial, but he resigned before it could convene and left the service bitter, scorned by the country he had thought he was serving. The question of whether the colonel was a hero or a scoundrel is still debated endlessly by the Western Americana experts. Certainly he was carrying out orders, but whether those orders—to "pursue and punish"—justified the coldblooded massacre of women and children appeared to be the crux of the matter. As in Minnesota after Little Crow's ravagers were caught, there was no complaint from the people of Denver and the Western settlements, who believed justice had been done. There was, indeed, a marked difference in the treatment of women captives by these Western tribes from those of the East, as the rapings in Minnesota had emphasized. In the Southwest, captured white women were not only raped casually but were passed along from one brave to another, and on occasion they were tortured as cruelly as were the men. Those who had known wives, sweethearts or friends to be so treated could not feel compassion for the slaughter of Indian women at Sand Creek, and no doubt many of the soldiers who did the killing were motivated by personal vengeance.

While Chivington was riding toward the end of his military career at Sand Creek, other commanders were busy mounting winter offensives in the Southwest, to escape the broiling sun and scanty water supplies of the summer. Columns rode out from forts everywhere in the territory, accepting snow and cold as a better alternative. One of those who commanded a column was Colonel Carson, conqueror of the Navajos. This time he was leading a force out of Fort Bascom to attack Kiowas and Comanches who had gathered at a place in northwest Texas called Adobe Walls.

Carson's force was potentially a far more effective one than he had commanded against the Navajos. There were 325 mounted volunteers from New Mexico and California, supported by two mountain howitzers, a large contingent of seventy-five Ute and Jicarilla Apache scouts and supplied by an ambulance and twenty-seven wagons loaded with supplies sufficient to last forty-five days. The line of march ahead of this army was 200 miles long, down the Colorado River to Texas. As the men marched, the brisk weather of the start yielded, as it so often did, first to cold weather and then to heavy snows. Nevertheless the Colonel was near his objective by November 24, and his scouts were reporting to him that Indians were in sight, whereupon Carson ordered his troops to make a forced march overnight, hoping to catch the enemy by surprise.

As it happened, the surprise failed because the Kiowas and Comanches had been doing the same thing. The two forces approached each other just about dawn, and in the haze of early morning, rode at each other in a savage charge. The Indians gave way, although fighting steadily, and the skirmish moved forward until the Indian village of Adobe Walls was in sight. At that Carson's cavalry sounded the charge and thundered into the little town of 170 lodges.

Those Indians who were still at home hurried out and tried to get to their ponies. Those who succeeded launched an immediate countercharge with rifles and lances. The cavalry fell back before it, and began to re-form. While they were doing it, Carson surveyed the situation and saw that he was outnumbered. Quickly he ordered his artillerymen, "Throw a few shells into that crowd over there."

As always, the bursting shells produced consternation among the Indians. Two more rounds were enough. The Indians wheeled their horses and galloped off. Carson's men did not pursue them, but stopped for a breathing space to eat breakfast. They were no sooner occupied with it than a giant dust cloud rose on the prairie and coming out of it the men saw, as they hurriedly formed their defenses, a force of 1,000 Indians in a wild, whooping charge. Overlooked somehow by the scouts, they had ridden over from a village three miles away when they heard the guns.

Now Colonel Carson had need of his howitzers as fast as they

Comanche warrior

could be reloaded and fired. The Indians encircled the village and
set the prairie grass on fire, an old trick. It was enough to send the
rearguard, gasping and choking, back into the main arena. Then the
Indians charged, again and again, while Carson's ranks wavered but
did not break, with the cavalry dismounted and fighting on foot. Helping himself to Indian strategy, Carson started a grass fire on his own
behalf, hoping to use the smoke as a screen to get his troops onto
higher ground. But again it was not so much maneuver as the sheer,
devastating power of the big guns that saved the day. The Indians

could not stand up to repeated hails of shell and canister. They melted away at last. Once more there was a field strewn with dead and dying Indians.

The battle had lasted from dawn, and it was now sunset. Since the troops and their horses had been on the move all the night before, they could hardly stand from fatigue. Moreover, the ammunition was low. Carson knew he must retreat or risk serious trouble if the Indians pulled themselves together and returned. Thus far his losses had been unbelievably low.

His fears were at least partly realized. It was a running, rearguard fight back to the wagon train and from there to Fort Bascom.

Clearly the Kiowas and Comanches had suffered a severe defeat, but it was equally obvious that their power was far from broken, much less ended. It would, in fact, be another long decade before this would occur.

A few months after Carson's campaign, the Civil War came to its belated, exhausted conclusion. The nation rested on its arms and began to talk about binding up the wounds. In the West, however, there was no peace. The whole area was still flaming with revolt, which was more or less out of hand. But the stilling of the guns at Appomattox foreshadowed the doom of the western tribes. Now there were troops available to man the weakened garrisons, and even to establish fresh ones. New infantry and artillery regiments appeared. With them came ten regiments of cavalry, and these were the instruments of the red man's final destruction.

# ★ 11 ★ ★ ★ ★ ★ ★

# Red Cloud Challenges
# the Cavalry

ONE OF THE MOST BIZARRE EPISODES of the Civil War, where the Indians were concerned, occurred after it was over. In a diplomatic move that can hardly be explained on rational grounds, Jefferson Davis, during the dying moments of the Confederacy, conceived the idea of holding a great council and bringing peace to the entire West.

To carry out his plan he dispatched what must surely have been one of the best Indian salesmen in history, a Creek brave named Tuk-a-Ba-Tche-Miko, to talk to the tribes and persuade them to attend the grand council. For months this emissary moved tirelessly among the Osages, Pawnees, Iowas, Kickapoos, Potawatomies, Wichitas, Kiowas, Comanches, Apaches, Southern Cheyenne, Arapahoes, Navajos, Mescalero Apaches, Northern Cheyennes, Unkpapas, Teton and Yankton Sioux. By the time he was finished, he had persuaded 20,000 Indians to heed the call of their Great White Southern Father and come to the council on the Washita River, on May 1, 1865. It was the largest such gathering ever seen west of the Mississippi and, by a choice irony, it was presided over by representatives of Jefferson Davis who had not yet heard that the war was over. Amazingly, they secured an agreement from these far-flung and disparate tribes that they would stop their depredations and keep the peace. So slowly did news of the war's end travel that many of the tribes kept their pledge for some time.

It was a short-lived truce, however. With the end of the war, the tide of westward migration was resumed along the four great routes to the Pacific—the Santa Fé Trail; the Kansas Trail, to Denver; the Oregon Trail, to Oregon and California by way of Nebraska and Salt Lake City; and the Bozeman Trail, from Wyoming to Montana. Where pre-war migration had been a trickle, the postwar surge was a flood, and the Plains Indians, sensing the inevitable, prepared for a last stand.

The new Army was prepared for it. Nothing like that Army has ever been seen in America. They were truly, as one writer has said, a Foreign Legion, made up of both Union and Confederate soldiers who could not adjust again to civilian life, as well as the usual run of adventurers. It was multi-lingual and multi-national—Irish, German, French, Italian and a half-dozen others. One crack regiment was the all-Negro 10th Cavalry, a companion to General Carpenter's Negro infantry regiment—"Carpenter's Brunettes," as they were known. This Indian-fighting army had Indian scouts—Pawnees, Crows, Shoshones—who had one thing in common: all of them hated the Sioux.

It was a hairy army, bearded and moustachioed, because so many of the men had grown beards in Civil War service, but most of them shaved when they reached the western deserts, where beards were miserably hot in the torrid summer heat, and were likely to gather hoarfrost or even icicles in the severe cold of winter. A compromise was the moustache, which sometimes almost seemed a part of the uniform. It was known as the Texas Ranger style.

Uniforms also had to be modified for western campaigning. Every General made his own modifications. General George Crook went so far that his soldiers began to look more like guerrillas than regular Army men, and an amazed Lieutenant, freshly arrived from West Point, wrote home: "The men frequently discard every item of dress and equipment prescribed or furnished."

If the soldiers looked like guerrillas, that was what, in effect, they were—a tough, mobile army which excited the admiration of military observers from other countries. All officers above the rank of second lieutenant were Civil War veterans. The spirit of the men was hard-working, hard-swearing, devil-may-care. They fought with each other when there were no Indians to fight, and the guardhouse was always jammed with prisoners on the morning after a payday. Crude and profane, alternately bored and belligerent, these western soldiers were particularly brave and loyal men, with a feeling for military tradition.

Cavalrymen were especially flamboyant and cocky. Knowing that they would be the target of civilians in the frontier settlements, they wore what they called their "drinking jewelry" when they went to town. These were rings on both hands made out of horseshoe nails, with the rough nailheads projecting. They were capable of doing fearful damage in a free-for-all.

A military staff of considerable distinction commanded these men, headed by General Grant himself, General William Tecumseh Sherman as his chief-of-staff and General Phil Sheridan as commander of the Department of the West. In the field were such officers as Alfred H. Terry, George Armstrong Custer, George Crook, John Gibbon, Nelson A. Miles and other names familiar in military history.

The men they directed over the vast terrain west of the Mississippi were no longer militia and volunteer units, except for a few remnants remaining here and there, but regular Army regiments. These were trained men, veterans of the Civil War and some of the Indian Wars as well, where before there had been mostly untrained, unpredictable and sometimes uncontrollable outfits.

During the conquest of the East there had been short campaigns interspersed by long periods of comparative quiet, and the clashes had been between relatively large forces on both sides. In the western war fighting was virtually continuous, and it was largely on the level of platoons, companies or battalions; few battles engaged forces as large as a regiment. In the first phase of these campaigns, from 1866 to 1875, more than 200 battles took place; most of them were with the Sioux nation. During the second phase, from 1875 to 1887, fewer engagements were fought, mostly with the Apaches.

As was customary in the Indian Wars, this final period in the long conflict began with a peace conference, held at Fort Laramie in 1866. The intention of General Sherman, who presided in the big tent erected outside the fort, was to persuade the Sioux and Northern Cheyennes to permit emigrants to pass over the lands ceded to them by the government only the previous year. Sherman also sought permission from the Indians for the construction of three forts to protect the Bozeman Trail. Apparently he did not see any incongruity in asking permission to build a military installation designed to defend against those from whom permission was sought.

The General was a powerful negotiator but he was matched by the forty-four-year-old chief who represented the Indians. Red Cloud, chief of the Oglalas and leader of both the Sioux and Cheyenne tribes, was in the tradition of Tecumseh, Black Hawk and other Indian statesmen. He was physically magnificent, proud in bearing, a natural leader, hardly to be distinguished from the white commanders in speech and manners. Later he would prove to be a military strategist of undoubted genius.

Red Cloud had come to the conference distrustful of its outcome. By this time he had discovered that the truce obtained through the Confederates was worthless since they could no longer guarantee it, and he viewed the demands of the northern negotiators as preposterous. He did not need the advice of the Great Spirit, with whom he sometimes claimed to be in direct touch, to tell him that if forts were built on the Bozeman Trail it could only mean a further diminution of Indian hunting lands and Indian rights. Probably he was also well aware that the white men intended to have their forts whether the Indians liked it or not, and the purpose of the conference was really to determine how high a price they were willing to pay for them.

But even Red Cloud had underestimated the white man's contempt for Indian rights. While the conference was going on, Colonel Henry B. Carrington was moving 2,000 troops up from Fort Kearney, and 700 of them marched through Laramie, a direct insult to the Indian negotiators. Everyone knew that the purpose of the troops was to occupy the Powder River country, which was supposed to be involved in the negotiations.

This action broke up the council. Red Cloud departed from it in anger, taking with him those leaders who agreed with his contention that the white men were seizing the land by force under their noses while they talked of peace and settlement. Three chiefs of the Brulé Sioux remained to sign the treaty, but in only two weeks they sent back a chill warning to General Sherman. The young men of their tribes had refused to acknowledge the document, they said, and warned that if any white men ventured very far away from Fort Laramie they should "go prepared, and look out for their hair." It was, in effect, an open declaration of war against Carrington's troops and any who tried to pass along the Bozeman Trail.

In the two years of warfare that followed, the cavalry took the brunt of the fighting against the mounted Indian warriors. Foot soldiers were at a disadvantage in this open warfare over large spaces. Cavalry was important to the white men for another reason, too. It removed, or at least countered, the element of surprise on which the Indians depended so much. Mobile forces could not be surprised so easily, and they could be shifted quickly.

Strangely, the regulars had had to fight an interior war against their own people while they battled the Indians. The West was well populated with riffraff—renegades, rustlers, peddlers of cheap whiskey, gun-runners, grafters, crooked politicians. They kept the Indians constantly stirred up, stole supplies wherever they could, rustled horses and mules and cheated the soldiers in their gambling houses and saloons.

It must be remembered that the soldiers were not there specifically to carry on a war against the Indians. Their mission was to enforce Federal law in the territories and protect the lives and property of citizens. (Indians, of course, were not considered citizens.) This mission had many faces. It meant trying to control the bandits who preyed on soldiers and civilians alike. It involved policing the cattle trails where they ran through Indian reservations, and in fairness it must be added that the troops were also charged with running settlers and squatters off Indian lands and to see that treaty terms were carried out. A modicum of attention was paid to this part of the mission.

Politically the Army was hampered in its administration of the western territories by conflicting directives from Washington, which created a great deal of confusion, and by a bad press, occasioned by the fact that the major eastern newspapers were a long way from the scene of action, and reporting from the West was scanty and often highly inaccurate. It was hard for people in the East, reading accounts of what was happening to settlers, miners, railroad builders and emigrants, to sort out rights and wrongs. All they could see was that progress was being impeded by the recalcitrant red men. They wanted something done about it, and complained frequently that the Army wasn't doing enough, or else that what it was doing was wrong. Whatever the Army did, as the commanders discovered, it was likely to be considered wrong by someone.

The first engagement of any consequence in the new war occurred in July, 1865. Its hero was not a regular, but a young Lieutenant of volunteers, Caspar W. Collins, of the 11th Ohio Cavalry, who was entrusted with carrying the mail along the dangerous reaches of the old Oregon Trail. Both Collins and the small detachment he led were experienced Indian fighters, so they proceeded cautiously. From a hilltop, after an uneventful progress, they saw Fort Dodge, then called Camp Dodge, standing near the Platte River. It was an extremely small, strong point, enclosed by a stockade and containing a meager cavalry station, a stagecoach station and a store. It was protected by a lone howitzer, situated to cover the bridge spanning the river. Camp Dodge was not a formidable thing to see, but it looked splendid to emigrant trains when they sighted it at the end of the 200 perilous miles from Fort Laramie.

Caspar and his men entered Camp Dodge, and the Lieutenant made a routine report. He did not know, nor did anyone at the fort, that 3,000 braves of the Sioux, Cheyenne and Arapaho tribes lay concealed behind the huge sandstone bluffs overlooking the tiny outpost. These were Indians with fresh memories of what had happened to the Sioux in Minnesota, and to the Cheyennes at Sand Creek.

At dawn the Indians tried to decoy the soldiers from the fort by sending a small party down from the bluffs, as though to attack. If the soldiers came out to fight them, scouts watching from the bluffs would give the signal and superior Indian forces would overwhelm the defenders. But the troops were not to be decoyed. The fort's commander fired his howitzer occasionally when the Indians got too close, but he sat quietly and awaited further developments. An unexpected one occurred. A detachment of cavalry coming up the river to the fort was spotted by the decoys, who whooped off to attack it. There were not enough of them, nor was there time to assemble reinforcements without giving the whole plot away. Helped by a covering fire from the walls, the troopers reached the fort safely and the decoys withdrew to the bluffs.

During the night, while the men in the fort remained under arms, the Indians moved down out of the hills, splitting their force above and below the bridge but remaining hidden in the timber and brush. Once more, in the early morning, decoys were sent out, but again it appeared that the troopers would not be lured until suddenly a cavalry detachment rode out of the gate toward the east. The decoys jubilantly drew away, believing that they were leading the white men into an ambush. They did not know that the sentries on the walls had seen a supply train approaching, with an escort, and had sent out a detachment to help it reach the fort. At the same time a charge was fired from the howitzer to put the train on its guard.

By this time the Indians had seen the approaching wagons and hurried to cut them off. Racing ponies streamed out of the brush and ravines in two long columns, one sweeping between the rescue troop and the bridge while the other moved in front of them to form a trap. Lieutenant Collins, who was in command of the cavalry column, galloped his troops straight ahead, hoping at first to break through the encirclement and reach the wagon train. But then he heard firing in the rear, and saw that a company had emerged from the fort, crossed the river and established a bridgehead to protect their comrades' retreat. The Indians at Collins' rear were already attacking this relief. Wheeling about, Collins and his men rode for the bridge, straight into the Indian force. It was hand-to-hand combat, with no time to reload. Using his saber and riding a powerful horse, Collins hacked his way toward the bridge, which fifteen of his men had already reached. Only a few steps from safety, Collins turned back to lift up one of his wounded men who had fallen from his horse and lay helpless on the ground. In an instant he was cut down and killed.

The supply train, meanwhile, was having its own difficulties as the Indians surrounded it. Five troopers riding ahead to protect it were cut down; two survived and reached the fort. The train's commander, Sergeant Amos J. Custard, a veteran non-commissioned officer, was a brave man who did what any commander would do in such a siege. He drew the wagons into a ring and placed his riflemen in them with instructions to cut loopholes.

But unfortunately for Custard he faced an Indian leader who was a better strategist than most. Roman Nose, a huge man (he weighed 230 pounds and stood six feet, three inches), had observed that the old method of galloping around a wagon train until one side or the other emerged as survivors was an inefficient piece of strategy. The white riflemen would be firing from fixed positions, and the advantage lay with them, unless they were overwhelmed by sheer force of numbers. Roman Nose had the numbers, but he also had a better plan. His braves dismounted and took cover, advancing slowly toward the train on their bellies. The chief was using only half his huge force for this operation; the other half was meanwhile besieging the fort, so that no troops could be sent to rescue the train.

Roman Nose could afford to take his time, and he did. For five hours the defenders of the wagon train held out, but their end was inevitable. Back in the fort the garrison heard with dismay the slow decrease of their rifle fire until at last there was silence. Only a few survivors had remained—Sergeant Custard and a few badly wounded men. They were burned to death by the triumphant Indians, after which Roman Nose inexplicably gave up his siege of the fort, which he could probably have captured without much trouble, and withdrew.

Only a year after this affair, the abortive conference at Fort Laramie took place, which ended when Carrington's troops marched into the fort, band blaring. The Colonel himself, entering the conference tent, was greeted by Red Cloud's outraged shout as he leaped to his feet, pointed at the officer's silver eagles and cried: "Look! Here is the white eagle who has come to steal a road through the Indians' land."

In justice, it must be remembered that the Army was in an uncomfortable position. Carrington and the other commanders knew the government was breaking its pledges to the Indians in trying to build the Bozeman Trail forts, and perhaps they believed that there was more than a little truth in the bitter charge of the Sioux leader, Spotted Tail, who declared flatly: "All men from Washington are liars!" But the Army commanders did not make policy; they only enforced the political decisions made back home. Thus they found themselves in the contradictory position of enforcing the terms of the Indian treaties, and at the same time protecting the rush of white settlers who were busy violating them. As one white man put it in another way, "The rights of savagery have been compelled to yield to the demands of civilization, ethics to the contrary notwithstanding."

The Army officers on the scene, entrusted with the enforcement of this totally cynical policy, had a different view of the demands of

scouts

civilization. "Civilization approached the Indian," wrote one officer, "with a Bible in one hand, a treaty in the other, a bludgeon under her arm, and a barrel of whiskey in her wagon."

Having precipitated an explosive situation along the Bozeman Trail and elsewhere, the government gave able commanders like Colonel Carrington precious little help in carrying out its policies. Jim Bridger, the mountain man, who probably knew more about the terrain and the Indians in it than any other living human being, was acting as a scout for the Colonel's 18th Infantry at a modest five dollars a day, but orders came from Washington to discharge him for reasons of economy. "Impossible to execute," Carrington replied curtly to this order. Government economy was already giving him enough trouble. His 700 men were badly equipped and, even worse, they possessed only a few howitzers and no cavalry whatever, making them virtually helpless in the Plains country. They were armed mostly with old Springfield single-shot muzzle-loaders instead of the new Spencer carbines. In vain Carrington had pleaded for replacements.

Nevertheless, the Colonel had to go about his business, and after the disintegration of the conference at Fort Laramie, he set out across the plains. It was a lengthy column. There were 226 wagons in it, with everything in them required to build and maintain a fort. Carrington would be able to set up a steam-powered sawmill, and to equip his installation with tools, forges, scythes and similar useful items. If the government was stingy with the implements of war, it was reasonably generous with the tools of peace and, moreover, it had recruited men who knew how to use them. They marched in the ranks with the other soldiers. Bringing up the rear of the train were light wagons called ambulances in Army jargon. In them for the moment were Army wives and children.

First stop on the journey was Fort Connor, 175 miles west of Laramie. There the 18th relieved some Michigan troops, acquired some of their horses, and established a garrison. Then they pushed on, but as the winding blue column began to penetrate these wilder regions an invisible cloud began to gather on its flanks. The Sioux were there, watching, waiting . . .

About sixty-six miles from Fort Connor, the column came to a stop on a plateau. Twin branches of Big Piney Creek, a tributary of the Powder River, flowed on both sides. It appeared to Carrington an ideal site for a fort, and the colonel concluded he would establish his first outpost in that spot. There was an abundance of water, grass and timber, but the forest was not near enough to provide cover for an enemy. The approaches to the plateau were commanded by two knolls, where sentries could be posted. Carrington posted some at once.

The column made camp and began to build the fort. Carrington was an excellent choice for the job; he was something more than a military man. As a graduate of Yale, he had been trained to be a draughtsman and engineer before he went to fight in the Civil War, and he meant to make his forts first-rate examples of the art. His first effort on the plateau turned out to be one of the finest strongholds ever constructed on the frontier. He called it Fort Phil Kearny, after the redoubtable General.

While it was being built, the Sioux did their best to prevent its construction, although they did not yet make a determined assault. They devoted themselves to picking off sentries on the lookout knolls, riding between them and the fort until the howitzers had to be employed to scare them off. At night Red Cloud's braves sniped away at sentries on the walls. Workers in the hayfields outside the fort had to use their rifles almost as often as their scythes. Every trip the wood train made from the rising fort to the forest where the wood was being cut was an adventure, because there was a seven-mile distance between them and the train was usually attacked either going or coming. Time after time the wagons had to be drawn into a circle and an Indian assault fought off until troops from the fort could come to the rescue.

Recognizing his essentially precarious position, Carrington persistently asked for more men, ammunition and guns from his superiors, but he got only ninety-five recruits for the infantry and sixty-five more for the cavalry. Nothing else was forthcoming. The government insisted that a state of peace existed in the Powder River country, notwithstanding that the Sioux were harassing wagon trains on the Bozeman Trail, running off cattle and scalping any travelers they could find, as well as slowing down the building of Fort Kearny.

In spite of every difficulty, morale at the new fort was high. The men were proud of what they had built—quarters, barracks, stables, a hospital, shops, storehouses and a laundry rising within a stockade 600 by 800 feet. The howitzers were grouped in a battery park and, as though Kearny had been in the midst of civilization, there was a well-tended grass parade ground and a bandstand. The first garrison flag was raised on October 31, 1866, there was a review of the troops and Colonel Carrington made a sententious speech, after which there was a celebration feast and a quadrille at headquarters.

Outside in the Wyoming hills, Red Cloud waited for the moment to strike. Because he had waited and, except for harassment, had made no spectacular moves, there was a certain amount of over-optimism among some of the fort's officers, in spite of the warnings of Jim Bridger and other experienced Indian fighters. One captain boasted he could march through the whole Sioux nation with eighty men, and another actually delayed his transfer East to do recruiting because he wanted to be the man to lift Red Cloud's scalp.

The end of this optimism came on December 21, 1866, when the wood train made one of its periodic trips down the valley, traveling in parallel columns. As usually happened, it was attacked and the pickets on the knolls informed the fort of this fact with warning shots. Carrington instantly mobilized a rescue force, giving the command to a dependable captain, James Powell. But Captain W. J. Fetterman, who had boasted he could conquer the Sioux with eighty men, asked for the opportunity and the Colonel reluctantly consented. He gave strict orders: "Relieve the wood train. Under no circumstances pursue the Indians beyond Long Trail Ridge."

Captain Fetterman accepted these orders, but he considered the Colonel far too cautious and departed with mental reservations. He headed a column of eighty men, by an odd coincidence. Two other fire-eaters rode with him, Captain Frederick H. Brown, the man who had delayed his transfer, and Lieutenant George W. Grummond, who had already been nearly killed in a skirmish yet still yearned for battle, although he had a bride of only a few months in the fort. There were also two civilians in the column, anxious to try out new Henry repeaters on the Indians. They approached the rescue in the spirit of a hunt.

As those on the stockade walls watched Fetterman's advance, they saw that he intended not simply to relieve the wood train but to attack the Indians from the rear and precipitate a fight. The Indians observed his movements too, sent out a few decoys and began to entice the column away. Fetterman was so entranced by the prospect of a battle that he forgot his orders, or ignored them, and pressed on across Long Trail Ridge.

It proved to be a disastrous mistake. For the decoys had drawn him into a place where 2,000 warriors, commanded by Red Cloud and another noted chief, Crazy Horse, waited behind the buttes and in the draws. There was no warning. The Indians fell upon Fetterman's column in a burst of fury. Meanwhile the wood train, suddenly relieved of pressure, made its way back to the fort, where Carrington, hearing the sound of guns in another direction, guessed what had happened to Fetterman and sounded the general alarm. A large rescue party was formed at once. Prisoners in the guardhouse, members of the band, cooks and everyone else available were summoned to defend the fort while the main body of troops was out of it.

On the ridge Fetterman had been climbing when the attack was unloosed upon him, the soldiers were even then beginning to justify the name later given to the place—Massacre Hill. A red tide of warriors began to flow over them. They fought on a slope that was slippery with snow and ice, and the weather was so cold the blood froze in their wounds. Carrington's worries about the old Springfields were being justified. It took much too long to reload them when the fight was at such close quarters. The civilians with their sixteen-shot Henry repeaters were at a better advantage. But even they were cut down, and in the last moments of the struggle both Captains Fetterman and Brown, seeing that they would be captured, shot themselves rather than face certain torture.

By the time Carrington and his rescue party reached the scene, it was too late. Grummond's cavalry, which had been leading Fetterman's column, had lasted a little longer because of its superior position higher on the ridge, where the men had dismounted and found cover behind rocks. But Grummond himself was dead, and the others soon met a horrible death as the Indians savagely slashed and hacked at their bodies, mutilating them even after they were dead.

It was all over in a remarkably brief time. At a cost of only sixty braves, Red Cloud had destroyed the entire column to the last man. Then he withdrew, leaving the white men to count their dead.

In the aftermath of this tragedy, Colonel Carrington felt it necessary to reassess his position. Plainly the Indian army outnumbered him, raising the question as to whether the fort could be held. Grimly he made preparations for a last-ditch stand. The explosives were placed in a magazine, to be blown up as a last necessity. Women and children were sent there, too. If the fort fell, it would be better to blow them up with the magazine than to permit them to fall into the clutches of Red Cloud's braves.

Carrington believed the Indians would attack that night, knowing that the garrison was now badly depleted, and probably could not be defended on all four sides. But the weather proved to be the Colonel's unexpected ally. A blizzard swept in from the Plains, instead of the Indians, and the temperature dropped to thirty degrees below zero. White men and Indians alike devoted the night to keeping themselves alive, Carrington changing his sentries every half-hour and the Indians huddling together for warmth in their tepees.

The blizzard gave the Colonel a little breathing space. He called for a volunteer to ride to Laramie for help. Only one man in the post was truly qualified for the job, and he was quite naturally the one who volunteered. John Phillips, whose nickname was "Portugee," was a civilian, a hard-bitten frontiersman who had long served as an Army scout. Few were any more familiar with terrain and Indians than Phillips. Even for such a man, the odds were a hundred to one that he could not get to Laramie alive through fierce weather and hostile country, but Phillips said he would try for the sake of the women and children. Carrington gave him the best horse available, his own Kentucky thoroughbred, and let him out the gate himself, calling after him as he vanished into the driving snow, "May God help you!"

It was one of the most incredible journeys in all frontier history, that dogged ride of 236 miles. It was, of course, not always a ride. Phillips encountered drifts so high sometimes that he had to get off and lead his horse through them. Protected though he was by layer upon layer of clothing under his thick buffalo robe, he was still almost paralyzed by the cold. Only his lengthy experience and sheer frontiersman's instinct saved him from traveling in a circle in the snow and darkness. When daylight came, he had to seek cover in case he was spotted by the Indians. Hiding all day, he started off again at nightfall and before long reached the tiny outpost of Fort Reno, too poorly manned to send any help and without any telegraph line to flash the news to Laramie. Phillips had no choice. He must remount and ride on.

As he rode, Phillips was congratulating himself that he had not seen any Indians, supposing them to be completely immobilized by the cold, but suddenly he came within sight of a band of them. They pursued him, and only his splendid horse saved him, carrying him to the summit of a hill where he was able to stand off the threatening braves until darkness came.

On his way again at dawn, he eluded the Indians with a burst of speed and before long he had reached Horse Shoe Station, where the call for help could be carried by wire. But Phillips did not trust the mechanical gadget. He was afraid his message might not get through, and it did not. There was only one way to make sure, and that was to carry it himself. Phillips rode on.

He staggered into Fort Laramie to interrupt the gay progress of a Christmas Eve ball, so exhausted at the end that he could barely deliver his message. The garrison, and in time the whole country, hailed this heroic exploit, which at first could scarcely be believed. Phillips nearly died from exposure and exhaustion as the result of his journey, but he recovered after a long illness and received a munificent reward from the government: $300. The Sioux did not forget him either. They raided his herd constantly in later years, when he left the service and became a cattleman. When he died in 1883, the Indians had damaged his herds so badly that the government, in a somewhat more beneficent mood, gave his widow $5,000 in compensation.

Phillips' ride saved Fort Kearny. The 1st Battalion of the 18th Infantry hastened to its rescue and reached the outpost before Red Cloud could organize another attack. Curiously, Army authorities blamed Carrington not only for Fetterman's massacre but for the precarious situation of his post, for which in fact *they* were responsible through their failure to man it and supply it properly. They relieved Carrington of his command, and ordered him to return with the women and children. Even the withdrawal had its price. It took place in another severe blizzard, at a cost of much suffering.

Now that the damage was done, the authorities gave Kearny everything Carrington had asked—men, supplies, ammunition and new rifles. They were going to be needed, as it turned out, because Red Cloud had by no means given up his intention of destroying the fort. He waited in the hills for a new opportunity. If he could not destroy Kearny by frontal assault, he decided, he would slowly deplete it by attacks on the parties which left it to get hay and wood from time to time, until it was weak enough to be assaulted.

Red Cloud's first attempt to carry out this policy occurred late in July, 1867, as the woodcutters began chopping away on Big Piney Creek, starting early to lay up enough firewood to last through the harsh winter on the Plains. The axmen were protected by a company of the 27th Infantry, under Captain Powell, who had already been saved from death by Fetterman's ill-considered bravado. Unlike the dead captain, Powell was a careful, thorough man who took no chances. His camp was on an open plain, protected by a fort in miniature made up of wagon bodies with their wheels removed, formed in the traditional circle and sandbagged at the spaces between by means of logs and filled grain sacks. A supply of arms, ammunition and provisions was laid by inside this makeshift fort in case of a siege. Powell was confident he would soon have to test these defenses. He believed the Indians would attack him at the first opportunity.

They chose the early morning of August 2. Fifteen hundred warriors under Red Cloud, and led by other noteworthy chiefs like Crazy Horse and American Horse, struck first at the herd of mules and horses, which they stampeded. In the resulting confusion the Indians wheeled away from Powell's fort and sought to pick off the guards in the forest, and after them the woodchoppers. But the axmen picked up their rifles, which were always at hand, and joined the guards to make a successful retreat to the safety of Kearny, leaving Powell to conduct his own defense, although a few of the woodsmen had joined him rather than retreat.

While it might have seemed logical to the woodsmen and their guards to retreat to the fort, it left Powell with only thirty-two men to face 1,500 Indians. Coolly, the Lieutenant assigned three rifles to each of his best marksmen, and designated other soldiers to load for them. He distributed all the available ammunition among these sharpshooters, and instructed them not to fire until he gave the order.

When the assault came, it was spearheaded by 500 Sioux and Cheyenne who came charging down the slopes at full gallop, brandishing their rifles and screaming warwhoops. Powell waited until they were only fifty yards away before he gave his order. A deadly fusillade burst against the Indians. It was followed by a steady rain of bullets as the marksmen fired the rifles as fast as they could pick them up from the re-loading relay.

At first the Indians did not understand what was happening. They split their force and began to circle Powell's small fortress, waiting for the firing to slacken so they could storm it. To their astonishment, it continued at a deadly and astonishingly uninterrupted pace. The Indians had never seen anything like it. Nor had they ever experienced such casualties. There were so many Indians and the besieged place was so small that the circling ring was thick with red horsemen, instead of being strung out as they more often were. Consequently the .50-caliber bullets sometimes passed through two or even three Indians.

Such firepower bewildered and demoralized the Indians. They

fled, after a slaughter which left the field heaped with rows of warriors and horses. Inside the fort there had also been casualties. Two men were dead, two others wounded. The twenty-eight remaining agreed among themselves that if the next charge looked as though it would be successful, they would shoot themselves.

Red Cloud now ordered a change in tactics. The next assault wave came on foot, whooping and firing but too high, as it proved. Splinters flew from the wood of Powell's homemade fort, but he lost no more men. To the main body of Indians watching on the slopes, however, it appeared that the fire from the fort was diminishing and, thinking their moment had come, they swept down past the dismounted attackers and came at the fort full tilt. A shot from Powell dropped one of their best chiefs, Red Cloud's nephew, and the steady barrage from his men cut away at the charging Indians like a giant scythe. Once more the charge faltered, slowed and broke.

But the Indians reformed and came on again, and again—six times in all, until the last one brought a few of them close enough for hand-to-hand fighting. Still they could not breach Powell's defenses, unbelievable as it must have seemed to them. Shaken and dazed, they broke off the engagement and retreated. Powell thought he had killed about 180 of them, but later estimates put the figure much higher, some as high as 1,137. In the aftermath, the Lieutenant understood how close he had come to annihilation. There was not enough ammunition remaining to withstand another charge. Soon a relief column came to his rescue with a hundred men and a howitzer, which was discharged after the retreating Indians to discourage them from a further attempt.

One of the repercussions of this remarkable feat, recorded in history as the "Wagon-Box Fight," in which thirty-two men had soundly defeated 1,500 of the Indians' finest, was its depressing effect on Red Cloud. He had lost considerable face as the result of his defeat, which he could hardly credit. Gloomy and dispirited, he withdrew into the hills and peace settled over the Powder River country for nearly a year.

But Red Cloud continued to threaten the white men by words, and occasionally by a few scattered deeds—enough to make the government anxious to come to terms with him. Negotiations were resumed late in 1867, but were broken off again. In the summer of 1868 they were picked up once more, and by November 8 a new treaty had been concluded, in which the government surprisingly reversed itself and agreed to close the Bozeman Trail and abandon both Fort Kearny and Fort C. F. Smith, which Carrington had built seventy miles farther north.

To the men who had suffered so much to defend them, and at such high cost, the order to abandon came as a stunning shock. Their commanders were incredulous, and the troops were angry. Good men had died for nothing, they said bitterly. But these were orders. They struck the flags, loaded the wagon trains and the blue columns marched out of the stockade for the last time. As they disappeared across the plains, the triumphant Sioux moved in to take charge of this unexpected gift from a government which had never done anything else for them. In a moment they had fired the buildings. Glancing back, the retreating columns could see the black smudges of smoke rising in the clear air, and knew that everything they had built was in ashes.

No doubt Red Cloud was too wise a man to believe that he had won anything more than a temporary advantage. The victory chants he heard rising from the lodges that night would turn before long to the wailing death cry. Red Cloud could not foresee the imminent coming of the railroads, or the discovery of gold in the Black Hills, but he knew that the white man had only retreated, not withdrawn.

# 12

★ ★ ★ ★ ★ ★

# The Reservation Policy
# and Its Results

THE CLOSING OF THE BOZEMAN TRAIL and its forts marked an important change in the government's Indian policy. Wars were too expensive and difficult, it was decided, and the way to stop them was to reduce the mobility of the Indians—that is, continue to put them on reservations. To make this idea more palatable, so it was believed, the Indians would be made gifts of these lands. No one inquired into how it might seem to the Indians to be given what they considered their own land.

There were some important omissions in the new policy. They were the same omissions that had caused so much trouble on the reservations already created. Nothing was said about how to prevent the encroachment of whites on these lands, nor whether the gifts were to be permanent or only an expedient, which obviously they were.

In 1868 the government began to carry out this policy seriously—and found itself in trouble for the next two decades, trying to implement it. From the beginning the difficulty could be foreseen. General Philip Sheridan, who had assumed command of the Department of the West, escaped the boring desk routine in 1868 and made a journey of inspection around the frontier posts. What he saw convinced him that, new policy or not, the Indians were once more in a highly restless state of mind. No matter where he went, he found his post commanders nervous about the tribes in their territory. There were ninety-three of these forts now, but they were all undermanned and devoted most of their time to staying alive rather than tracking down and punishing war parties.

Soldiers were justifiably cynical about government policy. It was "feed 'em in the winter and fight 'em in the summer," they said. Everyone resented the Indian commissioners who came out from Washington and rambled about the landscape, making absurd treaties which could never be enforced. These men were often political appointees who had no understanding whatever of Indian problems and were not particularly interested in learning. The more astute chiefs took shrewd advantage of them. These chiefs knew that winter was no time to fight, so when the cold winds began to blow, they signed a treaty which would ensure that they would not be molested during the winter while they ate at government expense and prepared to fight again in the spring.

Sheridan understood that the government's treaty policy was giving aid and comfort to the enemy, and in 1869 he persuaded President Grant to make a major step in its Indian relations. No more treaties were to be made, it was announced, because Indians were not tribes or nations any longer, but wards of the United States.

Matters were not immediately or radically changed by this doctrine. A major cause of friction had been removed by it, but the government did not yet know how it would assume its new obligation to its wards. Meanwhile, the beneficiaries of all this, the Indians, were still carrying on in the old ways, and they continued to be a threat to the garrisons charged with keeping them in hand.

Consequently General Sheridan was ready to listen in the fall of 1868 when one of his aides, Major George A. Forsyth, came to him with a plan for harassing the Indians without having to use troops from the garrisons, already so shorthanded. Forsyth, like his superior, was not a desk soldier. He had been a volunteer in the Civil War and worked his way up in the ranks from a Private of dragoons to Brevet Brigadier General. His idea was a simple one, but it sounded effective to Sheridan. A small, highly mobile force of scouts would be created, operating like the Indians themselves, using their tactics, tracking them, keeping constantly on their trail and forcing them to split up into smaller units, which would then be compelled to fight or surrender. In brief, it would be a war of attrition which would keep the Indians too busy to organize anything ambitious directed against the garrisons.

Sheridan gave his permission to try the plan, whereupon Forsyth asked for fifty volunteers. There was no lack of them. Frontiersmen were eager to get on the Army payroll and at the same time fight Indians. Forsyth enlisted them at a dollar a day in the quartermaster's division. The scouts were to use their own horses, while the Army agreed to supply them with weapons and provisions. Forsyth selected one other regular for his force—Lieutenant Frederick H. Beecher, from the famous New England family of that name. Beecher still limped from a wound he had suffered at Gettysburg.

About a third of the volunteers were also veterans of the war, many of them ex-officers, from both North and South. One, W. H. H. McCall had been a Brigadier General; now he was a First Sergeant in the new corps. The remainder were hunters and trappers.

In early September the scout corps got its first assignment when Sheridan heard that Indians were raiding not far away to the west. Armed with seven-shot Spencer repeating rifles and Army Colt revolvers, the corps marched away with a pack train of four mules. In six days they were well into Colorado, and had picked up the trail of a large Indian village on the move. Its size impelled several of the scouts to warn Forsyth that they might have bitten off too much this time, but the Major was not a particularly cautious man. He favored pushing on.

The trail led into a lush valley, where normally the Arakaree fork of the Republican River would have cut a broad, placid path, but the summer had been extremely dry and an island had risen from its midst, about twenty by sixty yards. Forsyth pitched his camp on the west bank, picketed his animals and posted sentries.

Next morning—it was September 17—Forsyth was making his usual dawn inspection when a sentry suddenly gave the alarm: "Indians!" There were Indians, certainly, Cheyennes, Sioux and Arapahoes, and they had taken the Major by surprise. Eight of them had already run off two pack mules carrying ammunition and all the medical supplies. Assessing the situation, Forsyth ordered his troops to make for the island. If the odds were going to be fourteen to one, as they appeared to be, that would be the only place he could hope to make a stand.

Having reached the island, the men tethered their horses and began hastily to dig slit trenches, using knives, tin cups or whatever came to hand. Meanwhile, they were under fire from both sides. Down the valley they could see the Indian horsemen massing for the attack, and soon they came dashing in their usual headlong assault, firing as soon as they were within range. Some marksmen dismounted to take more careful aim and pick off the horses, so the troops could not escape. Forsyth had instructed his men to hold their fire until he gave the signal and, as Lieutenant Powell had done, he waited until the Indians were no more than fifty yards away. As had been the case with Powell, the Indians were split by this barrage and had to circle the island.

Now, however, Forsyth was completely surrounded, and under heavy fire. The Major himself was wounded, with a bullet in his right thigh, another in his left leg between the knee and the ankle, and a third which creased his scalp. All around him other men were wounded or dead, and his entire force was pinned down by the Indians' fire. As the Indians withdrew from their first charge, Forsyth saw his second-in-command, Beecher, stagger and fall with a mortal wound. He had survived the Civil War, but he was to lose his life in this isolated skirmish thousands of miles from home.

There began another of the magnificent epics of the frontier, which would have been hard to match for endurance and heroism. As the only officer remaining, Forsyth knew he must command as long as he could in spite of his agonizing wounds. Observing the Indians, he saw that they appeared to be waiting, for what reason he could not guess. In fact they were expecting Chief Roman Nose, who had been delayed, the victim of his superstitions. Earlier in the day he had accidentally violated a taboo, not long before the fighting began, and he had had no time for the purification ceremonies necessary to restore his sacred talisman, his warbonnet, which he believed made him invulnerable. He had been reluctant to join the fight, therefore, but he was coming now because his people needed him. Talisman or no, he was prepared to fight, although he fully expected to be killed. At least he would go to his death like the great chief he was. Leaping on his pony, he gave the signal and 500 warriors followed him in a second attack on the island.

Again the scouts leveled their repeaters over the mounds of sand and their dead horses. They knew they would not have a chance to reload this time; every shot would count. As the Indians galloped toward them, their first and second volleys seemed to have no effect, however. The third staggered the oncoming horsemen and tore gaps in their ranks, but Roman Nose and his braves came on. The fourth volley opened even wider gaps, but the charge continued and now there were only three rounds left. Another crashing volley; still they came. As the sixth volley thundered, Roman Nose was almost upon the line and, as he had feared, a bullet struck him above the hips, throwing him out of the saddle, mortally wounded. Then the scouts stood up in their trenches and delivered the final volley squarely in the faces of the oncoming Indians. The warriors reeled back, on the brink of victory. Seeing Roman Nose fallen, they were thrown into confusion and fell away in a rush to reach the safety of the shore again.

By this time night was coming on, and Forsyth had his first breathing spell. His situation was truly desperate. Out of fifty-one men, seven were killed or mortally wounded. The company surgeon was among the dead. Seventeen others were less seriously wounded. Otherwise his force was in a condition just about adequate enough to survive for a short time unless it was starved out.

That, apparently, was what the Indians meant to do. Next day they made no effort to attack again, but waited patiently on the river banks. On the second night, Forsyth realized what the Indians' strategy was, and he knew it would succeed unless he could get help from Fort Wallace, 125 miles away. Calling for volunteers, he was gratified to see that every man who could walk stepped forward. He chose a veteran trapper named Dave Trudeau and, as insurance, a nineteen-year-old volunteer, Jack Stillwell. This pair slipped away in the darkness, the prayers of the company following them.

While they waited through the interminable hours of the next day, those who remained were beginning to find out that siege could be even worse than assault. The Indians kept up a desultory fire, just enough to prevent them from moving around, while the sun beating down on the wounded redoubled their suffering. Forsyth, without a surgeon, took his own razor and operated on his wounds, removing the bullets carefully.

The fourth day was the beginning of hell. The paralyzing heat continued, and as they saw the squaws break camp and disappear in the hills, leaving most of their men behind, the scouts knew that the Indians meant to sit quietly and let them starve. The rations had gone. On the fifth desperate day they were so wild with hunger that they cut pieces of the putrefying flesh of their dead horses and mules. One of the better marksmen was lucky enough to bag a coyote. Crawling around on their island, other scouts found a precious treasure of wild plums. But where was the relief? Had their two messengers been killed? Forsyth and his men were in an agony of doubt and misery, as they realized that they would soon die or be too weak to fight unless help came. Two more messengers were sent out after the first, and the waiting went on.

At last Forsyth, feeling himself weakening, ordered all the able-bodied men to leave him and the other wounded, and fight their way to safety if they could. The men flatly refused to obey his order. "We've fought together," said Sergeant McCall, for all of them, "and by God, if need be, we'll die together."

The first two messengers, however, had finally reached Fort Wallace, young Stillwell supporting the exhausted Trudeau, who died soon after he was inside the fort. The garrison sprung to action. A messenger was sent galloping after Captain Louis H. Carpenter, who was already in the field and not far from Forsyth's island. Another relief force was mustered quickly, and was about to set out when the major's second pair of messengers appeared to confirm that the beleaguered troops were still holding out.

Carpenter, riding with the Negro 10th Cavalry, got the message from Fort Wallace and pushed his men hard to the rescue. In two days he covered a hundred miles. As his column swept into the river valley, the Indians saw him coming, withdrew without a fight and, in a moment, the relief column was on the island. According to one story, Carpenter found his old friend Forsyth with his rifle across his knees, reading *Oliver Twist*. The major later told him, so the story goes, that he had made this gallant gesture so that he would not break down. In his case, help had come just in time. He was running a high temperature; blood poisoning had set in from his amateur operation under the most unsterile of conditions, and it was two years before he fully recovered from his wounds.

Forsyth's plan, then, had been tried and found sadly wanting. It had never made a great deal of sense. Sheridan continued to study the situation among the hostile tribes and try to think of some way to deal with it. For one thing, he was convinced that it would do no good to fight the Indians only in the fine weather of summertime, when conditions were at their best for them. By permitting them no rest during the winter, their attrition would be hastened, he believed, and besides they would not be nearly so mobile in ice and snow. A well-equipped winter army might well do them lasting harm.

Pursuing this idea, Sheridan issued the appropriate orders. One unit that responded to them was the 7th Cavalry, at Camp Supply, Indian Territory, which rolled out of its blankets on a sub-zero morning, November 23, 1868, and prepared to march, while its commander, Lieutenant-Colonel George Armstrong Custer, had a final interview with his friend, General Sheridan. Thus onto the stage of the Indian Wars stepped the man who was to become its most controversial and best-known figure.

The story of Custer's rise to fame and death has been so often told that it needs little rehearsal. Known as the "Boy General" of the Civil War, this handsome, dashing, impulsive and altogether strange young man had been under a year's suspension from the Army, following a court-martial on charges of cruelty and illegal conduct. Sheridan, who had always been his friend, had succeeded in getting him transferred from Fort Hays, Kansas, to the 7th Cavalry. His subsequent career, up to the time of his spectacular death, remains a matter for endless argument, but it can be said of him certainly that what he did was far more clear than his reasons for doing it.

The final phase of his career began on the frigid November morning when he rode at the head of his column out of Camp Supply, to carry out Sheridan's orders. It was a splendid outfit, superbly mounted on matched horses, with a regimental band and trumpeters and a special detachment of forty sharpshooters. The men had been trained to a highly effective pitch by Custer, who was good at it, but his personality had already caused a division in the ranks, as it seemed to everywhere. There were those of his men who adored him; the others hated him. Few, if any, were neutral, but they all followed him without question, although it was hard to say whether he was a brilliant military genius or a talented fool.

It was like Custer to march off on his winter campaign, on that biting cold morning, with the regimental band playing, "The Girl I Left Behind Me." Unfortunately, there were no girls at Camp Supply. It was also typical of Custer's tangled career that the column had not traveled far before the Indian scouts who were guiding it had to confess they were lost. Custer helped them by taking compass bearings, and the column pushed on into what is now Oklahoma, sustained on the freezing march every night by the supply train, which always caught up and prov.ded hot meals.

gen. Custer

After three days of travel, Custer thought he must be in hostile territory and sent out his second-in-command, Major Joel H. Elliott, with a reconnaissance squadron. A messenger returned from this squadron next morning to report that it had found the trail of a large war party. Disposing his troops, Custer galloped forward, caught up with Elliott that night and, next day, from the crest of a hill, where he had been guided by an Osage scout, he peered down upon the Indians encamped in the Washita River Valley.

Custer did not know it, but it was the village of Black Kettle, who had already suffered so much from the perfidy of white men. After

Sand Creek, he had raided white settlements in a desultory way for a time, but in the preceding year, he had appeared to be satisfied with the terms of a new treaty and seemed no longer anxious to fight. The trail Elliott had discovered leading to his village was not that of a war party, but merely late arrivals coming to his peaceful winter encampment, where he had already been joined by some Kiowas, Arapahoes and Apaches. In this camp were young braves who were not nearly as peaceful as Black Kettle. They had spent the summer raiding settlements in Kansas, and now, resting from their labors, they had with them certain trophies, including white captives, some scalps and dispatches which they had removed from Sheridan's couriers.

So one might say that there was guilt enough in Black Kettle's village to justify punishment, notwithstanding how peaceful the chief himself might be. Yet what followed did not make Custer any less controversial, and for Black Kettle himself it was the final blow. Custer might claim he was only carrying out Sheridan's orders, but later to many it seemed unnecessary to have repeated the Sand Creek Massacre. That, in effect, was what occurred. Custer assaulted the camp at dawn, although he missed a complete surprise when an early-rising brave spotted his troops. The cavalry converged on the village from several directions before it could rouse itself. Black Kettle and his wife were felled in the first volley, and his fourteen-year-old son was killed in a brief duel with Captain Frederick W. Benteen. Women and children fell indiscriminately in the attack. Custer also suffered some casualties, but the Indians were cut down wholesale.

After an hour's fighting, a startling development gave a new turn to the slaughter. Custer had thought he was alone with Black Kettle's village, but he did not know that it was only one of several Indian villages scattered up and down the valley, where thousands of red men were wintering. Some of Black Kettle's braves had fought their way out of the village and ridden off to spread the alarm. Now Custer learned that the Indians were massing farther up the valley, and he would soon be badly outnumbered. He swung his men into battle formation and prepared to fight it out, but his ammunition was beginning to run low and he was saved from virtually certain annihilation by the arrival of relief in the form of seven supply wagons, which came rushing up under heavy fire, with accompanying troops. The new threat was soon beaten back.

In the excitement of battle, no one had noticed until now that Elliott and his squadron had disappeared. Custer dared not look for him so late in the day, a failure for which he was later criticized. Moreover, although he still held the village, he would have to retreat as rapidly as possible. Before he left, he destroyed everything in sight, not only the lodges but all the precious supplies they contained—a thousand buffalo robes, 500 pounds of lead, 500 pounds of powder, 4,000 arrows. He even performed that most difficult of a cavalryman's tasks. His men shot a herd of 700 ponies so that they would not be pursued, at least on those mounts.

There remained the problem of how to extricate himself without bringing down the Indians on his rear. Custer decided on a typically unorthodox stratagem. The women and children who had been captured were loaded into wagons, the column formed, the band struck up "Ain't I Glad to Get Out of the Wilderness" and the troops began marching up the valley directly toward the other villages. For a moment the Indians hesitated, but believing that the white commander would never do such a foolish thing unless he was leading a great force against them, they withdrew.

Custer continued to look for Elliott as he continued his retreat, failing to find him. The mutilated bodies of that squadron were not found until much later, by another expedition. Their position in a field of tall grass told the story. They had been cut off somehow, had tried to hold out and were massacred.

As the troops proceeded down the valley, they found the first village they came to hastily evacuated, and paused there briefly before they continued their march. Ahead of them the Indians had prepared an ambush which they confidently expected Custer to walk into next morning, but at 2 A.M. he wheeled his troops around and made a forced march in the other direction. When dawn came, he was far away from the ambush.

If Custer's first campaign in the Indian Wars had proved nothing else, it had shown that Sheridan was right. The Indians could be hunted down in their winter quarters and hurt badly. Encouraged by Custer's success, Sheridan continued to pursue the tribes unrelentingly for some time until there were only a few centers of Indian resistance remaining. One was the still powerful encampment of the Sioux, near the Powder River in the valley of the Little Big Horn. Another encompassed the scattered villages of the Apaches, who continued to be the most merciless and recalcitrant of all the white man's foes. A third was the partnership of Kiowas and Comanches which, in the spring of 1871, was busy destroying and killing through Texas and Indian Territory. This was an embarrassment to the government, which had considered them safely confined on their reservation, and so they were not slow in responding to the complaints of the settlers.

These two southwestern tribes had, in fact, always been a particular source of trouble. In proportion to their numbers, the Kiowas had killed more white men than any other tribe west of the Mississippi, while the Comanches had accounted for thousands of Mexicans and a good many Texans, for whom they seemed to have a special hatred.

To wipe out at last these twin sources of devastation, Washington sent one of its most accomplished generals, Sherman. His entry on the scene of conflict was most unusual. Traveling as far as he could go by train, he was met at the railhead by a cavalry escort and a mule-drawn ambulance. With no more support, Sherman at once set out for the hills, where the Kiowa chief Satanta was presumed to make his headquarters, in the Red River region of Texas. Although Sherman did not know it, Satanta and a large war party were following him behind a screen of hills.

Before the chief could attack, however, an honor guard composed of fifteen men of the 4th Cavalry, under Lieutenant Robert G. Carter, met Sherman to escort him to the regiment's camp at Rock Station. The General observed that Carter's men looked tired after their ride, and he ordered the Lieutenant to stop and refresh them while the General's little entourage moved on ahead. Carter was dubious about such a splitting of forces in hostile country, but a Lieutenant does not argue with a General, and orders had been given.

Satanta observed this odd maneuver and must have been puzzled by it. Perhaps he thought it was some kind of trap. It would be difficult to explain otherwise his continued reluctance to attack. He permitted Sherman to go on to Rock Station, where the General paused overnight before going on next day to Fort Sill, in Indian Territory.

While Sherman was being welcomed by the garrison, Satanta informed the General of his presence by attacking a corn train on the Salt Creek prairie. Some of the teamsters escaped the massacre and reached Rock Station, and Sherman, informed soon after, ordered the 4th to the rescue. They were, of course, much too late. The train

Chief Satanta
Kiowas

was wrecked and plundered, its men massacred, the Indians long since returned to the reservation, where their expedition would not even have been known about if Satanta had been able to refrain from boasting about his exploit in the hearing of the Indian agent, who sent the word back to Fort Sill.

Instead of dispatching troops to the reservation on a punitive expedition, which would have meant a battle, Sherman decided to try a not unfamiliar deception. It led to a drama which would have done credit to any modern motion picture or television Western.

The General invited Satanta to bring a delegation of Kiowa chiefs to Fort Sill for a council. Some of the Indians were reluctant to accept his invitation, scenting treachery, but Satanta was a reckless braggart and utterly without fear. He insisted on accepting, and arrived one day at the head of a respectable delegation of chiefs.

As the Indians walked into the fort, a silence which they must have thought ominous hung over it. There were no women or children to be seen, and only a few soldiers. Satanta might have been less confident if he had known that Negro troopers of the 10th sat their horses just inside the stable doors, only waiting for a signal to emerge. In the fort's houses were squads of armed men, well concealed.

The headquarters of Colonel Benjamin H. Grierson, commanding at Sill, had a large, comfortable front porch on which the Colonel, Sherman and other officers were waiting for their guests. The white men sat on chairs; the chiefs sat on the floor. It was not difficult for the officers to guess that the Indians had not come entirely unprepared. The bulges under their blankets were certainly rifles, revolvers, and bows and arrows.

As the conference began, Satanta, with an astonishing lack of reticence, freely admitted the massacre of the corn train, and even boasted about it. Sherman was outraged. Bluntly he told the chief that he and everyone else responsible would be arrested at once and tried for murder. In answer, Satanta pulled a revolver from beneath his blanket and informed Sherman that he would rather be shot than arrested. In the abrupt silence, white men and red confronted each other tensely. Then Sherman gave his signal. All along the porch shutters flew back and carbines emerged, in the hands of Grierson's Negro troops. Simultaneously a trumpet call summoned the troops from the stables.

Again Indians and officers stared at each other in silence, each waiting for the next move. A chief broke the stillness with the defiant declaration that he had done nothing wrong himself, and he would never let the white men execute his people. Satanta, who had not yet risen from his squatting position, seconded this defiance by taking out a rifle and cocking it.

Sherman was a model of coolness. He began to walk up and down the porch, talking as he moved, trying to reason with the chiefs before blood was shed. But a Kiowa chief named Stumbling Bear was determined that, if he was going to die on the porch, the white man's big chief would go with him. Unobtrusively he slipped an arrow into his bow, and was bending it when one of the officers caught sight of his action and nudged his elbow. The arrow went wild. Grierson leaped on Stumbling Bear and began to wrestle with him, and it looked for a moment as though there would be another massacre on the porch, since the Indians had no chance whatever to escape.

But the General ordered the troopers to lower their guns and the chiefs sat down again. At that point the guard came up, handcuffed Satanta and two other chiefs and took them to the guardhouse. Later that day they were taken out again under guard, and a detail was delegated to escort them to Jacksboro, Texas, where they would be tried. Each chief rode in a separate wagon, with two soldiers on the driver's seat and two in the wagon. Satanta and his friend, Lone Tree, appeared to be resigned, but the third chief, Satank, an old man, began to wail his death chant. When he had finished, he somehow wrenched himself free of the handcuffs, pulled out a knife and stabbed one of his guards in the leg, while the other jumped from the wagon. Satank picked up the wounded man's gun and prepared to sell himself dearly.

From the front seat of the following wagon, Corporal John B. Charlton raised his carbine and hit Satank with the first shot. Wounded but trying to unjam his carbine for a return shot, the old chief was felled for good by Charlton's second shot. There were no further incidents on the trip. The other two chiefs were tried and sentenced to be hanged, but the Indian Bureau, apparently fearing a general uprising if the sentences were carried out, persuaded the Governor of Texas to commute the sentences, then release the chiefs on parole. Sherman, naturally, was furious. He expressed to the governor the pious hope that Satanta would lift his scalp when the chief got out.

While these events were taking place, the Kiowas were without their leader and remained quiet, but the Comanches made up for their inactivity during October, 1871, by assaulting Colonel Ronald S. Mackenzie, the commander at Rock Station, as he lay encamped for the night, getting away with seventy horses and narrowly missing an opportunity to massacre the entire party. The half-breed Comanche chief, Quanah Parker, led this attack, as he did several others against various elements of the troops who strayed far enough away from their forts.

Mackenzie was not one to forget the embarrassment and near

disaster Parker had caused him. In his cadet days, Mackenzie had been called "the most promising young officer in the army" by none other than General Grant, and he had indeed served with distinction in the Civil War, where he was wounded three times and acquired a reputation as a disciplinarian. His 4th Cavalry at Rock Station was a spit-and-polish outfit, with a desertion record of near zero because of his standing orders to bring back deserters dead or alive. He was harsh and not loved by his men, but he was highly respected.

As a commander whose post was in the midst of the continuing revolt, Mackenzie's agile brain was constantly devising ways to deal with the Indians, and in 1873 he conceived a plan so daring and yet so promising that both Sheridan and Secretary of War Belknap came down to Texas to confer with him about it. The Colonel pointed out to his superiors that the reason the Indians were having so much success in southern Texas was that they were able to retreat after their raids to the privileged sanctuary of Mexico, whose government tacitly permitted them to use their country as a base of operations. Mackenzie proposed that the cavalry follow them there. That, of course, accounted for the presence of the Secretary of War at the conference, since what Mackenzie was proposing was an act of war against Mexico.

If the contemporary overtones of this proposition sound more than familiar to the modern reader, the approach decided upon should be even more instructive. Belknap pointed out that written orders could not legally be issued by anyone to violate the Mexican border, but nonetheless he was sympathetic to the idea, and in effect indicated that he would pretend he knew nothing about it. With this tacit approval, Sheridan, who had been immediately enthusiastic about the idea, instructed Mackenzie to go ahead. The Colonel would have to take the risk, but he and Grant would accept the responsibility.

Consequently, Mackenzie and his 4th Cavalry began to march southward on March 17, 1873, under sealed orders whose contents only the Colonel knew. The men marched in intense heat, and wondered aloud where they were going. After nightfall they came to a river and were ordered to cross it and re-form on the other side. By that time they realized where they were, and that the river was the Rio Grande. On the other side lay Mexico.

In a hazy early spring moonlight the column rode along silently, tense and still wondering. When the mules carrying the rations began to slow down the march, their packs were cut loose and the rations distributed to be carried by the men.

Just before daylight scouts reported that a Kickapoo village lay ahead, asleep and unsuspecting. Orders were given, the charge was sounded, and the troop swept over the village with the fury of a tornado, stopped on the other side to dismount, and came back on foot to complete their slaughter. Only a few warriors survived. Mackenzie took some of the captured women and children along with him, and proceeded.

On into Mexico the column rode next day, but by this time one of the Kickapoo survivors had spread the word of their coming. Every village they encountered was deserted, and the Colonel ordered them all burned. Scouts brought back word that the Indians were on the run and apparently intended to put up no resistance, but the Mexicans were organizing for a fight. Mackenzie concluded that the raid had gone far enough. He turned his regiment around and headed for the river. His men had been traveling and fighting for two days and a night, and they could scarcely stay awake in the saddle. Amazingly, they recrossed the Rio Grande without the loss of a man, after a march of 160 miles in thirty-two hours.

As Belknap had anticipated, Mexico made an outraged protest but it came to nothing. The Mexican government was not about to fight another war with the United States. Texas was grateful, and Mackenzie was discreetly praised.

Like so many other military solutions of the Indian problem, however, Mackenzie's was hardly worth the risk involved. His raid had been successful, true, and the tribes put on notice that they could no longer regard themselves as safe in Mexico, but Texas and the Indian Territory were still seething with revolt. The Indian Bureau could no longer assert that the tribes were safely on reservations, and the government, once more in desperation, gave General Sheridan freedom to settle things any way he could.

Sheridan decided on a change of tactics. Instead of dealing with the Indians piecemeal, using small units, he would bring together all the strength he could command and smite the Kiowas in their heartland, which they called the Staked Plains. Cavalry and infantry were assembled under a half-dozen field commanders and poured in upon the Great Kiowa village from four directions. Satanta was among the first prisoners taken. Brought back to jail, he killed himself a little later by jumping out of an upper window. Mackenzie had to fight off a night raid, but he pursued the raiders next day and his advance scouts inadvertently stumbled on the Kiowas' secret refuge, Palo Duro, at the bottom of a deep, hidden canyon. Probably no white man had ever seen it before. John B. Charlton, Satank's slayer and now a Sergeant, was the man who made the discovery, but he could only report what he had seen, since his force was far too small to attack.

Mackenzie, however, brought his column to the rim of the canyon and peered over it far below to where the Indian encampment appeared like a village in miniature. Boldly he decided to ride straight down to the canyon floor and attack. It was a perilous descent, but it was accomplished successfully; the column formed on the canyon's floor, and charged headlong into the astonished Indian village. The Kiowas were routed and savagely reduced during a running five-mile battle. Worst of all, from the Indians' standpoint, Mackenzie destroyed 2,000 of their ponies. They were a long time recovering from this blow, and in fact, Mackenzie's raid marked the beginning of their decline as a threat to the white man.

These and other successes which followed appeared to justify Sheridan's change of tactics and more or less ended the government's warfare against the Kiowas and Comanches, who slowly subsided into the exile of their reservations.

The campaign against the Apaches did not go so expeditiously. Against them the government had begun by conducting a war of extermination. "I encouraged the troops to capture and root out the Apache by every means, and to hunt them as they would wild animals," wrote the commander of the Department of California in September, 1869. In this endeavor the Army was joined by civilians and even by other Indians who had particular reason to hate the Apaches. American and Mexican civilians, in combination with Papago Indians, destroyed an Apache village not far from Tucson in April, 1871. The Army surgeon from Fort Lowell who arrived with a detachment of troops a little later reported with some horror:

> . . . I found that I should have but little use for wagon or medicine; the work had been too thoroughly done. The camp had been fired, and the dead bodies of some twenty-one women and children were lying scattered over the ground; those who had been wounded in the first in-

stance had their brains beaten out with stones. Two of the best-looking of the squaws were lying in such a position, and from the appearance of the genital organs and of their wounds, there can be no doubt that they were first ravished and then shot dead. Nearly all of the dead were mutilated. One infant of some ten months was shot twice, and one leg nearly hacked off. While going over the ground, we came upon a squaw who was unhurt, but were unable to get her to come in and talk, she not feeling very sure of our good intentions.

The full horror of this raid was described next day by a lieutenant who came out with a detail to bury the dead.

Their camp was surrounded and attacked at daybreak. . . . So sudden and unexpected was it, that no one was awake to give the alarm, and I found quite a number of women shot while asleep beside their bundles of hay which they had collected to bring in on that morning. The wounded who were unable to get away had their brains beaten out with clubs or stones, while some were shot full of arrows after having been mortally wounded by gunshot. The bodies were all stripped. Of the whole number buried, one was an old man and one was a well-grown boy—all the rest women and children. Of the whole number killed and missing—about 125—only eight were men. . . .

The Apaches themselves could not have done worse than these white men, and thus atrocity begot atrocity in the Southwest.

It was only two months after this massacre that the government decided on an all-out campaign against the Apaches. On June 4, 1871, General George Crook took command of the Department of Arizona, and the settlers supposed that he would carry out the former policy of extermination to its logical conclusion. But Crook disabused them at once.

I think that the Apache is painted in darker colors than he deserves, [the general declared] and that his villainies arise more from a misconception of facts than from his being worse than other Indians. Living in a country the natural products of which will not support him, he has either to cultivate the soil or steal, and as our vacillating policy satisfies him we are afraid of him, he chooses the latter, also as requiring less labor and being more congenial to his natural instincts. I am satisfied that a sharp, active campaign against him would not only make one of the best Indians in the country but it would also save millions of dollars to the Treasury and the lives of many innocent whites and Indians.

Vincent Colyer, the President's representative on the scene, did not favor even a "sharp, active campaign." He wanted to try negotiation first. The Apache responded by a renewed outbreak of attacks, fifty-four of them within a year, after which Crook announced that he would "punish the incorrigibly hostile."

gen. George Crook

To his contemporaries, Crook was a baffling paradox. As one who believed the Indian problem ought to be solved by fair and equitable means rather than blood, he was excoriated by settlers as an "Indian lover." Government officials thought his idea of making the Indians self-supporting by dividing the reservations into farms was visionary, and even worse was his belief that Indians ought to be considered citizens of the United States, with all the rights and privileges of other citizens. Ordinarily such ideas would have led him straight into obscurity, but the undeniable fact remained that in the field, carrying out orders, he was the best Indian fighter in the Army, and was so rated by General Sherman. Moreover, he was a superb administrator, whose talents were constantly useful in a disorganized land.

The campaign Crook mounted against the Apaches in 1872 was a model of thorough preparation and efficient execution. He began by recognizing that a major reason for previous failures was an inability to catch the Indians. It was a common saying in Arizona that "only an Apache can catch an Apache." Very well, said Crook, he would hire some Apache scouts, since there were always a few disaffected Indians in any tribe. Realizing, too, that he was in pursuit of the most mobile and elusive of tribes, he made every effort to make his own troops as mobile as they. The mules for his expedition were hand-picked, fitted individually with pack saddles, and trained to march twenty miles farther a day than they had been used to doing, carrying 320 rather than the usual 175 pounds.

As for men, Crook had at his disposal the 5th Cavalry, units of the 3rd and 1st, and the 21st and 23rd Infantry. Like the mules, they were also trained for Apache fighting. They learned what would today be called survival tactics. Their packs contained only the essentials, and their training marches were merciless. Crook also believed in the advantages of a winter campaign, when the Indians were at their least mobile, and so he launched his operation on November 15, 1872.

The column began to move into the Tonto Basin on that day with only one specific order. If they found a trail, the men must follow it, no matter how long it took, until the Indians were compelled to fight.

On the day after Christmas, the Apache scouts flushed their first quarry, a cave stronghold of the Apaches in the Salt River Canyon of the Mazatal Mountains. A squadron of the 5th Cavalry, led by Major William H. Brown, was the unit which had struck this trail. Brown's men dismounted, marched through a night of severe cold to the mesa around the canyon and prepared for a surprise attack at dawn. A Lieutenant Ross, with a dozen sharpshooters, was dispatched down into the canyon, guided by the scouts.

Daylight, however, showed Brown that he was confronting a problem he had not anticipated in the darkness. The Apaches were not camped on the floor of the canyon, as he had supposed, but on a rock shelf projecting from a cave, and protected by great boulders. Before he could make another plan, Ross's sharpshooters opened fire, killing six warriors with their first volley. The Major had to move quickly. He sent forty men ahead to Ross's position on the canyon floor and followed with the others.

Brown had the Apaches bottled up in their cave in short order, but it was difficult to see how the battle could be brought to a decision. The Indians could not get out, but neither could the troopers get in.

When Brown told them to surrender, they yelled back a defiant refusal; when he promised to treat the women and children kindly if they sent them out, they refused as loudly.

Studying the situation, and rejecting the idea of an assault up the cliff face, Brown stationed three skirmish lines opposite the cave and told the men to fire so that their bullets would be deflected from the roof of the cave. From the cries and screams inside, he could tell that this strategy had been successful. Again he repeated his demand for surrender, and his promise to take care of the women and children. There was a moment of silence, then an eerie, blood-chilling chant rose in the thin air of the canyon. The major's Apache scouts told him it was the death chant. It meant they were about to charge.

In a moment warriors swarmed out of the cave, firing as they came, but the soldiers, aiming from behind rocks, drove them back. Only three Indians regained the cave. Brown resumed his fusillade at the cave roof, and the Indians returned the fire. The noise of the battle reached another column, under Captain James Burns, riding nearby, and it came dashing up to reinforce Brown's troops. Arriving at the rim of the canyon, Burns saw that the Indians had come out on the ledge to fire from behind the boulders, not only to get a better position but to escape the ricocheting bullets inside the cave. That made them perfect targets for anyone firing from above—or, better still, Burns had another idea. His men started rolling a cascade of large boulders down the side above the cave. Shrieks rose from the trapped Apaches, mingled with the rumble of the small avalanche Burns had started, and a huge cloud of dust rose, obscuring the cave. From below Brown signaled to stop the barrage of stones. He was ready to charge.

As the skirmish lines surged up the cliff wall to the ledge, they did not find it necessary to fire a shot. The Apaches were shattered. Seventy-five of them were dead or dying; eighteen were taken prisoner.

After this initial success, Crook pressed his multiple sorties relentlessly. When his horses and mules were decimated by epizootic fever, an equine disease, the tough, superbly conditioned men he commanded simply put the ammunition, rations and blankets the animals had carried on their own backs.

These foot soldiers scored a bold victory at a natural fortress called Turret Butte. There Major George M. Randall, with a battalion of the 23rd Infantry—one of five columns pursuing an Apache war party which had murdered a group of civilians—had cornered the marauders in their mountain plateau hideout. The slope up to it was steep and rock-strewn, impossible to assault in daylight. Artillery would have been the best answer, but Randall had none. There was only one alternative. With fingers numbed by the cold, these daring infantrymen scaled the face of the cliff at midnight, and charged the Indians at dawn in an attack that took them completely by surprise. The men had surrounded the camp, closing every exit, and they poured in their volleys from every direction. Some Apache warriors jumped from the heights to the rocks below rather than surrender. The survivors gave up.

Such victories, along with smaller skirmishes, eventually wore down the Apaches. Many of their leaders were killed or captured. In time most of these tribesmen were back on the reservation, where Crook made an earnest effort to carry out his idea of resettling them as farmers and herdsmen. With other Indians he might have been more successful, but the Apaches were too intractable. Crook was only moderately successful in turning them into peaceful agriculturalists. Nor did he get much help from the Arizona settlers, who wanted every last Indian killed. Eventually, in the early Eighties, everything he was able to accomplish was undone by stupid men.

At least Crook could employ his administrative talents and planning ability in the task of improving the territory. He built roads, established 700 miles of telegraph lines and improved the forts. For his work the government promoted him to Brigadier General, an unusual promotion for peacetime, and soon sent him north to deal with the Sioux.

The Apaches merely waited. They would be heard from again.

# 13 ★ ★ ★ ★ ★ ★

# The Modoc War, and the Sioux and Cheyenne Uprising

**C**ROOK'S EXPLOITS in chasing down the Apaches were briefly over-shadowed in 1872-73 by an outbreak of violence in northern California. This attracted wide public attention, more because of the colorful personalities involved with it than because of any major threat to white settlements. It was a tiny war, this Modoc War, but it cost the United States more in men and money, in proportion to the numbers of the enemy, than any it ever fought.

The terrain over which it was fought was as unusual as the men involved in the conflict. Seventy square miles of lava beds, tossed up by an ancient volcano, had made a weird natural fortress of virtually impregnable character. Like a frothy, frozen witches' brew, the flint-like lava provided naturally looped parapets, deep trenches, dangerous fissures which could be used as moats, and caves large enough to store large quantities of supplies and hide any number of men. Streams flowing through the beds supplied ample water. The rock itself was so hard that it was impossible to ride horses over it, and it would shred shoeleather in no time. Small wonder the Army came to call it "Hell with the fire out."

On this ground the Modocs made their stand. Keith A. Murray, a recent historian of the war, remarks of it:

The Modoc Indian War was the final desperate resistance to the impact of white man's culture on the ancient Indian folkways. It marks the concluding stages of the decline in vigor and numbers among a fierce people, beginning in the early years of the nineteenth century and ending when a band of beaten and spiritless prisoners was forced aboard a Central Pacific railroad train bound for exile on a tiny reservation in Oklahoma.

They were a strange tribe, these Modocs, proud and irascible. Their leaders bore such unlikely names as Captain Jack, Curley Headed Doctor, Bogus Charley, Shacknasty Jim, Scarfaced Charley, Steamboat Frank, Boston Charley, Ellen's Man George, One Eyed Watchman, Hooker Jim, Old Tail, William (the Wild Gal's Man), Old Chuckle Head, and One Eyed Mose—all testifying to an unassimilated dosage of the white man's culture.

The causes of the war were complicated. The Modocs had been badly treated by the early Oregonian settlers, and had resisted. Eventually, however, they had agreed to share a reservation with the Klamaths, their kinsmen with whom they maintained a running feud over land and hunting rights, an argument further complicated by the white administrators' inept handling of it. There was also a deep rivalry between the Modoc chief Sconchin, or Schonchin, and Captain Jack, his younger rival. This had resulted in a physical division of the tribe. Finally, there was the superstition generated by the medicine man, Curley Headed Doctor, who prompted the war with mystical fanaticism when reason must have told the other leaders they could not win.

Essentially the immediate cause of the war was the inability of the Modocs to find a place to live. The Klamaths did not want them on the reservation and, since the other tribe was larger, the Modocs were pushed back to their Oregon homelands. But then the Indian agent insisted that they return to the reservation. Caught between these forces, and increasingly angered by them, the Modocs flatly refused to move. The agent appealed for help.

His request came to General Edward R. S. Canby, a commander with a strong sense of justice, who examined the situation and suggested sensibly that the Modocs be given a reservation of their own. This was far too reasonable for the agent, who complained to Washington, with the result that Canby was ordered to make the Modocs comply with the agent's order.

The General had no choice. He sent a detail of the 1st Cavalry, thirty-eight men under Captain David Jackson, who rode into Captain Jack's camp on Lost River, early in the morning of November 29, 1872. As the troopers tried to disarm the Indians, one of the Modocs fired his rifle and a battle was on. In the brief flurry, a sergeant was killed and seven other men badly wounded, whereupon Captain Jack fled with his tribesmen.

Meanwhile, on the other bank of the river, Hooker Jim had confronted a posse of civilians and treated them even more harshly, killing three. He planned to join Captain Jack at the Lava Beds, but on the way there he seriously compounded his first crime by invading the homes of seventeen settlers and murdering them.

In the Lava Beds, sometimes called "The Stronghold," which lay south of Tule Lake near the Oregon border, Hooker Jim and Captain Jack merged their forces. There were seventy-five warriors, and about 150 women and children. Captain Jack was their leader. Whatever else might be said of this squat, short, moon-faced man— and he was a shifty character, probably involved in an Indian prostitution ring—he was a general of truly extraordinary ability, for he was able with this pitiful force to hold out for six months against an army of more than 1,000 soldiers and settlers, including detachments of the 1st Cavalry, 21st Infantry, artillerymen and California and Oregon volunteers.

The first attack on the Modoc fortress came on January 17, 1873. It was launched in a dense fog, two columns converging from east and west. Knowing how few the Modocs were, the soldiers were in almost a cheerful mood. They had reason to know better by nightfall, after firing all day at the flashes of Modoc fire in the mist. They could get no closer. Mountain howitzers were brought up, and shells hurtled away ineffectively into the mist. Infantry and dismounted cavalry tried to push forward in converging columns but they could make little progress over the flinty terrain, and against the murderous Modoc fire. As the columns came within hailing distance, English-speaking Indians yelled out confusing orders. When replies rose from both sides, the Modocs turned a shattering fire on the soldiers' flanks. In all this time the attackers had not seen a single Modoc, nor had they hit one.

medoc in lava beds

Near nightfall the Indians pinned the troops to the rocks with heavy fire, and they withdrew to count their losses. Sixteen enlisted men were dead. Forty-four others and nine officers were wounded. The others were so weary they could neither fight nor carry off their dead, and they had barely enough strength to help the wounded back to camp.

With this defeat, General Canby took personal command. It was somewhat surprising that a man of his fighting background had acquired a reputation for humane and fair treatment of the Indians. Canby had taken the field with Jackson against the Seminoles, and he had helped, although unwillingly, to remove the Cherokees. He had also fought in the Mexican War, in the so-called "Mormon War" of 1858, and had pursued the tribes of the Southwest in New Mexico, taken part in the Civil War's western battles and in 1865 was the conqueror of Mobile. After the war, he had been a military governor in four of the southern states, coming to Washington Territory from Virginia.

He hoped somehow to avoid further bloodshed against the Modocs. It was obvious that it would be almost impossible to get them out of the Lava Beds; therefore Canby hoped to persuade them to negotiate, and he would have succeeded, if it had not been for a single irrational, irresponsible act.

Since the January battle, Canby had patiently laid the groundwork for negotiation, and on April 11 he rode out to a prearranged peace tent with three other commissioners and an interpreter, Frank Riddle, whose Modoc wife Toby came along. Captain Jack and seven other Modocs were waiting for the delegation. It was said later that Hooker Jim, who was afraid of being executed for killing the settlers, had persuaded Captain Jack to use the occasion for treachery. In any event, the white men suspected nothing. In fact, the conversation was at first conciliatory, although it reached a snag when the heart of the problem was reached, namely, what land should be given to the Modocs for their reservation.

At this point one of the Modocs jumped up, and four more Indians, heavily armed, came out from behind some rocks. One of the negotiators, possibly Canby, shouted out, "What does this mean?" Captain Jack stood up. *"Atwe,"* meaning "all ready," he answered in Modoc, and with that he drew his pistol and fired pointblank at Canby, who stood only three feet away. The General was so stunned he could not move as the gun misfired. Captain Jack cocked it and fired again, this time dropping the General with a wound directly under one eye. Canby got up and tried to run, but Ellen's Man felled him again with a rifle shot. Captain Jack ran up and stabbed him in the neck, stripped him of his uniform and put it on.

Meanwhile, the Reverend Eleazer Thomas, one of the commissioners, was killed instantly, and another, A. B. Meacham, lost his life in a running duel while he tried to get to his horse. L. S. Dyer, the Indian agent from the Klamath reservation, and the interpreter and his wife escaped. Troops watching from the bluffs rode hastily to the rescue but they were too late, and lost a lieutenant to a Modoc sharpshooter in the process. The Modocs, it may be added, were expert shots, far above the Indian average.

This event had a profound effect on the white community, from the settlers on up to Washington itself. The atrocity was bad enough, but it was no worse than a hundred others. What rankled the white men was the fact that its victims had been two men, Canby and the Reverend Thomas, who were well known as friends of the Indians, had done a great deal for them, and were at the moment of their deaths trying to work out a better life for them. No one talked about negotiation any more. The old policy, extermination, was restored.

On April 14, 1873, Colonel Jefferson C. Davis, no relation to the Confederate President, took the field against the Modocs. In his force were 1,000 or more soldiers, civilians and a few renegade Modocs acting as scouts. His most potent weapon, however, was a battery of Cochorn mortars, fired by gun crews of the 4th Artillery. These little bronze cannon looked small but they sent seventeen-pound shells up in steep trajectories to distances of 1,200 yards. The Indians had never seen anything like them. They arched up so slowly that the Modocs had time to shoot at them, and one that fell unexploded was picked up curiously by a brave who managed to kill himself and two others when it exploded in his hands.

Davis laid down a barrage which drove back the Modocs slowly but steadily, in spite of occasional counterattacks. The mortars kept up a steady pounding through two days and two nights, while the troops advanced steadily, soon cutting off the Indians from the waters of Tule Lake. The advance was made at the cost of heavy casualties.

Trying to locate new mortar positions, Captain Evan Thomas, of the 4th Artillery, led eighty-five men into a trap, which was the result of his inexperience with Indians. The Modocs fell upon him as the men ate their noon mess in a rocky gorge. The troops, particularly the veterans, put up a stout fight, but relief columns reaching the gorge that night found five officers and eighteen men dead, another eighteen wounded. The survivors were taken out with difficulty through a driving sleet storm.

The Modocs might have resisted indefinitely if they had not fallen to quarreling among themselves. For one thing they were disillusioned with Curley Headed Doctor, whose influence with the Great Spirit had not seemed to do much for them. For another, Hooker Jim and his followers had lost heart, and in a frantic effort to save their own skins, had broken away and fled to Davis's camp, where they promised to turn state's evidence against Captain Jack if their crimes against the settlers were forgiven.

Hopelessly split and reduced in strength, sixty-five Modocs surrendered on May 22. Captain Jack, with two other braves and their women and children, refused to give in until June 1. As the scouts advanced toward him warily, he held out his arms for the handcuffs and muttered sullenly, "My legs have given out."

Captain Jack and five others were tried for murdering the commissioners. In reality it was a court-martial, since the government contended that the Modocs had violated the rules of war. All were sentenced to be hanged, but President Grant commuted two of the sentences to life. The other four were executed on October 3, 1873, Captain Jack full of hate and unrepenting to the last. "I am ready to go to the Great Father," he said as the trap was sprung.

It had been a most expensive war. In lives, it had cost eight officers, thirty-nine enlisted men, sixteen civilians and two scouts, in addition to the eighteen settlers Hooker Jim had killed. Sixty-seven others had been wounded. The Modocs had lost only five killed, besides a few women and children. In money, the war had required an expenditure of more than a half-million dollars. If the Modocs had been given what they asked, without war, it would have cost the government about $10,000, for 2,000 acres of land, and a new agency to govern the Modoc reservation, which might have cost $20,000 more.

While this futile and expensive conflict had been going on, events were moving toward a climax in the remaining tinderbox of the West, the Plains territory, where the Sioux constituted the last major stronghold of Indian resistance.

The Plains Indians stood squarely in the path of progress. When the Union Pacific and Central Pacific railroads came together in Utah on May 10, 1869, it was a fateful day for all the tribes, as well as a historic one for the United States. The transcontinental line cut through the Indians' lands, signaling the end of the buffalo, which was their meat staple and their protection from cold, and accelerating tremendously the flow of westward migration. The telegraph came with the railroad, giving the white men a communications advantage which would further shatter Indian resistance.

Then, in 1873, gold was found in the Black Hills of the Dakotas. The Sioux had been given that territory by treaty in 1868—willingly, because no one else wanted land which seemed good for nothing but as a place to shunt Indians. The Sioux took a different view of the Black Hills; in their religion, it was a sacred place.

Treaties, religion and every other consideration were forgotten in the madness which began in 1873. With the first gold strike, the government ordered Custer to move in with troops, find out whether the discovery was true, and control the area until the government could develop a policy. Custer reported that it was gold, well enough, and the rush was on. (His brother Tom, a captain in the Army, was on duty in the Black Hills the following year, in the first skirmishes with the Sioux. Tom captured the noted Chief Rain-in-the-Face, who slipped away from him with the promise that he would return one day and eat the Captain's heart.)

To the government's credit it must be said that it tried, through the Army, to hold back the gold rush until a new treaty could be worked out with the Sioux, but as the history of the world has shown, nothing can hold back greedy men. The sacred land was profaned by the flood of miners, and an accompanying tidewash of riffraff. Towns sprang up overnight. Within a year Deadwood was a bustling and soon to be historic community. The government offered to pay the Indians $6,000,000 for the Black Hills, but some of the tribes thought $30,000,000 would be a fairer price. Still others believed that no price would compensate for the sacred land and, putting on their warpaint, they rode away from the reservation. The government ordered them back by January 1, 1876, but the Sioux, who by this time had made common cause with the Cheyennes, bluntly refused. It was to be war.

Never had the government confronted so formidable a revolt. Fifty thousand Indians were involved, and nearly 15,000 of them were warriors, armed with good repeating rifles and plentifully supplied with ammunition. Moreover, they had in Crazy Horse a leader

Crazy Horse

to rank with the best of the past, a military genius to match any general the white men could put in the field. The Sioux also possessed in Sitting Bull a medicine man who was far more than a mystic invoking curses on the enemy's efforts. He was a planner and organizer, probably the only man the Western Indians had ever produced who could coordinate and direct the efforts of so many tribesmen.

Crazy Horse, whose unusual name came from an incident at his birth when a wild horse raced through his village, was no more than twenty-five, with the boldness of youth, the wisdom of a mature leader and an implacable hatred of white men and their governments. Because he was married to a Cheyenne woman, he commanded the loyalty of these allies as well. Sitting Bull was older, past forty at the time, a true politician by nature who had realized early in his career that it was better to be a medicine man than a war leader. Such leaders were likely to be killed and their reward was honor. Medicine men usually lived a long time and the emoluments along the way, of every variety, were impressive. For an Indian, Sitting Bull was already a rich man, and a powerful one as well, wheeling and dealing among the influential men of the Sioux, Cheyenne and Arapaho tribes. He had no special reason to hate white men. With him it was traditional. Dressed in store clothes and set down in a white community, Sitting Bull, except for his broad, swarthy countenance, could have passed as an alderman or a ward boss.

In the spring of 1876, with war imminent, the Sioux and their allies were gathered in a camp on the Rosebud River, in the Valley of the Little Big Horn. Their strength was 2,500 to 4,000 men and boys, all well armed, and new recruits were arriving constantly as the gold rush drove more and more outraged Indians into their encampment. Presiding as head of the war council, where his eminence had placed him, ahead of Crazy Horse and the other war chiefs, Sitting Bull waited for the incident which would precipitate a conflict.

It had, in fact, occurred a few months before, in December, 1875, when the Indian Commissioner in Washington had issued his order that all the Sioux must return to their reservation, even though it was now overrun by prospectors and was being rapidly settled. The messengers carrying this decree did not reach the Plains immediately, because of the terrible winter weather. It took one of them more than a month. When they did arrive, they found difficulty in delivering their message because the severity of the winter had driven many of the Sioux far away, searching for game. Consequently the deadline of January 31 came and passed, unobserved by the Indians.

The War Department sent its best man, General Crook, to carry out the order, and to put down the Sioux if they proved reluctant. He was given one of the largest concentrated forces yet to be sent against the Western Indians—ten troops of cavalry and two infantry companies. George Custer and Alfred H. Terry were to be the field commanders.

By March, Crook was ready to move. With ten troops of the 2nd and 3rd Cavalry and a part of the 4th Infantry, he set out from Fort

Fetterman, in Wyoming Territory, for the Powder and Big Horn Rivers. He left behind his eighty-six mule-drawn wagons and 400 more pack mules. To protect themselves against the snow and cold, the troops were equipped with heavy underwear, coats lined with blankets, fur caps and buffalo robes. The advance column moved ahead into the hills, pushing on rapidly by night marches. A lieutenant in that column wrote in his journal: "In the bright light of the moon and stars, our column of cavalry wound up steep hillsides like an enormous snake, whose scales were glittering revolvers and carbines."

The advance column halted when scouts came hurrying back to report to Colonel Joseph J. Reynolds, commander of the force, that an enemy encampment lay ahead. It was the village of Chief Two Moons, lying under the bluffs of the Powder River. Reynolds deployed his men and moved in rapidly for the kill, but an Indian herd boy saw them in time and gave warning. When Reynolds charged it was too late. His men were greeted with a curtain of rifle fire which forced them to fall back and gave the Indians time to get themselves into a commanding position on the bluff, from which they opened a ruinous fusillade.

Reynolds dismounted his men and dug in. Meanwhile, he had occupied the village and taken over the Indians' food and ponies. In short, he held a strong position and could hope for eventual victory, but for reasons never explained, he ordered a quick retreat instead— so rapid that a wounded man was left to the Indians. But because other wounded were brought back to the main column, Crook felt that he could advance no farther with these helpless men as an encumbrance, and returned to his base. For his inexplicable action, Reynolds was court-martialed, and permitted to retire for disability.

Crook now had to organize another campaign. The Indians, apprised of his presence and jubilant over their success in the first skirmish, were gathering a mighty army on the headwaters of the Rosebud River, according to reports which Crow scouts brought back to the General. Reinforced and with a new plan of battle, Crook was ready to set out again late in May. Once more he rode out of Fort Fetterman, with 1,200 men of the 2nd and 3rd Cavalry and the 4th and 9th Infantry, and a supply train which could also furnish armed teamsters and packers.

At the same time, according to a master plan devised by Sheridan, two other columns were to converge on the Sioux. While Crook was marching north into the Valley of the Rosebud, Colonel John Gibbon was to move eastward out of the Montana mountains until he made contact with General Alfred H. Terry, and the two would then set out from Fort Abraham Lincoln, in Dakota Territory, up the Missouri River. In the end, so the plan was outlined, these columns would split up the Sioux and prevent them from aiding each other.

With his scouts and advance force ahead, Crook pushed on by an interesting method. Two hours before the rest of the camp, the infantry marched on ahead. Later they would be overtaken and passed by the cavalry, but they would reach the next camp ahead of the supply train. Strung out along four miles, this leapfrogging expedition pushed through rivers, into clouds of choking prairie dust, and even an out-of-season snowstorm on June 1. They traveled over the Bozeman Trail and into the mountains, fighting a few inconsequential skirmishes along the way. They also acquired some Indian allies— 176 Crows, who wanted to help demolish their hated enemy, the Sioux; and eighty-six Shoshones, who were old friends of the white man.

Once he was deep in enemy territory, Crook began to move faster. Leaving his wagon train under a hundred-man guard, he put 200 other infantrymen on mules as makeshift cavalry—a maneuver not immediately successful until the mules, slow and stubborn learners, found out what was expected of them.

As the now unencumbered column reached the Tongue River, an Indian courier was waiting for them, carrying a message from Crazy Horse and Sitting Bull. Like small boys drawing a line in the dirt, but with deadly purpose, the chiefs warned Crook that if he crossed the river the resulting events would be on his head.

The General shrugged off this message impatiently. Avoiding combat was the last thing he wanted to do. On the morning of June 17, his troops broke camp in Dead Canyon Valley, on the Rosebud. Waiting on the bluffs were 1,500 fighting men of the Sioux and Cheyenne tribes, under Crazy Horse. Shortly after eight o'clock the battle was joined, with the Crows and Shoshones attacking the enemy's flanks. Captain Anson Mills was ordered to clear the bluffs in the center with his squadron, since Crook was a firm believer in the old military maxim, "Take the high ground or they'll bury you in the valley." Mills and his cavalry fought and clawed their way up the slope, which was so steep in places that the horses toppled over. When they were fifty yards from the top, the troopers who were still in the saddle let go with a volley from their revolvers, which scattered the Indians. Having attained the heights successfully, Mills dismounted and prepared to hold his position.

In the valley, meanwhile, squadrons under two captains, Guy V. Henry and Frederick Van Vliet, made another charge against the Indians who were countering the flank attack. Crazy Horse threw in wave after wave of his warriors. The floor of the valley was a maelstrom of smoke, dust and furiously moving masses of men and horses. Crook's horse was shot from under him but he found another quickly. Captain Henry's squadron found itself cut off at one point by a horde of Cheyennes, and the men had to fight their way back, with revolvers and carbines covering their retreat, and the rear guard countercharging from time to time. Henry himself was shot down and fell beneath the hoofs of the Cheyennes' horses. He was rescued by the Shoshone chief Washakie, who fought his way with some braves to Henry's side and surrounded the fallen officer, holding off the other Indians in hand-to-hand fighting until Henry's own men could help them. Captain Mills' squadron appeared at this point and cleared the field. Henry lived to fight again.

The armies broke apart after the long day's fighting. Crook occupied the battlefield and camped there, while Crazy Horse retired to his village nearby, which Mills' squadron would have destroyed if Crook had been able to lend him support. In one sense the contest had to be called a draw, since no real decision was reached, but it was Crook who had to retreat next day, with heavy losses, because he was short of both rations and ammunition. As it was, he had lost time and would not be able to meet the other two columns on schedule.

These columns were proceeding as planned. General Terry had departed from Fort Abraham Lincoln on May 17, a 7th Cavalry regimental band playing the traditional "Girl I Left Behind Me." At the head of his 7th Cavalry rode the unpredictable Lieutenant Colonel Custer, now a Brevet Major General. Terry's other officers included Major Marcus A. Reno, a Civil War veteran but with no experience in fighting Indians; Captain Frederick Benteen; Custer's brother Tom, and his brother-in-law, James Calhoun, among others. There were two lieutenants who would one day be generals: Edward S. Godfrey and Luther R. Hare.

Besides the 7th there were detachments of the 6th, 17th and 20th Infantry, a pack mule and wagon train of 150 vehicles, 175 civilians, three horse-drawn Gatling guns, a few Arickara scouts, and Custer's nephew, a newspaper correspondent named Mark Kellogg, whom Sheridan had specifically forbidden to come.

This army had nearly reached its goal by mid-June. Major Reno's squadron, riding south of the main body, had picked up an Indian trail leading toward the Big Horn Mountains, but he had failed to ride far enough on June 17. A few more miles and he would have been within earshot of Crook's battle; if he had, the course of the war might have been considerably different.

As planned, Colonel Gibbon, with the third column, met Terry at the junction of the Yellowstone and Rosebud rivers on June 21. Gibbon led the 17th Infantry and several squadrons of the 2nd Cavalry. At a conference following the meeting, Major Reno reported the trail he had discovered, and Custer was given written orders to circle the trail in an effort to find the Indian encampment, and sweep in on it from the headwaters of the Little Big Horn, while Terry and the other troops came at it from the other way to catch the Indians in a trap.

While the white men were maneuvering, Crazy Horse had hastened north from his indecisive battle with Crook and joined Sitting Bull and the main body of Indians at the Little Big Horn. There Sitting Bull sat in his tepee and planned the defense, which would be carried out by Crazy Horse and another noted chief, named Gall. The medicine man had his scouts out too, and they informed him that Custer and the 7th were coming up the Rosebud, looking for him.

Custer had specific instructions from Terry, who was willing to give his young subordinate officer some latitude because of his experience with Indians, but nevertheless he made it clear that if the Indian trail led to the Little Big Horn, Custer must wait for Terry's column to catch up.

Whether in a spirit of bravado or for some other reason, Custer declined to take the Gatling guns with him because, he said, they

would be too difficult to haul over the terrain, nor did he want reinforcements from the 2nd Cavalry which Terry offered. That was a
matter of simple pride. If there was to be a battle, he wanted it to be
the 7th Cavalry's alone. These were fatal decisions. The guns might
have saved his life.

Once he was on his own, Custer moved his column rapidly, covering thirty miles or more in a day. He would have gone faster if it had
not been for the pack train. He found the trail Reno had spotted
without difficulty—it was a half-mile wide—and after following it
for three days, it was plain to his scouts that it led directly into the
Valley of the Little Big Horn.

Now, under Terry's orders, he must wait for the others to catch up
so that the great Indian encampment could be attacked in force. But
instead of turning south, he pressed on. Why? Historians, professional
and amateur, have debated the point to this day. To some he was a
vainglorious man who decided to take the longest possible chance of
winning a victory that would make him famous and redeem him
from those who were always trying to bring his career to a close. To
others he was a brilliant tactician who attempted a maneuver which
ended in total failure. The question can never be decided.

What is clear, however, is that Custer *did* disobey written orders,
and *did* take a chance which, from the advantage of hindsight, seems
almost suicidal. After marching all night on the 24th, he was met by
his scouts who told him that an overwhelming number of Indians were
encamped ahead—far too many for him to cope with. Custer paid no
attention to this warning. One wonders if he would have gone on to
certain death had he known that there were more than 10,000 Sioux
and Cheyenne in the Valley of the Little Big Horn which lay on one
side of the divide, where he had paused. His own fighting strength
was 600 men.

In any case, it was too late to withdraw. The scouts reported that
the Indians knew he was there, and were on his trail. There was still
a way out, although by no means a certain one. He could wait for
Terry and Gibbon to come up, or try to retreat and join them. Neither
alternative would have been consistent with Custer's character.
Gathering his officers around him, he told them his decision, and in
retrospect it seems the worst one he could possibly have made. He
intended to divide his force, he told them. Benteen was to take three
troops and head south, to pinpoint the location of the Indian village.

Then he would advance with five troops, and Reno with three more. Reno would attack the village at once, while Custer came on in support.

With enough men, precise timing, a clear understanding of the enemy's strength and disposition and some knowledge of the battle-ground, Custer's strategy might have succeeded. As strategy, it was sound enough. But all these ingredients were lacking. The only man who truly understood the situation was Custer's half-breed scout, Mitch Bouyer, who tried to tell him what he faced, but Custer would not listen.

The three columns swung out on their separate paths. Even then Custer appears to have changed his mind, after they were out of sight of each other, and swerved his own men around to attack the place where he thought the rear of the enemy's camp might be.

Under the circumstances, the result could only be disastrous. Reno emerged from a defile and found the huge Indian village lying two miles straight ahead. He charged it with his pitifully inadequate force of 112 men. Immediately he was enveloped by more Indians than he had ever seen, as Chief Gall simply overwhelmed him. Reno knew he had to try to fight through, or else make a stand. There was no sign of the support that had been promised him, because Custer was now working his way around to the other side of the village.

Making a quick decision, Reno pulled away a little to a nearby stand of timber beside the river. Miraculously, he had lost only two men thus far, but the casualties were increasing. Again Reno had to decide. He could try to make his stand in the woods, or else fall back across the stream and dig in there, in a position that might possibly be stronger. He decided to fall back, and this decision, like all the others he made, has long been disputed by students of the affair. Some argue that this last decision was the worst, because Reno led the retreat himself and failed to organize a rearguard. The result was a pell-mell, desperate rush, in which some troopers were left in the timber, not having heard the order. Enemy fire also took a heavy toll of the men as they rode down a five-foot bank to the river. By this time the Indians were among the troops, dragging some of them from their saddles. One lieutenant wanted to stop and rally the men in an effort to save some of those in the rear, but Reno would not let him. The retreat plunged on.

Once across the river, the survivors climbed a low hill and Reno made a quick count of his strength. If an accurate count had been made, it would have shown three officers and twenty-nine troopers and scouts already dead, with seven others wounded and fifteen missing.

Custer, in the meantime, had come within sight of the village from the other direction, and had immediately sent back two couriers to Benteen, with instructions to rush up the pack train he had with him, which carried the ammunition. Obeying, Benteen reached the top of a rise and, looking down into the valley, he saw blue uniforms on a hill, surrounded by Indians, and instinctively sent his troops dashing to the rescue. In the dust and smoke he had not seen that this beleaguered force was Reno's, not Custer's. Benteen's added strength and ammunition beat off the attackers momentarily, although Gall was still besieging Reno. Both Majors heard the sound of volleys farther down the valley, and realized that Custer was now also engaged.

Reno had still another decision to make at this point—whether to go to Custer's aid, if he could, or hold his own position. His officers virtually demanded a rescue, and one captain began to move his troops in Custer's direction without orders. Reno gave the command to follow, but reluctantly, and his progress was slow. He not only had to fight off Gall's persistent attacks, but he had to carry his wounded in blankets, and so could move no faster than they could be moved on foot.

In any case, he was too late. Crazy Horse, in command of an army composed mostly of Cheyennes, had completely surrounded Custer. He was soon joined by Gall, who had left part of his force to harass Reno and taken the rest to help Crazy Horse. Little help was needed. The famous Last Stand had begun, and in the heat of the late afternoon it was over, within an hour. Custer and his command of 212 men were dead.

With that, Crazy Horse and Gall wheeled their yelling, triumphant army around to demolish the remainder of the 7th. They rolled Reno's men back to their hill, where they dug in and fought for their lives. Eighteen more men were killed and forty-three wounded by nightfall. Nor did darkness end the battle, so determined was Crazy Horse to annihilate the white man. In the night hours the besieged men could see the Indians silhouetted against their campfires in a frenzied scalp dance. Reno did get unexpected help during the night. The troopers who had been cut off in the timber earlier contrived to get out of their trap and join him.

When morning light came, the battle was still raging. Benteen was now the hero, leading repeated assaults to hurl back the Indians. But with every advantage in numbers, Crazy Horse and Gall still could not break through this stubborn defense and, during the afternoon, they decided to withdraw, strike their tepees and move off. They fired the prairie grass behind them. On the hill, Reno's exhausted men made no attempt to follow the enemy, thankful to survive and in any case suspecting the withdrawal was a ruse.

Next morning, Terry and Gibbon came into view. They were exactly on schedule. Their scouts had told them of the disaster, but Reno did not know of Custer's massacre until Terry relieved him on the hill. In a mood of deepest melancholy the dead were buried, and the sad journey back to Fort Abraham Lincoln began, the wagons bearing fifty-two wounded men.

When news of this defeat reached the public, there was a shocked outcry from newspapers, politicians and citizens. Everyone looked for a scapegoat. There were those who blamed everything on the Indian Bureau's shortsighted policies, and indeed they had contributed to the events that led up to the disaster. The Army was also blamed for what appeared to those back home as inept leadership, because of the lack of coordination among the three columns. Custer, who had been controversial enough while he was alive, was even more so dead. Reno, naturally, came in for a heavy share of censure. General Sherman observed moderately that if the 7th had not split it might have been able to defend itself successfully, although as an experienced officer he was not overly confident of it. President Grant was angry, wrote that he thought the slaughter was entirely unnecessary and blamed Custer for it.

In truth, there was enough blame to go around. But since Major Reno was alive and at the focal point of the dispute, he took the brunt. His career and his life were ruined. Haled before a Court of Inquiry, he defended himself and the Court returned a verdict remarkable for its ambiguity, in which it remarked that "while subordinates, in some instances, did more for the safety of the command than did Major Reno, there was nothing in his conduct that requires animadversion." It sounded like an acquittal, but was it? Certainly it left doubts, and there were many more in the mind of the public. Reno could not go anywhere without being conscious of what people were thinking and saying behind his back. The strain was so great that he fell increasingly into trouble. Once he slandered another officer's wife. Then he began to drink excessively, until at last he was court-martialed twice, and in 1880 was given a dishonorable discharge.

As everyone knows, the only survivor of Custer's last stand was "Comanche," sometimes mistakenly thought to be the General's horse, although he actually belonged to Captain Keogh. To the 7th he became a symbol. No one was permitted to ride him again, but he was led by the bridle in all the regiment's parades until he died in 1891. Today his remains, restored by the taxidermist's art, can be seen in the Smithsonian Institution. Even more durable is the argument over Custer's Last Stand. The literature on it, prickly with controversy, would fill several library shelves.

One thing was clear in the aftermath of the Battle of the Little Big Horn. It had been the Army's worst defeat by Indians since St. Clair's disaster which had so angered President Washington. President Grant was angry too. His orders went down the chain of command, to posts from the Canadian border to Mexico. Every available source of men and materials was to be drawn together in pursuit of the Sioux. Crook was already on their trail, and he was soon joined by Colonel Ronald Mackenzie, come up from the Southwest, and by Colonel Wesley Merritt, who joined in the chase.

Sitting Bull had anticipated this result, and he had evolved a plan to meet it. He had no intention of risking another major battle, because he suspected that the numbers were now on the other side. Instead, he split his triumphant army, which was imbued with a messianic fervor, into several strong bands, each led by able men, and spread them over a wide area.

One of these bands was encountered by Colonel Merritt, as he was riding from Fort Laramie with his crack 5th Cavalry to join Crook. He had been told there were Cheyennes, 1,000 in number, who had just broken away from the reservation and were on their way to join Crazy Horse. Intercepting them, Merritt reversed the usual order of business and set up an ambush, concealing his men in ravines and using the wagon train as bait with 200 infantrymen hidden under the canvas tops. This action took place in southeast South Dakota, near War Bonnet Creek.

The ambush was entirely successful. Hardly believing that a wagon train would be rolling along unescorted, the Cheyennes charged it anyway and fell headlong into the trap. There was a brief skirmish, in which one of Merritt's scouts, Buffalo Bill Cody, killed Chief Yellow Hand in a hand-to-hand fight, and then the Indians broke free and fled, so rapidly they could not be pursued.

Merritt reached Crook a few days later, bringing the General's strength to 2,000 men. These combined forces hurried toward another junction, with General Terry. On the way, what remained of the 7th Cavalry, still commanded by the unfortunate Reno, joined them. Terry's force was nearby, and in combination with Crook, made the army a formidable 4,000 men. There was to be no more splitting up into small units.

The Indians, however, had no intention of challenging so large a force. They moved away steadily while Crook's force endured first a season of heavy rain, then an unexpected cold snap at the end of August. Terry's command, already exhausted, could not endure further marching and had to withdraw, while Crook pressed on. His own men were weary, and their rations were low, but the General was determined. When he was asked if he really meant to march 200 miles with used-up horses and tired infantry and only two-and-a-half-days' rations, Crook replied grimly, "If necessary, we can eat our horses." He meant it.

Soon it came to that point. Captain Anson Mills, with 150 men and the fittest horses remaining, were dispatched toward Deadwood to get fresh supplies before the army succumbed to starvation. On the way, near Slim Buttes, in the northwest corner of South Dakota, Mills encountered a Sioux village and, hungry though he was, he waited through the night in steady rain, until he could strike the village at dawn. He dispatched a rider to Crook telling him of his intention to attack. Caught by surprise, the Indians fled into a dead-end gully, where they dug themselves in, meanwhile shouting that Crazy Horse would rescue them.

Mills had no reason to believe it might not be true, since the sound of firing could easily be heard if there were any Indians nearby. But he examined the village and found it amply stocked with the food the army needed, so he stood firm. Meanwhile, Crook, warned by Mills' message, was coming up. The General reached him before the besieged Sioux could get any reinforcement, and while pickets were posted to look out for Crazy Horse, Crook pressed the attack. The defenders were led by one of Sitting Bull's best chiefs, American Horse, who put up a stiff defense before he was overcome by superior firepower. Mortally wounded, he and his men surrendered.

The hungry soldiers had no more than started to eat from the supplies in the village before Crazy Horse and a Sioux army burst through the pine cover around the village, just as American Horse had promised. The chief was, however, too late. The whites were prepared for him, and after a day of heavy fighting, Crazy Horse had to withdraw. Crook made no effort to pursue. His command was in too depleted a condition. The supplies they had secured were only a stopgap, and he knew he must get to Deadwood. Once more Captain Mills and his squadron rode out ahead, and this time returned with wagons full of bacon, flour, hardtack, coffee and grain for the horses.

If Crook's campaign had thus far produced no decisive result, at least the Indians had made no progress either. Some of their confidence was leaving them. Washington wanted Crook to maintain pressure on them, and that was what Crook wanted to do. This meant a winter campaign. Crook prepared himself for it thoroughly, and for once the government gave him everything he needed. The Indians, on the other hand, were paralyzed by the unusually severe weather, and could scarcely move from their tepees.

Colonel Mackenzie, with ten troops of cavalry, opened the campaign. Riding across the snowy Wyoming prairie, he discovered the village of a Cheyenne chief named Dull Knife, another of Sitting Bull's principal leaders, in the canyon bed of Crazy Woman's Fork, on the Powder River. Mackenzie rode through bitter cold, until on the night of November 25 he was near enough to the canyon to hear victory drums beating. The Cheyennes had just diverted themselves by raiding a Shoshone village.

Following tradition, Mackenzie struck at dawn and achieved his hoped-for surprise. Fighting soon raged up and down the village, and along the sides and rim of the canyon. The Cheyennes were enraged to see their village burning and their pony herd being killed. They fought back with a passionate violence, and for a time seemed to be successful, but the battle was over by the time Crook reached it. He had marched all night—twenty-six miles in twelve hours. Searching the camp, he found several grisly trophies of Custer's debacle.

It was a shattering defeat for the Cheyennes. In winter weather they found themselves destitute, without ponies, food or shelter. Some sought Crazy Horse's village, only to be rebuffed; others holed up wherever they could find a welcome. Many of them died in the paralyzing cold. The majority of them surrendered.

There still remained the primary enemy, the man behind the Sioux revolt—Sitting Bull. In the autumn of 1876, Colonel Miles was on his trail, hanging on persistently while the chief kept moving. At one point Sitting Bull left a characteristic note for the Colonel. "I want to know what you are doing traveling on this road," it read. "You scare all the buffalo away. I want to hunt in this place. I want you to turn back from here. If you don't I'll fight you again. I want you to leave what you have got here, and turn back from here."

After these peremptory orders, the chief had the calm arrogance to sign himself, "I am your friend, Sitting Bull," and he added as an afterthought, "I mean all the rations you have got and some powder. Wish you would write me soon as you can."

Miles may have been bemused by this note, but he pressed on and soon the two forces were near enough so that a fight was inevitable. A parley was called. Sitting Bull and Miles confronted each other, each backed by his own delegation. The chief repeated his demand that the Colonel get out. "Surrender and return to your reservations," Miles replied. Sitting Bull had an answer difficult to top. "Almighty God made me an Indian," he said with dignity, "but not an agency Indian!"

Unable to think of any reply, Miles answered briefly that Sitting Bull had fifteen minutes to surrender or fight. The chief wheeled his pony and galloped away.

Miles was deterred neither by the prairie fire the Sioux set immediately to block his path, nor by the fact that Sitting Bull's forces outnumbered him three to one. He rode through the fire and struck hard at the Indians. In no time he was surrounded by warriors, and was compelled to form a hollow square, in the middle of which he placed his artillery. Once more it was these shells which broke the Indian attack and sent them flying. For forty miles the Colonel's men pursued them.

There was no doubt about this victory. When the battle was well over, 2,000 Sioux came in and surrendered. Sitting Bull fled all the way to Canada.

Crazy Horse was the last to be subdued, and Miles at once set out after him. In his wagon train he had devised another surprise for the Indians. Two of the vehicles concealed field guns, with their crews.

In pursuit of Crazy Horse, the Colonel's infantry had to make its way through deep snow, but at last it caught up with the Indians on January 7, 1877, capturing a few relatives of the principal chiefs, who were important enough to provoke a rescue attack that night. Miles beat off this attack, but next morning it was renewed. The cliffs above the Colonel swarmed with warriors, and one of them, probably Crazy Horse, shouted, "You have had your last breakfast."

The Colonel knew it might be true. There were at least a thousand Sioux, and he did not have the strength to outflank them. He would have to assault them frontally. The Sioux were so confident of the result that they let the charging soldiers get much closer than they would ordinarily, and at that point, Miles disclosed the surprise in his covered supply wagons. Only Crazy Horse's firm control of his men prevented them from bolting at the first volley.

The major assault was made by Major James S. Casey and his men, who were weighed down by their buffalo coats but nevertheless struggled up a steep bluff and met the Sioux in vicious hand-to-hand combat at the top. The battle swayed back and forth briefly, until Chief Big Crow, leading the Indians at that strong point, fell dead and the Sioux line broke.

It was like a signal. The whole Indian defense fell apart and the warriors began to disappear in a snowstorm which had enveloped the battlefield. Miles pursued them relentlessly. One by one, the bands gave up. Unbelievably, Crazy Horse himself surrendered, but he broke away again later and had to be recaptured. Thrown into the guardhouse, and realizing that his freedom had ended, he pulled out a knife and tried to hack his way to freedom again. In the ensuing scuffle, he was killed by his own knife, some say accidentally. "One of the great soldiers of this day and generation," remarked one of the officers who had fought him, and so he may have been.

The end of Miles' campaign was the end of the Sioux uprising. Only a year after the defeat at Little Big Horn, it was over. Sitting Bull, surrendering in July, 1881, after an escape to Canada and a later return, somehow became in the public eye the real Indian hero of these wars, although Crazy Horse deserved the honor far more. All this was small consolation to the medicine man, who brooded in his cabin on the Standing Rock Reservation for ten years after his surrender. Writers made up all manner of stories about him—that he was a West Point graduate, a scholar, a linguist, a Mason and a Catholic. In reality, he was a shrewd opportunist, an adroit politician and a near illiterate who could not even spell his own name. His bizarre and inglorious death waited for another event.

Meanwhile, night drew on for all the Indian nations.

# 14 ★ ★ ★ ★ ★ ★

# Last Stands

AMONG THE "LAST STANDS" of the Western tribes, nothing could match for pathos or waste of human resources the story of the Nez Percé Indians, which was unfolding while the narrative of the Sioux was coming to its melancholy closing chapter.

These were Indians who could say truthfully that they had always been the white man's friend. When Lewis and Clark met them on the way West, they were welcomed rather than menaced, and so it was when Frémont passed their way. The Nez Percé had never killed a white man nor broken a promise.

In 1863 the government sought to move the tribe from its homeland in the Wallowa Valley, in eastern Oregon, to the Lapwai Reservation in northwest Idaho. Their chief, Hinmaton-Yalakrit, whose name meant "thunder coming from the water up over the land," known as Joseph, protested the move, but at the same time entered a claim arguing that the Stevens Treaty of 1855 had extended the boundaries of this reservation all the way to the tribe's Oregon home. President Grant conceded this was true, in an executive order signed on June 16, 1873, but only two years later the order was revoked, the Wallowa Valley declared in the public domain, and therefore open to settlers.

Unlike other tribes when such flagrant treaty-breaking occurred, Joseph did not lead his people in an uprising. He tried to persuade the government by every peaceable means possible to restore the tribe's rights, but he reached an impasse in 1877 when brutal settlers, impatient because the Indians still occupied the land, killed two of them. That was too much for the young braves, although Joseph would have endured even this cruelty. These young men, without authorization from the chief, went on the warpath and massacred a score of settlers, whereupon General O. O. Howard was instructed "to occupy the Wallowa Valley in the interest of peace." Joseph believed he now had no honorable alternative but to fight.

The young leader, who had been chief since his father died in 1873, was only thirty-seven years old. Growing up in a peaceful tribe, he had never so much as seen a battle. The forces available to him were sadly inadequate, no more than 300 men. Joseph, however, was a natural leader, a military man of remarkable native talents, like so many of the Indian chiefs. In his first skirmish with General Howard, his little force beat off a much superior army of white men. But even after he had repeated these small victories, Joseph understood that it would be futile to try to confront the American Army for long. He was well aware of what had happened to the Plains Indians. The alternative was retreat—not to a better strategic position, but out of the country, to Canada, where he could hope to reestablish the tribe in the wild, unsettled Western wilderness.

Thus began what must be one of the most extraordinary retreats in military history. It started when Captain David Perry, with three officers and ninety troopers of the 1st Cavalry, rode out of Fort Lapwai, Idaho, to punish the Nez Percé for the massacre and drive them out of the Wallowa Valley. In two days they had marched seventy miles when they camped on the night of June 17, 1877, near White Bird Canyon. Joseph, whose camp was in the gorge, had been apprised of their approach by his scouts, and had already sent the women, children and pony herd down the Salmon River. When Perry made his expected dawn attack, Joseph was waiting in ambush for him. When the troopers deployed after the first volley, Joseph would have enveloped the column's flanks if Perry had not quickly ordered a retreat. At that, he lost more than fifty per cent of his men and barely made his escape. Joseph pursued only a short way. His strategy was retreat.

General Howard now took the field, with 277 men supported by a howitzer and two Gatling guns. Arriving at the Salmon River, they found Joseph in position on the mountains opposite. That left Howard in a dilemma. If he tried to cross the river he would be exposed on the other side to Joseph's direct assault. Moreover, the chief's auxiliary, another band of Nez Percé under Chief Looking Glass, might well slip in behind him. The General decided to take the chance, but after his troops had crossed the river and struggled up the muddy, slippery slopes on the other side in a drenching rain, they found their quarry gone. It was an exasperated Howard who took up the trail once more.

Chief Joseph

Meanwhile, he had dispatched Captain Stephen S. Whipple, with two troops and a Gatling gun, to hunt down Looking Glass. By accident the captain stumbled upon this chief and managed to capture 600 of his ponies, but Looking Glass escaped. Before Whipple could follow, he was trapped by Joseph, who had worked around behind him and nearly overwhelmed the troops before Howard came up. Joseph resumed his retreat.

It was slowly dawning on Howard and the other white commanders that in Joseph they were facing a leader worthy of their best talents. The chief was always tantalizingly out of their reach except when he chose to turn and fight, and then it was always at a place of his choosing, and naturally the most advantageous for the Indians.

One of these places was reached on July 11, when Howard caught up again and, for the first time, was able to fight something like a regulation battle. It was not a heartening experience. Like the Modocs, the Nez Percé were expert shots and they proved it in this engagement. Not only did they repulse Howard's men with considerable loss, but pinned them down when they sought cover. Again, Joseph launched his favorite flanking maneuver, on both sides. In one of these the General lost his pack train. The other attack overran the artillery, which Joseph dragged away and left useless.

In the morning the Indians began their fire again, but the complexion of the struggle changed when Lieutenant Charles F. Humphrey and eleven men made a heroic dash to recapture the cannon, and returned dragging them behind, along with four wounded men. Three others had been killed.

As always, artillery was decisive. Howard drove off the Nez Percé while his cavalry under Captain Marcus P. Miller turned the left flank of the Indians and bore down on their rear. Joseph did not panic. His braves countercharged and drove off the horsemen, while his riflemen prevented Howard from taking advantage of the situation and provided a cover until the Indians could get across the river and into new positions.

Thus ended the Battle of Clearwater, as it was later called. The Nez Percé had been damaged, but they were able to resume their retreat in good order, while Howard was once more cast in the role of pursuer. Joseph's rearguard fought a continuing series of skirmishes as the Indians made their way through the Kamai Valley, then up the Lo-Lo Trail into the Bitter Root Mountains, where the terrain was, in General Sherman's words, "one of the worst trails for man or beast on this continent." Deep ravines cut through it, and boulders and fallen trees made a tangled mass.

It was much easier for Indians to traverse this kind of territory and Joseph got away to a two- or three-day lead while Howard and his men struggled over the rough country. There was one enemy, however, that Joseph could not control. By this time the telegraph had penetrated even this wild region, and Howard sent ahead orders to intercept the Nez Percé.

This task fell to Captain Charles C. Rawn, who had fifty regulars and a hundred civilian volunteers in the force which he rushed to the pass where the Nez Percé would have to come out of the Bitter Root Mountains. There he put up a fortification and waited. When Joseph appeared, he sent a courier ahead to demand passage, promising at the same time that he would not harm any settlers in his path. Rawn refused, and Joseph instructed his sharpshooters to pin down the whites in their fortification, while the remainder of his band circled it by secret trails and came down into the valley beyond. He kept his word about the settlers who lived there.

In relatively open country again, Joseph moved rapidly now. He came out of the Rockies and stopped in Big Hole Basin, Montana, for a few days' rest, confident that he had left Howard far behind. He did not yet understand that the General was again telegraphing ahead.

The second officer to respond to these messages was Colonel John Gibbon, who rode out of Helena with 200 infantry in wagons, and one howitzer. His campaign proved to be nearly a disaster for Joseph, who had posted no sentries, thinking he was safe.

Joseph found himself surprised by Gibbon in the customary dawn attack. In twenty minutes he had lost his camp. But the resourceful chief managed to get his sharpshooters into the thickets beside the river, and from there they poured in such a deadly fire that the troops could not advance, and in fact had to stand off repeated counter-charges from the Nez Percé, which soon became hand-to-hand combats.

Suffering heavy losses, Gibbon retreated to a knoll and sent a messenger to Howard for help. All afternoon he held off Joseph's repeated assaults until nightfall. His wagon train, carrying the howitzer, had not reached him. It was camped five miles away that night and, when it started to join Gibbon on the following morning, Joseph discovered it and sent thirty braves, who beat off the gunners and captured the howitzer, which they disabled. Then they departed, taking 2,000 rounds of precious ammunition with them.

On the knoll, Gibbon's plight was desperate. His men were reduced to eating raw horsemeat, until a Sergeant, Milton K. Wilson,

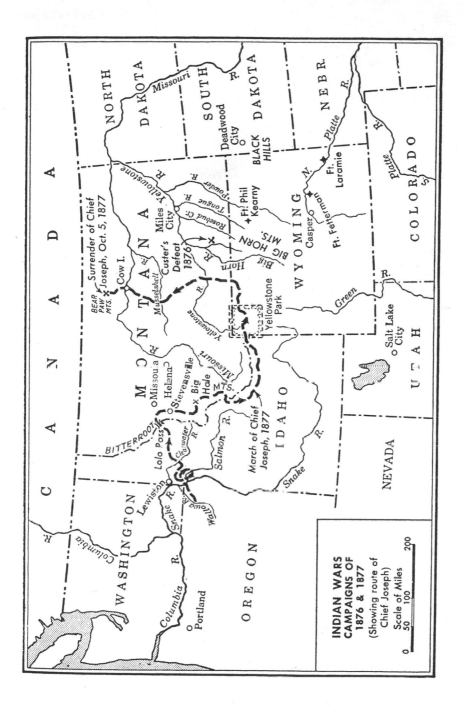

INDIAN WARS
CAMPAIGNS OF
1876 & 1877
(Showing route of
Chief Joseph)

Scale of Miles

0   50   100   200

penetrated the Nez Percé lines and was able to bring up the wagons. The siege dragged on through the following day. Gibbon could not move under the penetrating fire of the Indian sharpshooters, and the Colonel himself was hit in the thigh. When a strong wind came up, Joseph took advantage of it to fire the grass, and when fire and smoke rolled up the knoll, with the Indians behind it, the prospects for another massacre seemed almost inevitable. But then Joseph's luck deserted him. The wind died suddenly, then shifted, and began to blow the other way, killing the fire in its own ashes.

Howard reached the besieged troops on the third day, but Joseph's scouts had warned him. The retreat was under way again. It had been an expensive siege for the Indians. Joseph had lost eighty-nine of his people, some of them women and children, while the Army counted twenty-nine killed and forty wounded. But the Nez Percé had escaped, and were on their way to Canada, while Gibbon's force was too exhausted to pursue and Howard had to take the trail again.

Trying to anticipate where the Indian leader would go, the General decided the chief would travel by way of Yellowstone Park. In an attempt to cut him off, Howard sent a detachment under Lieutenant George R. Bacon on ahead to Tacher's Pass. The Lieutenant reached the pass, held it for two days and retired without seeing an Indian. Once more Joseph had outsmarted his pursuers. His scouts had reported Bacon's maneuver, and when he learned that Howard was encamped, with his army depleted, the chief executed a truly brilliant deception. Forming forty-five of his warriors in columns of fours, just like a cavalry troop, he moved up to Howard's lines in the middle of the night, and the sentry, thinking Bacon was returning, permitted them to go through. They were well beyond him before he realized what he had done and gave the alarm.

By that time Joseph and his party had fallen on the camp, driven off all the pack mules and a good part of the horses and galloped off. Three troops, saddling hastily, gave chase, as Joseph had anticipated. Dividing his forces in three, he let his pursuers ride into a trap. Two of the troops managed to retreat. The third was cut off and surrounded, and nearly exterminated before Howard and the others could get there. And again Joseph had slipped off and headed for the pass which Bacon had now vacated. Howard could not follow him until he had rounded up his pack mules.

Joseph and his column rode rapidly through the Yellowstone. Odd as it may seem, the region was already a place where camping parties came to hunt and enjoy the scenery. The retreating Nez Percé encountered two of them, killing three men and wounding two others. This, as it proved, was a mistake because it told Howard, who was following, where the chief was and in what direction he was headed. That gave the General the opportunity to use the telegraph lines again, and now troops began to close in on Joseph from every direction. The 5th Cavalry was on its way from the Little Big Horn country, and Colonel Samuel D. Sturgis hurried up with six troops of the 7th, reconstituted by this time. As for Howard, he still followed doggedly along Joseph's trail.

The Nez Percé were now not far from the Canadian border, but Joseph's scouts reported to him erroneously that the shortest and best trail was blocked by a concentration of troops, although it was actually only a small cavalry detachment. This proved to be a vital mistake. Joseph made a spectacular maneuver, turning his warriors into a long, difficult detour, leaving a twisting, tangled trail behind him. This trick, while it was successful, slowed him down just enough so that he was compelled to halt at Canyon Creek and do battle once more with his pursuers. Through the long day of September 13, he stood off Howard and Sturgis and their 350 troops, but in the process he lost twenty-nine more men, besides 900 ponies. Nevertheless, when night came he was able to slip away again, leaving his exhausted attackers behind. His destination now was the Bear Paw Mountains, only thirty miles from the border. When he reached them, he paused on the northern slope of the mountains, on Snake Creek.

With victory in sight, Joseph had overlooked one possibility, and it proved to be fatal. He believed that all his pursuers were directly behind him, but there was another he did not know about. It was a column out of Fort Keogh, Wyoming, under the command of that veteran Indian fighter, Colonel Miles. Sturgis had sent couriers to Miles, apprising him of Joseph's possible route and urging him to cut off the chief if he could. Miles was on the march at once with an impressive force consisting of six companies of the 5th Infantry, some mounted; two troops of the 2nd Cavalry; three troops of the 2nd Infantry; two field guns; and a covey of white and Indian scouts. For such a large command, it moved incredibly fast—267 miles in twelve days. On September 30, in the cold, stormy morning light, he came upon Joseph's camp, in a ravine shaped like a crescent. Without any preliminaries, the Colonel attacked.

There has since been speculation that Joseph had misjudged his position and thought he was already in Canada. Otherwise one could not account for the failure of this magnificent strategist to post sentries. The Indians never saw the attacking troops until they were almost upon them. They had only time to reach the adjacent ridges, leaving behind what remained of their pony herd. A charge by the 7th up one ridge was repulsed with heavy loss; two officers who had survived the Little Big Horn were severely wounded, and all but one officer was killed or wounded. There were fifty casualties all told among the 115 who made the assault.

While he was repulsing the 7th, Joseph converted his position into a fort, his warriors digging in with knives, tomahawks, even frying pans. He managed to slip out a messenger to Sitting Bull's camp, only a day's march away, urging him to come and help. Miles, too, had sent for reinforcements, scenting the kill. Meanwhile he brought up his field gun. Joseph held out stubbornly, hoping that Sitting Bull would arrive and fall upon the enemy's rear, but the medicine man, who was already in Canada, had no taste for further conflict at the moment, and merely moved farther away, out of danger.

Hopelessly outnumbered and trapped at last, Joseph nevertheless held out stubbornly for four days. Then a white flag appeared above his trenches and a brave brought down a surrender message.

Tell General Howard that I know his heart [Joseph wrote]. What he told me before I have in my heart. I am tired of fighting. Our chiefs are killed. Looking Glass is dead. Too-hul-sul-suit is dead. The old men are all dead. It is now the young men who say yes or no. He who led the young men [Joseph's brother, Ollicut] is dead. It is cold and we have no blankets. The little children are freezing to death. My people— some of them have run away to the hills, and have no blankets, no food. I want to have time to look for my children and see how many of them I can find; maybe I shall find them among the dead. Hear me, my chiefs, my heart is sick and sad. From where the sun now stands, I will fight no more forever.

A present-day historian describes how Joseph looked as he rode into Miles' camp on October 5:

His scalp lock was tied with otter fur. The rest of his hair hung in thick plaits on each side of his head. He wore buckskin leggings and a gray woolen shawl through which could be seen the marks of four or five bullet-holes received in the last fight. His head and wrist were also scratched by bullets. He gave his rifles to Miles, then smiled as he shook hands with Howard.

Howard had little reason to return the smile at that moment. Miles had lost 20 per cent of his command, while only seventeen of the Nez Percé had died in the last battle. Nevertheless the General gave his adversary a military man's tribute: "Chief Joseph was the highest type of Indian I have ever known, very handsome, kind, and brave." The white commanders could not help but have the highest respect for what Joseph had done, in a military sense. He had traversed more than 2,000 miles of the most difficult terrain in the country, meanwhile holding off more than 2,000 white soldiers. In doing so, he had killed 176 of them and wounded 140 others. Of his own meager force, which had never exceeded 300 warriors, he had lost 151 killed and eighty-nine wounded, and had won three of the five battles in which he had been engaged. One of the other two was a stalemate.

The Nez Percé were taken to a reservation in a part of the country strange to them, in Indian Territory. Many of them became sick and died there. Joseph continued to do everything he could for them as long as he lived, and in time the government permitted him the privilege of meeting President Theodore Roosevelt. But it did not do for him what would have been far easier, to let him and his people live out their years in their own beloved valley. It was one more expression of the government's reservation policy, which can only be called barbaric. In the West, the attitude toward Indians was cruel and vindictive. In the East, it was largely one of indifference. Consequently the reservations became the ghettoes they remain today.

After Joseph's defeat, there were only a few pockets of Indian resistance remaining, but they seemed inordinately troublesome in 1878. Carl Schurz was the new head of the Indian Bureau, and he was instituting long-overdue reforms in it, but they had not yet had time to take effect. There were still 375,000 Indians under Army control, and in places that control was precarious. In the Northwest, for example, the Bannock Indians were pushed into revolt by a clerk's error in transcribing a treaty which removed the Bannocks, so the clerk

nez Percé

wrote, from "Kansas Prairie" country. It should have read "Camas Prairie," from the camas root, which was the chief food supply of these Indians. To remove them from it might mean starvation, but the Bureau did not see or understand its error and insisted the Bannocks be removed. Revolt was inevitable.

It was a small war, as the Indian Wars went, but the Bannocks were encouraged by what Chief Joseph had done to the white man, and with the addition of several hundred Piutes, they thought their chief, Buffalo Horn, might do as much for them. General Howard was called to put out that brush fire, too. This time he moved quickly enough to prevent any consolidation of the revolt with other restless tribes in the Northwest.

His pursuit of the Bannocks was interrupted briefly by an episode strange to these wars. Captain Reuben F. Bernard, of the 1st Cavalry, was approached one day by the daughter of a Piute chief, Sarah Winnemucca, known both to him and Howard as a bright, pretty Indian girl of good education. She told Bernard that her father and part of his tribe had changed their minds about fighting the army, but were being held by the Bannocks. She wanted Bernard to help her arrange the escape of these Piutes, and thwart the Bannocks if they tried to follow. She outlined her plan, the Captain approved it and Sarah carried it off without a hitch. That exploit was enough to earn her a job as Howard's interpreter. Later she married an Army lieutenant and in time came to be well known in the West as a lecturer, writer and teacher.

Howard was able to subdue the Bannocks after two heavy skirmishes, one of which was distinguished by a miniature naval action as the fleeing tribesmen tried to cross the Columbia River into Washington Territory. Three small steamers interrupted the Indians' fording of the river, landed troops as though they were Marines, and did considerable damage to the refugees before they got away.

Eventually the Bannocks returned to their reservation, with a loss of eight warriors in their war. It had cost the United States nine soldiers, thirty-one civilians and a half-million dollars.

The Bannocks were no more than subdued before there was another outbreak in 1879, an obscure conflict known as the Sheepeaters' War. A small contingent of Bannocks was involved in this episode, too, along with Shoshones and outcasts from other tribes who lived in central Idaho, in a mountain wilderness. These people were called Sheepeaters because they were celebrated as hunters of the splendid and wily mountain sheep. As long as they stayed among the crags, these Indians were inconspicuous enough, but in 1879 they began to raid the valleys, with the usual result.

Again it was General Howard who undertook the job, this time with only two small columns at his disposal. Captain Bernard led one of the columns and suffered a miserable experience in the mountains when his men came down with fever and a variety of afflictions, which he had to doctor himself because there was no surgeon in the party. The second column, under Lieutenant Henry Catley, was trapped by the Sheepeaters on a narrow trail and narrowly escaped.

Bernard finally made his way through the mountains and abruptly descended the other side—as he put it, "from ten feet of snow to roses and rattlesnakes." He fought a sharp skirmish with the Sheepeaters, and other units of the cavalry came on to harass the Indians so mercilessly that they surrendered in September.

In that same year, the Army was also busy in Colorado, where the Utes were the troublesome tribe at the moment. It had been a question of the discovery of silver and lead on their lands, a sudden influx of miners and war when the government attempted to move the Indians. The Indian agent there, N. C. Meeker, who had done much to convert the Utes to self-supporting status as stock raisers and farmers, was renounced by the Indians in spite of all his efforts. A column commanded by Major Thomas T. Thornburg came to put down the revolt, and was set upon in Red Canyon by 400 Utes, who killed the Major and inflicted heavy casualties, firing from the ridges down into the column. Besieged on three sides and with the river behind them, the troops were nearly burned to death when the Utes set the sagebrush on fire. They beat out the flaming wagons and had barely caught their breath when the Utes launched another attack at dusk, which came within forty yards of the defenders before it was beaten back. Four volunteers slipped through the Indian lines to get help. After they had gone, the Utes shot all the remaining horses and next day skirmished their way to within fifty yards of the defenders. But all four volunteers got through, and Captain Francis S. Dodge, with a troop of the Negro 9th Cavalry, arrived in time to bolster the defense. Then they, too, were pinned down in the blistering heat, with the stench of three hundred dead horses in their nostrils and the moans of forty-one wounded men in their ears. They broiled in the sand pit where they lay, and waited for more help.

Colonel Wesley Merritt, at Fort D. A. Russell, in Wyoming, got their call and came to the rescue, in a forced march that covered 160 miles in forty-eight hours. His arrival broke the siege and scattered the Utes. When Merritt moved on to the agency, he found Meeker and his male employees dead and mutilated. The women and children had been carried away, but were finally returned by the Indians. Those who had ravished the women, in the manner of these southwestern tribes, were sent to Leavenworth prison. The other Utes were removed to another reservation.

Not unexpectedly, the Apaches were nearly the last Indians to be conquered. They had been quiet for some time, under the beneficent influence of George Crook, but after the General left as commander of the Department of Arizona, corruption set in. Indians and white men combined in what was called the "Tucson Ring," composed of thieving contractors, dishonest Indian agents, peddlers of whiskey and gun-runners. The Apaches, of course, were the recipients of both the rifles and liquor. This Tucson Ring, or Indian Ring, as it was also called, had influence all the way up to the Indian Bureau itself. As a result, the Apaches were not only corrupting but were the victims of corruption. Bands began to break away from the reservations, and the territory began to slip into its former bloody state. Plunder, torture and indiscriminate murder were once more the order of the day.

Victorio, a new and talented Apache chief, led the Army on a chase almost as spectacular as Joseph's, through Arizona, New Mexico and Texas. Five cavalry troops were pursuing him in constant frustration. Posses of Texas Rangers and cowboys failed to trap him. Victorio was always mobile, because he was constantly stealing fresh horses from ranches. He never turned to fight unless there was no way to avoid it, and then he chose his own ground and fought on his own terms. The cavalrymen began to have a reluctant affection for their adroit adversary, and called him "Old Vic." When the troops got too close, "Old Vic" simply crossed into Mexico and reappeared somewhere else along the border. The Mexicans did not tolerate him; they, too, sent punitive expeditions after him, with no better success. Victorio annihilated one such party, waited for the relief to show up, and destroyed that one too.

It took two years of the most concentrated effort to trap Victorio, by a combined American-Mexican expedition which finally brought him to bay in a box canyon of the Tres Castillos Mountains of

Mexico. Before the trap was sprung, the Mexican commander insisted on doing the job himself. The American troops could not go, he said; their Apache scouts could not be trusted not to join the enemy. Since it was Mexican territory, the American commander had to comply. It mattered little to "Old Vic" in the end. He and his men died fighting.

Victorio was succeeded by an entirely different personality, Nana, a grizzled seventy-year-old Apache who was troubled with rheumatism but little else. From July, 1881, to April, 1882, he emulated his predecessor and led the Army another chase of 1,000 miles, fighting eight battles with them en route, and leaving behind him a bloody wake of murdered ranchers, prospectors and settlers. He, too, fled to Mexico, and there made common cause with the toughest chief of them all, Geronimo.

Other chiefs began to emulate Victorio's and Nana's example, and they were joined by Nock-ay-del-Klinne, a medicine man who asserted he could bring the dead to life. His camp was filled with a fanatical, wild-eyed band of converts who fought for him with madness in their eyes. He was captured at last on the reservation by a young lieutenant who was attacked while he was trying to get his prisoner back to Fort Apache, after his own Apache scouts mutinied. Acting on the specific instructions of his superiors, a sergeant shot the medicine man through the head when the attack occurred. After it had been beaten off, a burial detail was about to bury the victims when Sergeant Joseph A. Smith, in charge of it, witnessed the grisly spectacle of the medicine man, who appeared to be resurrected by his own boasted powers, with three bullets in his head, trying to drag himself away through the brush. Smith prepared to shoot him, but rather than alarm the camp, he picked up an axe and finished the old man with two blows.

The column returned to find Fort Apache itself under siege. A sortie from the fort, after being warned of the column's approach by a brave sergeant, saved both the troops and the installation. Some of the mutinous Apache scouts were hanged; the others were sent to Alcatraz.

Thus the war against the Apaches went on. The exploits of both sides have been recounted in literally hundreds of books and stories. In the lengthy, drawn-out struggle, lives and dollars were poured into the campaigns until, in 1882, the government called on General Crook to put an end to it. Returning to his old post in Arizona Territory, the General was now in effect the chief representative of the Army, the Indian Bureau and Federal law.

From the vantage point of his famous riding mule, "Apache," Crook began by learning everything he could about the situation through riding from reservation to reservation and listening to the grievances of the Indians—something nobody else had done. Protected only by a small escort, he even rode boldly into the mountains to talk to known hostile chiefs in their villages. Only his reputation for fair dealing saved him from death.

When he had heard everyone's story, Crook took the actions that should have been taken long before. He used his troops to remove all the miners, squatters and ranchers who were trespassing on the reservations. Using his governmental powers, he extinguished the corruption in the Indian agencies. Then he turned the Apaches back to their crops and stock.

By these humane and sensible steps, Crook put down the revolt without bloodshed, except for 500 diehards who would never have anything to do with white men under any circumstances. These were the Chiricahuas, led by such chiefs as Geronimo, Chatto and Natchez. They made their headquarters in the Sierra Madre Mountains of Mexico, and came out only to conduct raids across the border, and to try to persuade other tribes to revolt.

Crook's campaign against these holdouts was conducted with the aid of the pack trains he had made famous before, and several companies of Apache scouts which he organized and placed under the command of experienced officers. It was a highly mobile army, this "native infantry," and in the summer of 1883, Crook made effective use of it, aided by a treaty with Mexico which enabled him to cross the border freely. It was a short, sharp campaign, but it ended with the surrender of 285 Indians and, in the end, the collapse of Geronimo and his band. Later they bolted from the reservation, after getting drunk on beer they had made themselves, and fled back to Mexico.

Geronimo at liberty was, as General Miles once put it, "the worst Indian who ever lived," and certainly one of the most dangerous. Crook went after him and ran him to earth. In the surrender parley that followed, the General informed Geronimo that if he refused to

come in, he meant to destroy him if it took fifty years. An agreement
was made and the march back began, but in the night a bootlegger
made his way into the camp, and got Geronimo and his band drunk.
They changed their minds again, sneaked out of camp and fled back
to the Sierra Madres.

geronimo

General Miles was called to the command, after a dispute between
Sheridan and Crook over the terms that the General had made with
Geronimo. Miles had 5,000 men and a signaling device, the helio-
graph, which the Apaches had seen before but not in such quantity.
Until now they had hacked down the Army's telegraph poles and

stolen the wire. Miles circumvented them by setting up twenty-seven interlocking heliostations on mountain peaks, a system of communication so efficient that the General could proceed with confidence.

In spite of Miles' formidable force, the hunt for Geronimo soon became old-fashioned guerrilla warfare. These thousands of troopers were in pursuit of no more than eighty Indians. At that, it took sixteen months to trap Geronimo. But surrender he did, after Miles sent him an ultimatum, on the promise that the Apaches would not be separated from their families. This agreement was promptly repudiated by the government, and while Miles protested, as Crook had before him, he was simply ignored.

As though to signal the end of all Indian resistance, there was a solar eclipse on January 1, 1889. "The day the sun died," the Indians called it, in their terror at the event. The phenomenon excited the superstitious everywhere, including Wavoka, the medicine man of the Nevada Piutes, who chose the moment to announce that this was a sign from the Great Spirit that he, Wavoka, had been chosen to lead the Indians out of bondage, into a new world free of white men, where the Indian dead would be resurrected and the buffalo restored to the plains. In anticipation of that day, Wavoka prescribed a ghost dance, a ceremonial dance. Those who participated in the dance could be sure, he said, that white men's bullets would never pierce the shirts they wore when they danced.

Like the twist and its infinite variations in our own time, the ghost dance spread among the Indians until it became a cult. It was particularly seized upon by the Sioux, who danced until they fell in an exhausted frenzy or went into trances, muttering messages from their ancestors.

Sitting Bull, who had returned from Canada to brood in defeat and retirement, saw in Wavoka and his ghost dance a final opportunity to confound the white man. He had no real faith in such superstition himself, but he knew how to use it to play upon the minds of the gullible and excite their emotions. In his camp on the Grand River, he fanned the flames of the new religion until by November, 1889, it had taken on the alarming proportions of an uprising, serious enough for President Harrison to order the War Department to take whatever steps were necessary. The Indian agent at the Standing Rock Reservation counseled doing nothing. Let the Indians dance themselves out, he said, and the fad would pass. As usual, no one listened to this sensible advice. General Miles was ordered to move a large number of troops into the area.

It was Miles' idea to arrest Sitting Bull, and circumvent the trouble he was sure the old medicine man was causing. McLaughlin, the agent, agreed but it would not be an easy task, with several thousand fanatical Sioux about. On December 14, 1890, forty uniformed Indian police, under Lieutenant Bull Head, came to Sitting Bull's camp, surrounded his cabin and arrested him.

Sitting Bull permitted himself to be led out of the cabin quietly enough, but outside there were 160 armed ghost dancers who appeared to be waiting for some sign from him. That was all he needed. He yelled to them for help. At that moment one of the crowd, an old enemy of Bull Head's named Catch-the-Bear, seized his opportunity and shot the Lieutenant. As he fell, and following instructions, Bull Head put a slug into Sitting Bull's body, and at the same time another policeman, Red Tomahawk, who was walking behind the prisoner, put another shot in his head. A shot from the crowd killed a second policeman, Shave Head. The other Indian police held their ground against the ghost dancers until help came up—two troops of the 8th Cavalry.

The death of any other chief might have meant a more serious revolt, but Sitting Bull had lost so much of his influence and prestige that there was no immediate, violent response to his death. Nevertheless Miles moved all the troops he had available into the Sioux country. In spite of these precautions some of the Sioux began to slip away from the reservations into the Badlands. One of these bands was a substantial force under Chief Big Foot, but a column of cavalry pursued him and compelled him to surrender. Most of his band escaped, and were hunted down by the 7th Cavalry. Rounded up once more, they were about to be marched back to the reservation, but in the morning as the squaws were packing up, it was not clear whether they were really preparing to go back to the reservation or laying the groundwork for another escape, even though the camp was surrounded by troops and under the guns of a battery. Colonel James W. Forsyth, who was commanding, decided to take no chances and ordered the band disarmed.

Instructed to turn over their weapons, the sullen warriors produced only a few broken carbines, and Forsyth could get nothing more out of them. He ordered the camp searched. That produced a quantity of guns and ammunition which the squaws were hiding, and Forsyth was led to believe there might be more beneath the blankets of the warriors. He ordered them searched.

What followed might have been inspired by simple resentment on the part of a proud people. Most likely it was a result of the fanaticism generated by the ghost dancers; there were many of them in the tribe. Jumping to his feet, a medicine man shrieked the litany of the dancers: no white man's bullets could penetrate their ghost shirts. At that four braves jumped up, tossed off their blankets and brandished rifles. Others followed, one Sioux fired a shot, and with that the troopers sent a fusillade crashing into the Indians. Almost toe-to-toe, the Sioux and the soldiers shot it out. When this first exchange was over, nine troopers were killed and eleven wounded. Big Foot was dead, too, and so was the medicine man. Only inaccurate firing on both sides prevented a worse slaughter, but even so, women and children began to fall as the Sioux broke through the soldiers' lines and the battle spread out over the prairie.

Forsyth unlimbered his artillery and, as might be expected, the temper of the contest changed. It had begun at nine in the morning. Six hours later it was over, with thirty killed and thirty-four wounded on the Army's side. For the Sioux, it amounted to a massacre. They had lost 143 killed and thirty-three wounded.

There was an immediate public controversy over this event. Newspapers called it the 7th Cavalry's revenge for Custer, and there were several official investigations. The wide variance in what they concluded depended on who was conducting the inquiry. The Army investigated itself, and General E. D. Scott, reviewing the evidence, wrote:

> There is nothing to conceal or apologize for in the Wounded Knee Battle—beyond the killing of a wounded buck by a hysterical recruit. The firing was begun by the Indians and continued until they stopped—with the one exception noted above. That women and children were casualties was unfortunate but unavoidable, and most must have been from Indian bullets . . . The Indians at Wounded Knee brought on their

own destruction as surely as any people ever did. Their attack on the troops was as treacherous as any in the history of Indian warfare, and that they were under a strange religious hallucination is only an explanation, not an excuse.

On the other hand, a government investigator who was certainly not an Indian partisan, reported:

The terrible effect may be judged from the fact that one woman survivor, Blue Whirlwind, with whom the author conversed, received fourteen wounds, while each of her two little boys were also wounded by her side. In a few minutes two hundred Indian men, women and children, with sixty soldiers, were lying dead and wounded on the ground, the tepees had been torn down by the shells and some of them were burning above the helpless wounded, and the surviving handful of Indians were flying in wild panic to the shelter of the ravine, pursued by hundreds of maddened soldiers and followed up by a raking fire from the Hotchkiss guns, which had been moved into position to sweep the ravine. There can be no question that the pursuit was simply a massacre, where fleeing women, with infants in their arms, were shot down after resistance had ceased and when almost every warrior was stretched dead or dying on the ground.

A noted historian of the Indian in our own time, Oliver La Farge, has remarked that it was entirely typical of the white man that the incident in the Battle of the Little Big Horn has become famous in American history as the Custer massacre, but the slaughter by Forsyth's men is known officially as the Battle of Wounded Knee.

There were scattered repercussions among the Indians. An agency was attacked by a force of Sioux under Two Strike, and another band attacked Forsyth before he could return from Wounded Knee. He was saved from annihilation by the timely arrival of the Negro 9th Cavalry, under Major Guy V. Henry. There were sporadic outbreaks for a month after the massacre, and then resistance among the Sioux ended abruptly.

Wavoka, the man who started it all, was aghast at the bloody consequences of his new religion. He took off his broad-brimmed black hat and replaced it with a blanket over his head, in the traditional Indian gesture of mourning. His people had "twisted things," he said. It was better to forget. Like a prophet of old, Wavoka walked among his people, a pathetic, frail figure, crying out: "Hoo-oo! My children, my children. In days behind many times I called you to travel the hunting trail or to follow the war trail. Now those trails are choked with sand; they are covered with grass, the young men cannot find them. My children, today I call upon you to travel a new trail, the only trail now open—the White Man's Road . . ."

With few exceptions, that was the road they traveled. Ironically, the last uprising to be recorded, in 1911, involved the Shoshones, who had the most peaceful history of all the tribes, and who had always been the white man's friend. Their brief flurry, in Humboldt County, Nevada, ended with another massacre. A sheriff's posse hunted down the small band which had killed several stockmen, and slaughtered every one of them except a squaw and two children. Why they were overlooked is not recorded.

As late in this century as 1915 there were occasional threats of revolt, but by that time no one took them seriously. The Indians were already well along the dreary white man's road. Scarcely a year has gone by since then that has not recorded at least one instance of the white man's continuing disregard of the Indian as a human being and a citizen. The comparatively recent ruthless grab of land in Nevada by politicians and speculators is a matter of documented history. The shameful taking of Iroquois land in upper New York State in 1960 produced a brief flurry of indignation, but in the end the white man got what he wanted, and with the sanction of the Supreme Court, at that.

Having kept them in reservation ghettoes for a hundred years, the Indian Bureau decided recently that Indians were not truly Indians any more but must be considered as white men. Stimulated by this absurdity, Congress passed an incredible law "terminating" Indian tribes. Translated into practicalities, this meant that they would no longer be entitled to Federal welfare services, and were permitted to have the privilege of starving like everyone else. The first tribe to be terminated was the Menominees, in Wisconsin. They woke up one morning to find their reservation designated as a county. The Bureau, of course, had to abrogate old treaties to accomplish it but then white governments had been doing that in America for nearly 300 years.

The Indians, who have fought in the nation's great wars of this century, who have helped to build its skyscrapers and bridges and contributed to its arts, have much to be proud of. But the plight of many tribes is still pitiful. Assimilation has not really replaced extermination. The white man's road, for the Indian, had no ending. He has, as the government so aptly puts it, been terminated.

# Selected Bibliography

Abel, Annie Heloise. *The American Indian as Slaveholder and Secessionist*. Cleveland: The Arthur H. Clark Co., 1915.
———. *The American Indian as Participant in the Civil War*. Cleveland: The Arthur H. Clark Co., 1919.
Arnold R. Ross. *Indian Wars of Idaho*. Caldwell, Idaho: Caxton Printers, 1932.
Bandel, Eugene. *Frontier Life in the Army, 1854–1861*. Glendale, California: The Arthur H. Clark Co., 1932
Beirne, Francis F. *The War of 1812*. New York: E. P. Dutton and Co., 1949.
Boatner, Maj. Mark M., III. *The Civil War Dictionary: A Concise Encyclopedia*. New York: David McKay Co., 1959.
Bourke, Capt. J. G. *On the Border with Crook*. New York: Charles Scribner's Sons, 1892.
Brimlow, George Francis. *The Bannock Indian War of 1878*. Caldwell, Idaho: The Caxton Printers, 1938.
Britt, Albert. *Great Indian Chiefs*. New York: Whittlesey House, 1938.
Britton, Wiley. *The Civil War on the Border*. 2 vols. New York: G. P. Putnam's Sons, 1899.
Burt, Struthers. *Powder River*. New York: Farrar & Rinehart, 1939.
Byrne, P. E. *Soldiers of the Plains*. New York: Minton, Balch & Co., 1926.
Carter, Maj. Gen. William Harding. *The Life of Lieutenant General Chaffee*. Chicago: University of Chicago Press, 1917.
Cashin, Herschel V., and others. *Under Fire, with the 10th U. S. Cavalry Regiment*. Chicago: F. T. Neely, 1899.
Catlin, George. *Letters and Notes on the Manners, Customs, and Condition of the North American Indians*. New York: Wiley & Putnam, 1842.
———. *North American Indians*. 2 vols. Philadelphia: Leary, Stuart & Co., 1913.

Clark, George Rogers. *Papers, 1771–1781 and 1781–1784*. Collections of the Illinois State Historical Library, vols. 8 and 19. James Alton James, ed., Springfield, Ill., 1912, 1926.

Clarke, T. Wood. *The Bloody Mohawk*. New York: The Macmillan Co., 1940.

Cleaves, Freeman. *Old Tippecanoe*. New York: Charles Scribner's Sons, 1939.

Collier, John. *Indians of the Americas*. New York: W. W. Norton, 1947.

Colton, Ray C. *The Civil War in the Western Territories*. Norman: University of Oklahoma Press, 1959.

Commager, Henry Steele, and Morris, Richard B., eds. *The Spirit of 'Seventy-Six*. 2 vols. Indianapolis: The Bobbs-Merrill Co., 1958.

Company of Military Collectors & Historians. *Journal*. Files.

Cook, Frederick. *Journals of the Military Expedition of Major General John Sullivan Against the Six Nations of Indians in 1779*. Auburn, N.Y.: Knap, Peck & Thompson, 1887.

Cooke, Philip St. George. *Cavalry Tactics*. 2 vols. Philadelphia: J. B. Lippincott Co., 1862.

Coutant, C. G. *History of Wyoming*. 3 vols. Laramie: Chaplin, Spafford and Mathison, 1899.

Crockett, David. *Autobiography*. New York: Charles Scribner's Sons, 1923.

Croghan, Col. George. *Army Life on the Western Frontier*. F. P. Prucha, ed. Norman: University of Oklahoma Press, 1958.

Cunningham, Frank. *General Stand Watie's Confederate Indians*. San Antonio, Texas: The Naylor Co., 1959.

Custer, Col. George A. *Wild Life on the Plains*. St. Louis: Royal Publishing Co., 1891.

Debo, Angie. *The Road to Disappearance*. Norman: University of Oklahoma Press, 1941.

Douglas, Marjory Stoneman. *The Everglades: River of Grass*. New York: Rinehart & Co., 1947.

Downes, Randolph Chandler. *Frontier Ohio, 1788–1803*. Columbus: Ohio State Archeological Society, 1935.

Downey, Fairfax. *Indian-Fighting Army*. New York: Charles Scribner's Sons, 1941.

——. *Indian Wars of the U. S. Army, 1776–1865*. New York: Charles Scribner's Sons, 1963.

——. *General Crook, Indian Fighter*. Philadelphia: The Westminster Press, 1957.

Du Bois, Col. John Van Deusen. *Campaigns in the West, 1856–1861*. Tucson: Arizona Pioneers Historical Society, 1949.

Dupuy, Col. R. Ernest. *The Compact History of the United States Army*. New York: Hawthorn Books, 1961.

Elkins, Capt. John M. *Indian Fighting on the Texas Frontier*. Amarillo: Russell & Cockrell, 1929.

Eliott, Charles Winslow. *Winfield Scott, the Soldier and the Man*. New York: The Macmillan Co., 1937.

English, William Hayden. *Conquest of the Country Northwest of the River Ohio, 1778–1783, and Life of Gen. George Rogers Clark*. Indianapolis: The Bobbs-Merrill Co., 1896.

Fiske, John. *The American Revolution*. 2 vols. Boston: Houghton Mifflin Co., 1891.

Foreman, Grant. *Advancing the Frontier*. Norman: University of Oklahoma Press, 1933.

————. *The Five Civilized Tribes*. Norman: University of Oklahoma Press, 1934.

Freeman, Douglas Southall. *George Washington*, vols. 2, 4 and 6. New York: Charles Scribner's Sons, 1948-54.

Ganoe, William. *History of the United States Army*. New York: D. Appleton & Co., 1932.

Garland, Hamlin. *The Book of the American Indian*. New York: Harper & Bros., 1928.

Green, James A. *William Henry Harrison: His Life and Times*. Richmond: Garrett & Massie, 1941.

Hafen, LeRoy R. and Ann W. *Relations with the Indians of the Plains*. Glendale, Calif.: The Arthur H. Clark Co., 1961.

———— *Powder River Campaigns and Sawyer's Expedition*. Glendale: The Arthur H. Clark Co., 1961.

Hafen, LeRoy R. and Young, Francis Marion. *Fort Laramie and the Pageant of the West*. Glendale: The Arthur H. Clark Co., 1938.

Halsey, Francis Whitney. *The Old New York Frontier*. New York: Charles Scribner's Sons, 1901.

Hamilton, Holman. *Zachary Taylor, Soldier of the Republic*. Indianapolis: The Bobbs-Merrill Co., 1941.

Haskin, W. L. *History of the 1st Regiment of Artillery*. Portland, Me.: R. Thurston & Co., 1879.

Hebard, Grace Raymond, and E. A. Brininstool. *The Bozeman Trail*. 2 vols. Cleveland: The Arthur H. Clark Co., 1922.

Henry, Will. *From Where the Sun Now Stands*. New York: Random House, 1960.

Hollon, W. Eugene. *The Lost Pathfinder: Zebulon Montgomery Pike*. Norman: University of Oklahoma Press, 1949.

Hulburt, Archer Butler. *Military Roads of the Mississippi Basin; the Conquest of the Old Northwest*. Cleveland: The Arthur H. Clark Co., 1904.

Hunt, Aurora. *The Army of the Pacific*. Glendale: The Arthur H. Clark Co., 1951.

Hyde, George E. *Red Cloud's Folk: A History of the Oglala Sioux.* Norman: University of Oklahoma Press, 1937.

———. *Indians of the High Plains.* Norman: University of Oklahoma Press, 1959.

Jacobs, J. R. *The Beginning of the U. S. Army, 1783–1812.* Princeton: Princeton University Press, 1947.

James, Marquis. *Life of Andrew Jackson.* Indianapolis: The Bobbs-Merrill Co., 1938.

King, Capt. Charles. *Campaigning With Crook.* Harper & Bros., 1890.

Kreidberg, Lt. Col. Marvin A., and Henry, 1st Lt. Merton G. *History of Military Mobilization in the United States Army, 1775–1945.* Dept. of the Army Pamphlet No. 20-212. 1955.

Leach, Douglas Edward. *Flintlock and Tomahawk.* New York: The Macmillan Co., 1958.

Lewis, Oscar. *The War in the Far West: 1861–1865.* Toronto: Doubleday & Co., 1961.

Lockwood, Frank C. *The Apache Indians.* New York: The Macmillan Co., 1938.

Manring, B. F. *The Conquest of the Coeur d'Alenes, Spokanes, and Pelouses.* Spokane: John W. Graham & Co., 1912.

McConnell, W. J. *Early History of Idaho.* Caldwell: The Caxton Printers, 1918.

Merritt, Gen. Wesley. "Three Indian Campaigns," in *Harper's* Magazine, April, 1890.

Miles, Gen. Nelson A. *Personal Recollections and Observations.* Chicago: The Werner Co., 1896.

Montross, Lynn. *Rag, Tag and Bobtail, the Story of the Continental Army, 1775–1783.* New York: Harper & Bros., 1952.

Murray, Keith A. *The Modocs and Their War.* Norman: University of Oklahoma Press, 1959.

Nelson, Bruce. *Land of the Dacotahs.* Minneapolis: University of Minnesota Press, 1946.

Nye, W. S. *Carbine and Lance, The Story of Old Fort Sill.* Norman: University of Oklahoma Press, 1937.

Okison, John M. *Tecumseh and His Times.* New York: G. P. Putnam's Sons, 1938.

*Order of Indian Wars of the United States.* Files. In Historical Section, Army War College, Washington, D.C.

Parker, James. *The Old Army, 1872–1918.* Philadelphia: Dorrance & Co., 1920.

Parkman, Francis. *France and England in North America.* Boston: Little, Brown & Co., 1905.

Peckham, Howard. *Pontiac and the Indian Uprising.* Princeton: Princeton University Press, 1947.

Pelzer, Louis. *Marches of the Dragoons in the Mississippi Valley*. Iowa City: State Historical Society of Iowa, 1917.

Pike, Cpl. James. *Scout and Ranger*. Princeton: Princeton University Press, 1932.

Richardson, Rupert Norval. *The Comanche Barrier to South Plains Settlement*. Glendale: The Arthur H. Clark Co., 1933.

Riegel, Robert E. *America Moves West*. New York: Henry Holt & Co., 1930.

Rister, C. C. *The Southwestern Frontier*. Cleveland: The Arthur H. Clark Co., 1928.

Rodenbaugh, Gen. Theo. F. *From Everglade to Canon with the Second Dragoons*. New York: D. Van Nostrand, 1875.

St. Clair, Arthur. *Papers*. 2 vols. William H. Smith, ed. Cincinnati: Robert Clark Co., 1882.

Sargent, Winthrop. *Diary*. In Ohio Archeological and Historical Society Publications, vol. 33.

Schlesinger, Arthur M., Jr. *The Age of Jackson*. Boston: Little, Brown & Co., 1945.

Scott, Gen. Hugh L. *Some Memories of a Soldier*. New York: The Century Co., 1928.

Seymour, Flora. *Indian Agents of the Old Frontier*. New York: D. Appleton & Co., 1941.

Sheridan, Lt. Gen. P. H. *Record of Engagement with Hostile Indians Within the Military Division of the Missouri from 1868 to 1882*. Washington, 1882.

Sherman, Gen. W. T. *Memoirs*. 2 vols. New York: C. I. Webster & Co., 1891.

————. *Official Letters*, vol. 1, 1866–1878.

Smith, Justin H. *The War With Mexico*. 2 vols. New York: The Macmillan Co., 1919.

Spring, Agnes Wright. *Caspar Collins*. New York: Columbia University Press, 1927.

Starkey, M. I. *The Cherokee Nation*. New York: Alfred A. Knopf, 1946.

Tebbel, John, and Keith Jennison. *The American Indian Wars*. New York: Harper & Bros., 1960.

Thornbrough, Gayle, ed. *Outpost on the Wabash, 1787–1791*. Indiana Historical Society Publications, vol. 19.

Tucker, Glenn. *Poltroons and Patriots, a Popular Account of the War of 1812*. Indianapolis: The Bobbs-Merrill Co., 1954.

————. *Tecumseh, Vision of Glory*. Indianapolis: The Bobbs-Merrill Co., 1956.

Underhill, Ruth M. *The Navajos*. Norman: University of Oklahoma Press, 1956.

————. *Red Man's America*. Chicago: University of Chicago Press, 1953.

United States Adjutant General's Office. Chronological List of Actions, etc., with Indians from Jan. 1, 1866, to Jan., 1891.

United States Army, Military Division of the Missouri. Reports of officers in the West and Southwest, 1874–1875.

————. *The Medal of Honor of the United States Army.* Washington: Government Printing Office, 1948.

————. Surgeon General's Office, Official Circular No. 8. *Report of Hygiene, U. S. Army, with a Description of Army Posts.*

Verrill, A. Hyatt. *The Real Americans.* New York: G. P. Putnam's Sons, 1954.

Vestal, Stanley. *New Sources of Indian History, 1850–1891.* Norman: University of Oklahoma Press, 1934.

————. *Sitting Bull.* Boston: Houghton Mifflin Co., 1932.

Wallace, Ernest, and E. Adamson Hoebel. *The Comanches, Lords of the South Plains.* Norman: University of Oklahoma Press, 1952.

Ward, Christopher. *The War of the Revolution.* 2 vols. New York: The Macmillan Co., 1952.

Ware, Capt. Eugene F. *The Indian War of 1864.* New York: St. Martin's Press, 1960.

Wellman, Paul I. *Death in the Desert.* New York: The Macmillan Co., 1935.

————. *Death on Horseback.* Philadelphia: J. B. Lippincott Co., 1947.

————. *Death on the Prairie.* New York: The Macmillan Co., 1934.

Wesley, Edgar Bruce. *Guarding the Frontier.* Minneapolis: University of Minnesota Press, 1935.

Whitman, S. E. *The Troopers.* New York: Hastings House, 1962.

Wildes, Harry Emerson. *Anthony Wayne.* New York: Harcourt, Brace & Co., 1941.

Williams, T. Harry. *Americans at War.* Baton Rouge: Louisiana State University Press, 1960.

Wilson, Frazer E. *Arthur St. Clair.* Richmond: Garrett & Massie, 1944.

Young, Otis E. *The West of Philip St. George Cooke, 1809–1895.* Glendale: The Arthur H. Clark Co., 1955.

————. *The First Military Escort on the Santa Fe Trail.* Glendale: The Arthur H. Clark Co., 1952.

# Index

# The Author and His Book

JOHN TEBBEL, *who is descended from Michigan pioneer Indian-Irish-English stock, was educated at Central Michigan University (A.B., 1935; Litt. D., 1948) and the Columbia School of Journalism (M.S., 1937). After a long career in the newspaper business, on such papers as the Detroit* Free Press, Providence Journal *and* The New York Times; *and on magazines* (Newsweek *and* The American Mercury), *he entered book publishing as associate editor of E. P. Dutton Co. He joined the faculty of New York University in 1949, and served as chairman of the Department of Journalism from 1954 to 1965, except for four years (1958-1962) when he was on leave as director of the University's Graduate Institute of Book Publishing. He resigned the chairmanship in 1965 to devote more time to teaching and writing. Among his many books, Dr. Tebbel lists four in the field of Americana besides the present volume,* The Battle for North America *(Doubleday, 1948),* George Washington's America *(Dutton, 1954),* The Compact History of the American Newspaper *(Hawthorn, 1963), and (with Keith Jennison),* The American Indian Wars *(Harper, 1960); three historical novels,* The Conqueror *(Dutton, 1951),* Touched with Fire *(Dutton, 1952), and* A Voice in the Streets *(Dutton, 1954); seven biographies,* An American Dynasty *(Doubleday, 1947),* The Marshall Fields *(Dutton, 1947),* George Horace Lorimer and the Saturday Evening Post *(Doubleday, 1948),* The Life and Good Times of William Randolph Hearst *(Dutton, 1952),* The Inheritors *(Putnam, 1961),* From Rags to Riches *(Macmillan, 1963), and* David Sarnoff *(Encyclopaedia Britannica Press, 1963). He has also written two books in the field of popular medicine,* Your Body *(Harper,*

*1951), and* The Magic of Balanced Living *(Harper, 1956); a textbook with Kenneth N.* Stewart, Makers of Modern Journalism *(Prentice-Hall, 1950), and (with Ann Seranne) an anthology,* The Epicure's Companion *(McKay, 1962). Mr. Tebbel has written for many national magazines, and is a regular contributor to the Communications section of* Saturday Review.

THE COMPACT HISTORY OF THE INDIAN WARS *was set in type by the Pyramid Composition Co., Inc., of New York City, printed by the Halliday Lithographic Corporation of West Hanover, Mass., and bound by The Book Press of Brattleboro, Vermont. The text type is Linotype Times Roman, a face originally designed by Stanley Morison for use by the London* Times.

A HAWTHORN BOOK